The Effortless Tower Air Fryer Cookbook

365

Affordable and Delicious Tower Air Fryer Recipes for Beginners
with Tips & Tricks to Fry, Grill, Roast, and Bake.

William Adkins

All Rights Reserved:

The content contained within this book may not be reproduced, duplicated, or transmitted without direct written permission from the author or the publisher. Under no circumstances will any blame or legal responsibility be held against the publisher, or author, for any damages, reparation, or monetary loss due to the information contained within this book, either directly or indirectly.

Legal Notice: This book is copyright protected. It is only for personal use. You cannot amend, distribute, sell, use, quote or paraphrase any part, or the content within this book, without the consent of the author or publisher.

Disclaimer Notice:

Please note the information contained within this document is for educational and entertainment purposes only. All effort has been executed to present accurate, up to date, reliable, complete information. No warranties of any kind are declared or implied. Readers acknowledge that the author is not engaged in the rendering of legal, financial, medical, or professional advice. The content within this book has been derived from various sources. Please consult a licensed professional before attempting any techniques outlined in this book. By reading this document, the reader agrees that under no circumstances is the author responsible for any losses, direct or indirect, that are incurred as a result of the use of the information contained within this document, including, but not limited to, errors, omissions, or inaccuracies.

Table of Contents

Table of Contents 3

Introduction 8

Basics about the Tower Air Fryers 8

How the Tower Air Fryer Works 8
Benefits of the Tower Air Fryers 8
Foods that Can Cook Straight Away in Your Tower Air Fryer 9
Cleaning and Caring for Your Tower Air Fryer 9
Tower Air Fryer Tricks and Tips You Should Know 9

Vegetable Side Dishes Recipes 11

Roasted Brussels Sprouts 11
Goat Cheese Stuffed Portobellos 11
Buttered Garlic Broccolini 11
Smooth & Silky Cauliflower Purée 11
Southwestern Sweet Potato Wedges 12
Speedy Baked Caprese With Avocado 12
Savory Brussels Sprouts 12
Stunning Apples & Onions 12
Turkish Mutabal (eggplant Dip) 12
Hasselbacks 13
Ricotta & Broccoli Cannelloni 13
Garlicky Bell Pepper Mix 13
Roasted Heirloom Carrots With Orange And Thyme 13
Roasted Bell Peppers With Garlic & Dill 14
Broccoli Tots 14
Steamboat Shrimp Salad 14
Pecorino Dill Muffins 14
Roasted Broccoli And Red Bean Salad 15
Asparagus Fries 15
Crispy Noodle Salad 15
Steak Fries 16
Roasted Peppers With Balsamic Vinegar And Basil 16
Breaded Artichoke Hearts 16
Perfect French Fries 16
Cheesy Potato Pot 17
Crispy, Cheesy Leeks 17
Roast Sweet Potatoes With Parmesan 17
Almond-crusted Zucchini Fries 18
Smoked Avocado Wedges 18
Spicy Fried Green Beans 18
Stuffed Avocados 18
Cheese Sage Cauliflower 18
Italian Breaded Eggplant Rounds 19
Pork Tenderloin Salad 19
Smoky Roasted Veggie Chips 19
Polenta 19
Parsnip Fries With Romesco Sauce 20
Yukon Gold Potato Purée 20
Vegetable Roast 20
Herb Roasted Jicama 20
Homemade Potato Puffs 21
Crispy Cauliflower Puffs 21
Green Dip With Pine Nuts 21
Five-spice Roasted Sweet Potatoes 21
Roman Artichokes 22
The Ultimate Mac`n´cheese 22
Lemony Green Bean Sautée 22
Salt And Pepper Baked Potatoes 22
Air-fried Potato Salad 23
Dauphinoise (potatoes Au Gratin) 23
Stuffed Onions 23
Baked Shishito Peppers 24
Grilled Lime Scallions 24
Perfect Broccolini 24
Tofu & Broccoli Salad 24

Appetizers And Snacks 25

Muffuletta Sliders 25
Garlic Wings 25
Jalapeño & Mozzarella Stuffed Mushrooms 25
Prosciutto Mozzarella Bites 26

Avocado Fries	26
Buffalo Bites	26
Mouth-watering Vegetable Casserole	26
Spicy Chicken And Pepper Jack Cheese Bites	27
Vegetarian Fritters With Green Dip	27
Rich Egg-fried Cauliflower Rice	27
Cheesy Spinach Dip(2)	28
Warm And Salty Edamame	28
Barbecue Chicken Nachos	28
Spicy Pearl Onion Dip	28
Mozzarella Sticks	29
Balsamic Grape Dip	29
Basil Feta Crostini	29
Fried Apple Wedges	29
Tasty Roasted Black Olives & Tomatoes	30
Honey-lemon Chicken Wings	30
Shrimp Egg Rolls	30
Za'atar Garbanzo Beans	31
Beef Steak Sliders	31
Skinny Fries	31
Rich Clam Spread	31
Cauliflower "tater" Tots	32
Brie-currant & Bacon Spread	32
Cayenne-spiced Roasted Pecans	32
Roasted Jalapeño Salsa Verde	32
Bbq Chips	33
Roasted Red Pepper Dip	33
Crunchy Spicy Chickpeas	33
Plantain Chips	33
Artichoke Samosas	34
Onion Ring Nachos	34

Sandwiches And Burgers Recipes 35

Inside Out Cheeseburgers	35
White Bean Veggie Burgers	35
Philly Cheesesteak Sandwiches	35
Chili Cheese Dogs	36
Chicken Club Sandwiches	36
Perfect Burgers	36
Sausage And Pepper Heros	37
Chicken Gyros	37
Thanksgiving Turkey Sandwiches	37
Mexican Cheeseburgers	38
Salmon Burgers	38
Dijon Thyme Burgers	39
Chicken Spiedies	39
Inside-out Cheeseburgers	40
Black Bean Veggie Burgers	40

Desserts And Sweets 41

Sweet Potato Donut Holes	41
Oatmeal Blackberry Crisp	41
Cheese Blintzes	41
Fall Pumpkin Cake	41
Oreo-coated Peanut Butter Cups	42
Fried Twinkies	42
Mixed Berry Pie	43
Coconut Cream Roll-ups	43
Blueberry Crisp	43
Nutty Cookies	43
Pumpkin Brownies	44
Fast Brownies	44
Apple Crisp	44
Wild Blueberry Sweet Empanadas	45
Sugared Pizza Dough Dippers With Raspberry Cream Cheese Dip	45
Baked Caramelized Peaches	46
Strawberry Pastry Rolls	46
Vanilla Butter Cake	46
Fruit Turnovers	47
Roasted Pears	47
Famous Chocolate Lava Cake	47
Donut Holes	47
Fried Pineapple Chunks	48
Spiced Fruit Skewers	48
Holiday Peppermint Cake	48
Black And Blue Clafoutis	49
Coconut-custard Pie	49
Spanish Churro Bites	49
Guilty Chocolate Cookies	49
Struffoli	50

Vegetarians Recipes 50

- Honey Pear Chips 50
- Pizza Portobello Mushrooms 50
- Green Bean Sautée 51
- Tropical Salsa 51
- Veggie Burgers 51
- Cheesy Eggplant Rounds 52
- Rigatoni With Roasted Onions, Fennel, Spinach And Lemon Pepper Ricotta 52
- Home-style Cinnamon Rolls 52
- Tortilla Pizza Margherita 52
- Vegetarian Paella 53
- Colorful Vegetable Medley 53
- Spaghetti Squash And Kale Fritters With Pomodoro Sauce 53
- Egg Rolls 54
- Golden Breaded Mushrooms 54
- Meatless Kimchi Bowls 54
- Farfalle With White Sauce 55
- Sushi-style Deviled Eggs 55
- Quick-to-make Quesadillas 55
- Spicy Bean Patties 55
- Pineapple & Veggie Souvlaki 56
- Vegetarian Eggplant "pizzas" 56
- Authentic Mexican Esquites 56
- Bell Pepper & Lentil Tacos 56
- Spinach And Cheese Calzone 57
- Tomato & Squash Stuffed Mushrooms 57
- Effortless Mac `n´ Cheese 57
- Curried Potato, Cauliflower And Pea Turnovers 57
- Fennel Tofu Bites 58
- Tex-mex Stuffed Sweet Potatoes 58
- Easy Cheese & Spinach Lasagna 59
- Mushroom Bolognese Casserole 59
- Cauliflower Steaks Gratin 59
- Bite-sized Blooming Onions 60
- Spring Veggie Empanadas 60
- Tex-mex Potatoes With Avocado Dressing 60
- Roasted Veggie Bowls 61
- Cheddar Bean Taquitos 61
- Spicy Vegetable And Tofu Shake Fry 61
- Quinoa & Black Bean Stuffed Peppers 61
- Sicilian-style Vegetarian Pizza 62
- Veggie-stuffed Bell Peppers 62
- Sweet Roasted Carrots 62
- Italian-style Fried Cauliflower 62
- Crispy Apple Fries With Caramel Sauce 63
- Roasted Vegetable, Brown Rice And Black Bean Burrito .. 63

Bread And Breakfast 64

- Egg Muffins 64
- English Scones 64
- Oat & Nut Granola 64
- Peppered Maple Bacon Knots 64
- Favorite Blueberry Muffins 65
- Smoked Salmon Croissant Sandwich 65
- Peach Fritters 65
- Chorizo Sausage & Cheese Balls 66
- Orange-glazed Cinnamon Rolls 66
- Shakshuka-style Pepper Cups 66
- Bread Boat Eggs 67
- Spring Vegetable Omelet 67
- Breakfast Sausage Bites 67
- Morning Potato Cakes 67
- Cheddar-ham-corn Muffins 68
- Cinnamon Pumpkin Donuts 68
- Country Gravy 68
- Holiday Breakfast Casserole 68
- Strawberry Streusel Muffins 69
- Pumpkin Empanadas 69
- English Muffin Sandwiches 69
- Vegetarian Quinoa Cups 69
- Crustless Broccoli, Roasted Pepper And Fontina Quiche ... 70
- Morning Chicken Frittata Cups 70
- Carrot Orange Muffins 70
- Flank Steak With Caramelized Onions 70
- Roasted Vegetable Frittata 71
- Cinnamon Banana Bread With Pecans 71
- Broccoli Cornbread 71
- Zucchini Hash Browns 72

Poultry Recipes 72

- Chicken Tenders With Basil-strawberry Glaze 72
- Thai Chicken Drumsticks 72
- Turkey Tenderloin With A Lemon Touch 73
- Country Chicken Hoagies 73

Recipe	Page
Parmesan Chicken Fingers	73
Indian Chicken Tandoori	73
Cheesy Chicken Tenders	74
Hazelnut Chicken Salad With Strawberries	74
Saucy Chicken Thighs	74
Chicken Wellington	74
Mexican Chicken Roll-ups	75
Mexican-inspired Chicken Breasts	75
Greek Gyros With Chicken & Rice	75
Southern-style Chicken Legs	76
Yogurt-marinated Chicken Legs	76
Chipotle Chicken Drumsticks	76
Enchilada Chicken Quesadillas	76
Buttered Chicken Thighs	77
Chicken Cordon Bleu Patties	77
Pecan Turkey Cutlets	77
Spiced Mexican Stir-fried Chicken	77
Spicy Black Bean Turkey Burgers With Cumin-avocado Spread	78
Maewoon Chicken Legs	78
Farmer's Fried Chicken	78
Za'atar Chicken Drumsticks	79
Granny Pesto Chicken Caprese	79
Chicken & Rice Sautée	79
Greek Chicken Wings	80
Air-fried Turkey Breast With Cherry Glaze	80
Yummy Maple-mustard Chicken Kabobs	80
Peachy Chicken Chunks With Cherries	80
Mom's Chicken Wings	81
Chicken Cordon Bleu	81
Party Buffalo Chicken Drumettes	81
Crunchy Chicken Strips	82
Daadi Chicken Salad	82
Buttered Turkey Breasts	82
Quick Chicken For Filling	82
Jerk Turkey Meatballs	82
Chicken Meatballs With A Surprise	83
Kale & Rice Chicken Rolls	83
Chicken Salad With Roasted Vegetables	83
Buttery Chicken Legs	84
Gruyère Asparagus & Chicken Quiche	84
Tortilla Crusted Chicken Breast	84
German Chicken Frikadellen	84
Bacon & Chicken Flatbread	85
Sweet Chili Spiced Chicken	85
Chicken Breasts Wrapped In Bacon	85
Mushroom & Turkey Bread Pizza	86

Fish And Seafood Recipes 86

Recipe	Page
Timeless Garlic-lemon Scallops	86
Catalan-style Crab Samfaina	86
Herb-rubbed Salmon With Avocado	86
Caribbean Skewers	87
Family Fish Nuggets With Tartar Sauce	87
Chili Blackened Shrimp	87
Breaded Parmesan Perch	87
Maple Balsamic Glazed Salmon	88
Salmon Croquettes	88
Fish Tacos With Hot Coleslaw	88
Cheesy Tuna Tower	89
King Prawns Al Ajillo	89
Fried Shrimp	89
Holliday Lobster Salad	89
Southeast Asian-style Tuna Steaks	90
Shrimp Patties	90
Fish Tacos With Jalapeño-lime Sauce	90
Fish Cakes	91
Mediterranean Salmon Burgers	91
Blackened Red Snapper	91
Shrimp & Grits	92
Sriracha Salmon Melt Sandwiches	92
Restaurant-style Breaded Shrimp	92
Fish Goujons With Tartar Sauce	93
Horseradish Tuna Croquettes	93
Catalan Sardines With Romesco Sauce	93
Crunchy Clam Strips	93
Saucy Shrimp	94
Tuna Nuggets In Hoisin Sauce	94
Beer-battered Cod	94
British Fish & Chips	95
Black Olive & Shrimp Salad	95
Fried Scallops	95
Chinese Fish Noodle Bowls	95
Catfish Nuggets	96
Hot Calamari Rings	96
Parmesan Fish Bites	96
Coconut Shrimp	97

Buttered Swordfish Steaks ... 97	Honey Pecan Shrimp ... 98
Fish Nuggets With Broccoli Dip ... 97	Hazelnut-crusted Fish ... 99
Lime Bay Scallops ... 97	Super Crunchy Flounder Fillets ... 99
Maple-crusted Salmon ... 98	Tex-mex Fish Tacos ... 99
Californian Tilapia ... 98	Quick Shrimp Scampi ... 100
Lemon-dill Salmon Burgers ... 98	Spiced Shrimp Empanadas ... 100

Beef, pork & Lamb Recipes ... 101

Sausage-cheese Calzone ... 101	Easy Carnitas ... 109
Crispy Steak Subs ... 101	Cheeseburger Sliders With Pickle Sauce ... 109
Greek Pork Chops ... 101	Spanish-style Meatloaf With Manzanilla Olives ... 109
Lemon-garlic Strip Steak ... 102	Stuffed Pork Chops ... 110
Mustard And Rosemary Pork Tenderloin With Fried Apples 102	Marinated Rib-eye Steak With Herb Roasted Mushrooms 110
Beef Al Carbon (street Taco Meat) ... 102	Pepperoni Pockets ... 110
Flank Steak With Roasted Peppers And Chimichurri ... 102	Minted Lamb Chops ... 110
Herby Lamb Chops ... 103	Pork Chops ... 111
Italian Sausage Rolls ... 103	French-style Steak Salad ... 111
Paprika Fried Beef ... 103	Hungarian Pork Burgers ... 111
Italian Sausage & Peppers ... 104	Steak Fajitas ... 111
Calzones South Of The Border ... 104	Beef Brazilian Empanadas ... 112
Meat Loaves ... 105	Sirloin Steak Bites With Gravy ... 112
Rosemary Lamb Chops ... 105	Greek-style Pork Stuffed Jalapeño Poppers ... 112
Provençal Grilled Rib-eye ... 105	Tarragon Pork Tenderloin ... 113
Balsamic London Broil ... 105	Beef Meatballs With Herbs ... 113
Lazy Mexican Meat Pizza ... 105	Rosemary T-bone ... 113
Perfect Pork Chops ... 106	Bourbon Bacon Burgers ... 113
Red Curry Flank Steak ... 106	Homemade Pork Gyoza ... 114
Greek Pita Pockets ... 106	Tender Steak With Salsa Verde ... 114
German-style Pork Patties ... 107	Fried Spam ... 114
Beef And Spinach Braciole ... 107	Jerk Meatballs ... 115
Seedy Rib Eye Steak Bites ... 107	Bacon, Blue Cheese And Pear Stuffed Pork Chops ... 115
Beef & Barley Stuffed Bell Peppers ... 108	Canadian-style Rib Eye Steak ... 115
Sloppy Joes ... 108	Steak Fingers ... 116
Friendly Bbq Baby Back Ribs ... 108	Crispy Five-spice Pork Belly ... 116
Smokehouse-style Beef Ribs ... 108	Tacos Norteños ... 116
	Vietnamese Beef Lettuce Wraps ... 117

RECIPE INDEX ... 118

Introduction

The air fryer is a dream machine. That may sound like hyperbole, but it's true. It's hard to resist the taste and texture of fried foods—there's nothing like that crispy mouthfeel when you first bite into a French fry or fried chicken, only to meet the melting and tender interior. We all know unhealthy fried foods are not meant to be a mainstay in our diet. That's where the air fryer comes in. This appliance produces crisp, moist, and tender foods with little or no oil. With an air fryer, you can eat fried chicken, potato chips, croquettes, doughnuts, egg rolls, shrimp, and tater tots that aren't laden with grease from trans fats. Air-fried foods have the traditional crunch and classic texture of perfectly fried foods, but you can enjoy them guilt-free.

But that's not all the air fryer can make. In addition to fried favorites, you can bake, grill, steam, and roast in your air fryer—and in less time than it takes to cook foods using traditional methods. It's possible to serve risotto, stir-fries, pizzas, casseroles, and desserts from your air fryer in record time, with fabulous results.

In this book, you'll not only learn how to use your air fryer in new and interesting ways but also get acquainted with how the appliance works, the benefits of it and find useful tricks and tips to get the most from your new dream machine. Let's get frying!

Basics about the Tower Air Fryers

How the Tower Air Fryer Works

The technology of the Tower Air Fryer is very simple. Fried foods get their crunchy texture because hot oil heats foods quickly and evenly on their surface. Oil is an excellent heat conductor, which helps with fast and simultaneous cooking across all of the ingredients. For decades cooks have used convection ovens to try to mimic the effects of frying or cooking the whole surface of food. But the air never circulates quickly enough to achieve that delicious surface crisp we all love in fried foods.

With this mechanism the air is circulated on high degrees, up to 200° C, to "air fry" any food such as fish, chicken or chips etc. This technology has changed the whole idea of cooking by reducing the fat up to 80% compared to old-fashioned deep fat frying.

The Tower air fryer cooking releases the heat through a heating element which cooks the food in a healthier and more appropriate way. There's also an exhaust fan right above the cooking chamber which provides the food required airflow. This way food is cooked with constant heated air. This leads to the same heating temperature reaching every single part of the food that is being cooked. So, this is only grill and the exhaust fan that is helping the Tower air fryer to boost air at a constantly high speed in order to cook healthy food with less fat.

The internal pressure increases the temperature that will then be controlled by the exhaust system. Exhaust fan also releases filtered extra air to cook the food in a much healthier way. Tower air fryer has no odor at all and it is absolutely harmless making it user and environment friendly.

Benefits of the Tower Air Fryers

1. Safer to Use

As compared to other cooking devices, air fryers are safer since they are self-contained cooking appliances which ensure that the user is protected from the heating element and any form of oil that may splatter when cooking. Air fryers ensure that the immediate space is safe and no one gets burned. Moreover, apart from mitigating the risk of personal injury, air fryers have little chance of starting fires which can lead to damage of property and sometimes even death. The main reason for their safety is that they come with auto-shutdown safety features so that when the timer is done, they immediately turn off. This is a huge plus as compared to convection ovens and grills which do not have such a safety feature.

2. Economical to Use

Cooking oil is an expensive commodity especially in the instance when you need to use a gallon or more to cook either for a friend, guests or even colleagues from work. To cook food with a countertop deep fryer, you will need to purchase a gallon or so of cooking oils which can be a tad bit expensive and this is where an air fryer comes in since it uses a very little amount of oil.

3. Fewer Calories and Fats

When cooking with an air fryer, you will need to factor in that one tablespoon of commonly used cooking oil only has about one twenty calories and ten to fourteen grams of fat. Depending on the type of oil you are using, this translates to fewer calories when using an air fryer. When cooking with an air fryer, you only need to use a tablespoon or so of cooking oil. We can then safely say that one's intake of calories will be lower when using an air fryer compared to food prepared using a deep fryer. It also means that you will get fried, tasty, textured and crunchy food all without having to intake large amounts of calories.

4. Take Up Less Space in Your Kitchen

Typical air fryers are 1 foot cubed which is a relatively small size for a cooking appliance in your kitchen. To put this into perspective, they are only a little bit bigger than a typical coffee maker but in essence smaller than a toaster oven. Their small sizes come with several advantages.

Foods that Can Cook Straight Away in Your Tower Air Fryer

For the ultimate in quick cooking and convenience, some foods can be dropped into the air fryer as is. You can cook frozen French fries (curly fried or straight), tater tots, bread dough, puff pastry, vegetables (such as cauliflower florets, bell pepper strips, and carrot sticks), baby potatoes, frozen waffles and pancakes, and whole nuts in the air fryer, just as they come out of the bag or box. Meats and fish that you can drop into the air fryer include frozen chicken nuggets, chicken drumsticks, and chicken wings, fish sticks, fish fillets, salmon fillets and steaks, beef steaks, and pre-marinated meats (after patting them dry). In fact, many air fryers have automatic cooking times set into the appliance for each food, so you don't have to guess about the time or temperature.

Cleaning and Caring for Your Tower Air Fryer

Remember that the air fryer is not a toy, but cooking equipment, and should be treated with care.

Let the machine cool down before attempting to clean. Remove the basket and pan and wash with soap and water and a plastic scrubbing brush. If food is stuck on these pieces, let them soak in warm water for 10 to 20 minutes, then clean. Some parts may be dishwasher-safe; check the instruction manual.

Make sure that you always check inside the appliance for stray crumbs or bits of food and remove them. Wipe the appliance—turned off, unplugged, and cooled down—both inside and outside with a damp towel, sponge, or paper towel. If grease or oil has fallen to the bottom of the pan, soak it up with paper towels, then wipe clean.

Tower Air Fryer Tricks and Tips You Should Know

Although an Air Fryer is easy to use, please follow these tips for getting the most out of your new, fancy device. Once you get into it, crispy and delicious foods are just minutes away.

1. How to keep the rendered fat drippings from burning? Simply pour a little water into the bottom of the air fryer drawer. In this way, the fat drippings can't reach smoking temperatures.
2. If you miss the traditional fried food, try melting butter and sprinkling in your favorite herbs and spices to shake things up. Then, you can whip up a healthy avocado mayo and a few drizzles of hot sauce for a custom dip. You can use a tablespoon or two of extra-virgin olive oil and add whatever aromatics you like (garlic, herbs, chili, etc.); the result is veggies with a crisp texture and fewer calories. Win-win!

3. As for cooking times, always test your food for doneness before removing it from the cooking chamber, even if you are an experienced cook. As for meats and poultry, use a meat thermometer to ensure that meat is cooked thoroughly. The quantity and quality of food, as well as its thickness or density, may affect actual cooking time. It is recommended to cook food in smaller batches for the best results. Remove the frying basket drawer halfway through the cooking time to check your food. Most foods need to be shaken or turned over several times during the cooking time.
4. How to achieve that delicious, crispy surface? Pat your food dry before adding spices and oil. A tablespoon or two of oil should be brushed onto foods; experts recommend using oil sprays or misters with your favorite oil (olive, vegetable, or coconut oil). Avoid aerosol spray cans because they have harsh agents that can damage the coating on Air Fryer baskets. Although most foods need some oil to help them crisp, there are certain foods that naturally have some fat such as fatty cuts of meat; therefore, you do not have to add extra fat to these foods, but anyway, do not forget to grease the cooking basket.
5. Allow your food to rest for 5 to 10 seconds before removing them from the cooking basket unless the recipe indicates otherwise.
6. If you want to shake or add ingredients during the cooking cycle, simply remove the cooking basket; the machine will automatically shut down. Place the cooking basket back into the Air Fryer drawer and the cooking cycle will automatically resume.
7. Use your Air Fryer to reheat leftovers by setting the temperature to 300 degrees F for up to 10 minutes.
8. For crunchy, bright cruciferous vegetables, you can place them in boiling water for 3 to 5 minutes before adding them to the Air Fryer basket. Lightly toss your veggies with olive oil or an herbed vinaigrette and place in the preheated Air Fryer basket. Always remember not to over-fill the cooking basket. It is also important to keep air-fried veggies warm until ready to serve.
9. As for French fries, baking this favorite food is much healthier cooking method than deep-frying. Here's the secret to perfect fries. Cut your potatoes into 1/4-inch lengthwise pieces; make sure that the pieces are of uniform size; now, soak them in cold water for 30 minutes. You can add the vinegar to the water as well. Your fries will turn out slightly crispier and vinegar can improve their flavor too. When ready to eat, drain and pat them dry with a kitchen towel. Choose oil with a high smoke point such as olive oil, canola oil or clarified duck fat. Try not to crowd the fries in the Air Fryer basket. Afterwards, place them on a cooling rack set over a baking sheet – it is a little trick to keep your fries crispy until ready to serve. Salt your fries while they are still hot.

Vegetable Side Dishes Recipes

Roasted Brussels Sprouts

Servings: 4
Cooking Time: 25 Minutes
Ingredients:
- ½ cup balsamic vinegar
- 2 tablespoons honey
- 1 pound Brussels sprouts, halved lengthwise
- 2 slices bacon, chopped
- ½ teaspoon garlic powder
- 1 teaspoon salt
- 1 tablespoon extra-virgin olive oil
- ¼ cup grated Parmesan cheese

Directions:
1. Preheat the air fryer to 370°F (185°C).
2. In a small saucepan, heat the vinegar and honey for 8 to 10 minutes over medium-low heat, or until the balsamic vinegar reduces by half to create a thick balsamic glazing sauce.
3. While the balsamic glaze is reducing, in a large bowl, toss together the Brussels sprouts, bacon, garlic powder, salt, and olive oil. Pour the mixture into the air fryer basket and cook for 10 minutes; check for doneness. Cook another 2 to 5 minutes or until slightly crispy and tender.
4. Pour the balsamic glaze into a serving bowl and add the cooked Brussels sprouts to the dish, stirring to coat. Top with grated Parmesan cheese and serve.

Goat Cheese Stuffed Portobellos

Servings: 4
Cooking Time: 35 Minutes
Ingredients:
- 1 cup baby spinach
- ¾ cup crumbled goat cheese
- 2 tsp grated Parmesan cheese
- 4 portobello caps, cleaned
- Salt and pepper to taste
- 2 tomatoes, chopped
- 1 leek, chopped
- 1 garlic clove, minced
- ¼ cup chopped parsley
- 2 tbsp panko bread crumbs
- 1 tbsp chopped oregano
- 1 tbsp olive oil
- Balsamic glaze for drizzling

Directions:
1. Brush the mushrooms with olive oil and sprinkle with salt. Mix the remaining ingredients, excluding the balsamic glaze, in a bowl. Fill each mushroom cap with the mixture. Preheat air fryer to 370°F (185°C). Place the mushroom caps in the greased frying basket and Bake for 10-12 minutes or until the top is golden and the mushrooms are tender. Carefully transfer them to a serving dish. Drizzle with balsamic glaze and serve warm. Enjoy!

Buttered Garlic Broccolini

Servings: 2
Cooking Time: 20 Minutes
Ingredients:
- 1 bunch broccolini
- 2 tbsp butter, cubed
- ¼ tsp salt
- 2 minced cloves garlic
- 2 tsp lemon juice

Directions:
1. Preheat air fryer at 350ºF. Place salted water in a saucepan over high heat and bring it to a boil. Then, add in broccolini and boil for 3 minutes. Drain it and transfer it into a bowl. Mix in butter, garlic, and salt. Place the broccolini in the frying basket and Air Fry for 6 minutes. Serve immediately garnished with lemon juice.

Smooth & Silky Cauliflower Purée

Servings: 4
Cooking Time: 25 Minutes
Ingredients:
- 1 head cauliflower, cut into florets
- 1 rutabaga, diced
- 4 tbsp butter, divided
- Salt and pepper to taste
- 3 cloves garlic, peeled
- 2 oz cream cheese, softened
- ½ cup milk
- 1 tsp dried thyme

Directions:
1. Preheat air fryer to 350ºF. Combine cauliflower, rutabaga, 2 tbsp of butter, and salt to taste in a bowl. Add veggie mixture to the frying basket and Air Fry for 10 minutes, tossing once. Put in garlic and Air Fry for 5 more minutes. Let them cool a bit, then transfer them to a blender. Blend them along with 2 tbsp of butter, salt, black pepper, cream cheese, thyme and milk until smooth. Serve immediately.

Southwestern Sweet Potato Wedges

Servings: 4

Cooking Time: 30 Minutes

Ingredients:

- 2 sweet potatoes, peeled and cut into ½-inch wedges
- 2 tsp olive oil
- 2 tbsp cornstarch
- 1 tsp garlic powder
- ¼ tsp ground allspice
- ¼ tsp paprika
- ⅛ tsp cayenne pepper

Directions:

1. Preheat air fryer to 400°F (205°C). Place the sweet potatoes in a bowl. Add some olive oil and toss to coat, then transfer to the frying basket. Roast for 8 minutes. Sprinkle the potatoes with cornstarch, garlic powder, allspice, paprika, and cayenne, then toss. Put the potatoes back into the fryer and Roast for 12-17 more minutes. Shake the basket a couple of times while cooking. The potatoes should be golden and crispy. Serve warm.

Speedy Baked Caprese With Avocado

Servings: 4

Cooking Time: 15 Minutes

Ingredients:

- 4 oz fresh mozzarella
- 8 cherry tomatoes
- 2 tsp olive oil
- 2 halved avocados, pitted
- ¼ tsp salt
- 2 tbsp basil, torn

Directions:

1. Preheat air fryer to 375°F. In a bowl, combine tomatoes and olive oil. Set aside. Add avocado halves, cut sides up, in the frying basket, scatter tomatoes around halves, and Bake for 7 minutes. Divide avocado halves between 4 small plates, top each with 2 tomatoes and sprinkle with salt. Cut mozzarella cheese and evenly distribute over tomatoes. Scatter with the basil to serve.

Savory Brussels Sprouts

Servings: 4

Cooking Time: 15 Minutes

Ingredients:

- 1 lb Brussels sprouts, quartered
- 2 tbsp balsamic vinegar
- 1 tbsp olive oil
- 1 tbsp honey
- Salt and pepper to taste
- 1 ½ tbsp lime juice
- Parsley for sprinkling

Directions:

1. Preheat air fryer at 350°F. Combine all ingredients in a bowl. Transfer them to the frying basket. Air Fry for 10 minutes, tossing once. Top with lime juice and parsley.

Stunning Apples & Onions

Servings: 4

Cooking Time: 30 Minutes

Ingredients:

- 2 peeled McIntosh apples, sliced
- 1 shallot, sliced
- 2 tsp canola oil
- 2 tbsp brown sugar
- 1 tbsp honey
- 1 tbsp butter, melted
- ½ tsp sea salt

Directions:

1. Preheat the air fryer to 325°F (160°C). Toss the shallot slices with oil in a bowl until coated. Put the bowl in the fryer and Bake for 5 minutes. Remove the bowl and add the apples, brown sugar, honey, melted butter, and sea salt and stir. Put the bowl back into the fryer and Bake for 10-12 more minutes or until the onions and apples are tender. Stir again and serve.

Turkish Mutabal (eggplant Dip)

Servings: 2

Cooking Time: 40 Minutes

Ingredients:

- 1 medium eggplant
- 2 tbsp tahini
- 2 tbsp lemon juice
- 1 tsp garlic powder
- ¼ tsp sumac
- 1 tsp chopped parsley

Directions:

1. Preheat air fryer to 400°F (205°C). Place the eggplant in a pan and Roast for 30 minutes, turning once. Let cool for 5-10 minutes. Scoop out the flesh and place it in a bowl. Squeeze any excess water; discard the water. Mix the flesh, tahini, lemon juice, garlic, and sumac until well combined. Scatter with parsley and serve.

Hasselbacks

Servings: 4
Cooking Time: 41 Minutes

Ingredients:
- 2 large potatoes (approx. 1 pound each)
- oil for misting or cooking spray
- salt, pepper, and garlic powder
- 1½ ounces sharp Cheddar cheese, sliced very thin
- ¼ cup chopped green onions
- 2 strips turkey bacon, cooked and crumbled
- light sour cream for serving (optional)

Directions:
1. Preheat air fryer to 390°F (200°C).
2. Scrub potatoes. Cut thin vertical slices ¼-inch thick crosswise about three-quarters of the way down so that bottom of potato remains intact.
3. Fan potatoes slightly to separate slices. Mist with oil and sprinkle with salt, pepper, and garlic powder to taste. Potatoes will be very stiff, but try to get some of the oil and seasoning between the slices.
4. Place potatoes in air fryer basket and cook for 40 minutes or until centers test done when pierced with a fork.
5. Top potatoes with cheese slices and cook for 30 seconds to 1 minute to melt cheese.
6. Cut each potato in half crosswise, and sprinkle with green onions and crumbled bacon. If you like, add a dollop of sour cream before serving.

Ricotta & Broccoli Cannelloni

Servings: 4
Cooking Time: 35 Minutes

Ingredients:
- 1 cup shredded mozzarella cheese
- ½ cup cooked broccoli, chopped
- ½ cup cooked spinach, chopped
- 4 cooked cannelloni shells
- 1 cup ricotta cheese
- ½ tsp dried marjoram
- 1 egg
- 1 cup passata
- 1 tbsp basil leaves

Directions:
1. Preheat air fryer to 360°F (180°C). Beat the egg in a bowl until fluffy. Add the ricotta, marjoram, half of the mozzarella, broccoli, and spinach and stir to combine. Cover the base of a baking dish with a layer of passata. Fill the cannelloni with the cheese mixture and place them on top of the sauce. Spoon the remaining passata over the tops and top with the rest of the mozzarella cheese. Put the dish in the frying basket and Bake for 25 minutes until the cheese is melted and golden. Top with basil.

Garlicky Bell Pepper Mix

Servings: 4
Cooking Time: 30 Minutes

Ingredients:
- 2 tbsp vegetable oil
- ½ tsp dried cilantro
- 1 red bell pepper
- 1 yellow bell pepper
- 1 orange bell pepper
- 1 green bell pepper
- Salt and pepper to taste
- 1 head garlic

Directions:
1. Preheat air fryer to 330°F (165°C). Slice the peppers into 1-inch strips. Transfer them to a large bowl along with 1 tbsp of vegetable oil. Toss to coat. Season with cilantro, salt, and pepper. Cut the top of a garlic head and place it cut-side up on an oiled square of aluminium foil. Drizzle with vegetable oil and wrap completely in the foil.
2. Roast the wrapped garlic in the air fryer for 15 minutes. Next, add the pepper strips and roast until the peppers are tender and the garlic is soft, 6-8 minutes. Transfer the peppers to a serving dish. Remove the garlic and unwrap the foil carefully. Once cooled, squeeze the cloves out of the garlic head and mix into the peppers' dish. Serve.

Roasted Heirloom Carrots With Orange And Thyme

Servings: 2
Cooking Time: 12 Minutes

Ingredients:
- 10 to 12 heirloom or rainbow carrots (about 1 pound), scrubbed but not peeled
- 1 teaspoon olive oil
- salt and freshly ground black pepper
- 1 tablespoon butter
- 1 teaspoon fresh orange zest
- 1 teaspoon chopped fresh thyme

Directions:
1. Preheat the air fryer to 400°F (205°C).
2. Scrub the carrots and halve them lengthwise. Toss them in the olive oil, season with salt and freshly ground black pepper and transfer to the air fryer.

3. Air-fry at 400°F (205°C) for 12 minutes, shaking the basket every once in a while to rotate the carrots as they cook.
4. As soon as the carrots have finished cooking, add the butter, orange zest and thyme and toss all the ingredients together in the air fryer basket to melt the butter and coat evenly. Serve warm.

Roasted Bell Peppers With Garlic & Dill

Servings: 4

Cooking Time: 30 Minutes

Ingredients:

- 4 bell peppers, seeded and cut into fourths
- 1 tsp olive oil
- 4 garlic cloves, minced
- ½ tsp dried dill

Directions:

1. Preheat air fryer to 350°F (175°C). Add the peppers to the frying basket, spritz with olive oil, shake, and Roast for 15 minutes. Season with garlic and dill, then cook for an additional 3-5 minutes. The veggies should be soft. Serve.

Broccoli Tots

Servings: 24

Cooking Time: 10 Minutes

Ingredients:

- 2 cups broccoli florets (about ½ pound broccoli crowns)
- 1 egg, beaten
- ⅛ teaspoon onion powder
- ¼ teaspoon salt
- ⅛ teaspoon pepper
- 2 tablespoons grated Parmesan cheese
- ¼ cup panko breadcrumbs
- oil for misting

Directions:

1. Steam broccoli for 2minutes. Rinse in cold water, drain well, and chop finely.
2. In a large bowl, mix broccoli with all other ingredients except the oil.
3. Scoop out small portions of mixture and shape into 24 tots. Lay them on a cookie sheet or wax paper as you work.
4. Spray tots with oil and place in air fryer basket in single layer.
5. Cook at 390°F (200°C) for 5minutes. Shake basket and spray with oil again. Cook 5minutes longer or until browned and crispy.

Steamboat Shrimp Salad

Servings: 4

Cooking Time: 4 Minutes

Ingredients:

- Steamboat Dressing
- ½ cup mayonnaise
- ½ cup plain yogurt
- 2 teaspoons freshly squeezed lemon juice (no substitutes)
- 2 teaspoons grated lemon rind
- 1 teaspoon dill weed, slightly crushed
- ½ teaspoon hot sauce
- Steamed Shrimp
- 24 small, raw shrimp, peeled and deveined
- 1 teaspoon lemon juice
- ¼ teaspoon Old Bay Seasoning
- Salad
- 8 cups romaine or Bibb lettuce, chopped or torn
- ¼ cup red onion, cut in thin slivers
- 12 black olives, sliced
- 12 cherry or grape tomatoes, halved
- 1 medium avocado, sliced or cut into large chunks

Directions:

1. Combine all dressing ingredients and mix well. Refrigerate while preparing shrimp and salad.
2. Sprinkle raw shrimp with lemon juice and Old Bay Seasoning. Use more Old Bay if you like your shrimp bold and spicy.
3. Pour 4 tablespoons of water in bottom of air fryer.
4. Place shrimp in air fryer basket in single layer.
5. Cook at 390°F (200°C) for 4 minutes. Remove shrimp from basket and place in refrigerator to cool.
6. Combine all salad ingredients and mix gently. Divide among 4 salad plates or bowls.
7. Top each salad with 6 shrimp and serve with dressing.

Pecorino Dill Muffins

Servings:4

Cooking Time: 25 Minutes

Ingredients:

- ¼ cup grated Pecorino cheese
- 1 cup flour
- 1 tsp dried dill
- ⅛ tsp salt
- ¼ tsp onion powder
- 2 tsp baking powder
- 1 egg
- ¼ cup Greek yogurt

Directions:

1. Preheat air fryer to 350ºF. In a bowl, combine dry the ingredients. Set aside. In another bowl, whisk the wet ingredients. Add the wet ingredients to the dry ingredients and combine until blended.
2. Transfer the batter to 6 silicone muffin cups lightly greased with olive oil. Place muffin cups in the frying basket and Bake for 12 minutes. Serve right away.

Roasted Broccoli And Red Bean Salad

Servings: 3

Cooking Time: 14 Minutes

Ingredients:
- 3 cups (about 1 pound) 1- to 1½-inch fresh broccoli florets (not frozen)
- 1½ tablespoons Olive oil spray
- 1¼ cups Canned red kidney beans, drained and rinsed
- 3 tablespoons Minced yellow or white onion
- 2 tablespoons plus 1 teaspoon Red wine vinegar
- ¾ teaspoon Dried oregano
- ¼ teaspoon Table salt
- ¼ teaspoon Ground black pepper

Directions:
1. Preheat the air fryer to 375°F (190°C).
2. Put the broccoli florets in a big bowl, coat them generously with olive oil spray, then toss to coat all surfaces, even down into the crannies, spraying them a couple of times more.
3. Pour the florets into the basket, spreading them into as close to one layer as you can. Air-fry for 12 minutes, tossing and rearranging the florets twice so that any touching or covered parts are eventually exposed to the air currents, until light browned but still a bit firm. (If the machine is at 360°F (180°C), you may need to add 2 minutes to the cooking time.)
4. Dump the contents of the basket onto a large cutting board. Cool for a minute or two, then chop the florets into small bits. Scrape these into a bowl and add the kidney beans, onion, vinegar, oregano, salt, and pepper. Toss well and serve warm or at room temperature.

Asparagus Fries

Servings: 4

Cooking Time: 5 Minutes Per Batch

Ingredients:
- 12 ounces fresh asparagus spears with tough ends trimmed off
- 2 egg whites
- ¼ cup water
- ¾ cup panko breadcrumbs
- ¼ cup grated Parmesan cheese, plus 2 tablespoons
- ¼ teaspoon salt
- oil for misting or cooking spray

Directions:
1. Preheat air fryer to 390°F (200°C).
2. In a shallow dish, beat egg whites and water until slightly foamy.
3. In another shallow dish, combine panko, Parmesan, and salt.
4. Dip asparagus spears in egg, then roll in crumbs. Spray with oil or cooking spray.
5. Place a layer of asparagus in air fryer basket, leaving just a little space in between each spear. Stack another layer on top, crosswise. Cook at 390°F (200°C) for 5 minutes, until crispy and golden brown.
6. Repeat to cook remaining asparagus.

Crispy Noodle Salad

Servings: 3

Cooking Time: 22 Minutes

Ingredients:
- 6 ounces Fresh Chinese-style stir-fry or lo mein wheat noodles
- 1½ tablespoons Cornstarch
- ¾ cup Chopped stemmed and cored red bell pepper
- 2 Medium scallion(s), trimmed and thinly sliced
- 2 teaspoons Sambal oelek or other pulpy hot red pepper sauce (see here)
- 2 teaspoons Thai sweet chili sauce or red ketchup-like chili sauce, such as Heinz
- 2 teaspoons Regular or low-sodium soy sauce or tamari sauce
- 2 teaspoons Unseasoned rice vinegar (see here)
- 1 tablespoon White or black sesame seeds

Directions:
1. Bring a large saucepan of water to a boil over high heat. Add the noodles and boil for 2 minutes. Drain in a colander set in the sink. Rinse several times with cold water, shaking the colander to drain the noodles very well. Spread the noodles out on a large cutting board and air-dry for 10 minutes.
2. Preheat the air fryer to 400°F (205°C).
3. Toss the noodles in a bowl with the cornstarch until well coated. Spread them out across the entire basket (although they will be touching and overlapping a bit). Air-fry for 6 minutes, then turn the solid mass of noodles over as one piece. If it cracks in half or smaller pieces, just fit these back together after turning. Continue air-frying for 6 minutes, or until golden brown and crisp.

4. As the noodles cook, stir the bell pepper, scallion(s), sambal oelek, red chili sauce, soy sauce, vinegar, and sesame seeds in a serving bowl until well combined.

5. Turn the basket of noodles out onto a cutting board and cool for a minute or two. Break the mass of noodles into individual noodles and/or small chunks and add to the dressing in the serving bowl. Toss well to serve.

Steak Fries

Cooking Time: 20 Minutes

Servings: 4

Ingredients:

- 2 russet potatoes, scrubbed and cut into wedges lengthwise
- 1 tablespoon olive oil
- 2 teaspoons seasoning salt (recipe below)

Directions:

1. Preheat the air fryer to 400°F (205°C).
2. Toss the potatoes with the olive oil and the seasoning salt.
3. Air-fry for 20 minutes (depending on the size of the wedges), turning the potatoes over gently a few times throughout the cooking process to brown and cook them evenly.

Roasted Peppers With Balsamic Vinegar And Basil

Servings: 6

Cooking Time: 12 Minutes

Ingredients:

- 4 Small or medium red or yellow bell peppers
- 3 tablespoons Olive oil
- 1 tablespoon Balsamic vinegar
- Up to 6 Fresh basil leaves, torn up

Directions:

1. Preheat the air fryer to 400°F (205°C).
2. When the machine is at temperature, put the peppers in the basket with at least ¼ inch between them. Air-fry undisturbed for 12 minutes, until blistered, even blackened in places.
3. Use kitchen tongs to transfer the peppers to a medium bowl. Cover the bowl with plastic wrap. Set aside at room temperature for 30 minutes.
4. Uncover the bowl and use kitchen tongs to transfer the peppers to a cutting board or work surface. Peel off the filmy exterior skin. If there are blackened bits under it, these can stay on the peppers. Cut off and remove the stem ends. Split open the peppers and discard any seeds and their spongy membranes. Slice the peppers into ½-inch- to 1-inch-wide strips.
5. Put these in a clean bowl and gently toss them with the oil, vinegar, and basil. Serve at once. Or cover and store at room temperature for up to 4 hours or in the refrigerator for up to 5 days.

Breaded Artichoke Hearts

Servings: 2

Cooking Time: 25 Minutes

Ingredients:

- 1 can artichoke hearts in water, drained
- 1 egg
- ¼ cup bread crumbs
- ¼ tsp salt
- ¼ tsp hot paprika
- ½ lemon
- ¼ cup garlic aioli

Directions:

1. Preheat air fryer to 380°F (195°C). Whisk together the egg and 1 tbsp of water in a bowl until frothy. Mix together the bread crumbs, salt, and hot paprika in a separate bowl. Dip the artichoke hearts into the egg mixture, then coat in the bread crumb mixture. Put the artichoke hearts in a single layer in the frying basket. Air Fry for 15 minutes.
2. Remove the artichokes from the air fryer, and squeeze fresh lemon juice over the top. Serve with garlic aioli.

Perfect French Fries

Servings: 3

Cooking Time: 37 Minutes

Ingredients:

- 1 pound Large russet potato(es)
- Vegetable oil or olive oil spray
- ½ teaspoon Table salt

Directions:

1. Cut each potato lengthwise into ¼-inch-thick slices. Cut each of these lengthwise into ¼-inch-thick matchsticks.
2. Set the potato matchsticks in a big bowl of cool water and soak for 5 minutes. Drain in a colander set in the sink, then spread the matchsticks out on paper towels and dry them very well.
3. Preheat the air fryer to 225°F (160°C) (or 230°F (165°C), if that's the closest setting).
4. When the machine is at temperature, arrange the matchsticks in an even layer (if overlapping but not compact) in the basket. Air-fry for 20 minutes, tossing and rearranging the fries twice.

5. Pour the contents of the basket into a big bowl. Increase the air fryer's temperature to 325°F (160°C) (or 330°F (165°C), if that's the closest setting).
6. Generously coat the fries with vegetable or olive oil spray. Toss well, then coat them again to make sure they're covered on all sides, tossing (and maybe spraying) a couple of times to make sure.
7. When the machine is at temperature, pour the fries into the basket and air-fry for 12 minutes, tossing and rearranging the fries at least twice.
8. Increase the machine's temperature to 375°F (190°C) (or 380°F (1955°C) or 390°F (200°C), if one of these is the closest setting). Air-fry for 5 minutes more (from the moment you raise the temperature), tossing and rearranging the fries at least twice to keep them from burning and to make sure they all get an even measure of the heat, until brown and crisp.
9. Pour the contents of the basket into a serving bowl. Toss the fries with the salt and serve hot.

Cheesy Potato Pot

Servings: 4
Cooking Time: 13 Minutes
Ingredients:
- 3 cups cubed red potatoes (unpeeled, cut into ½-inch cubes)
- ½ teaspoon garlic powder
- salt and pepper
- 1 tablespoon oil
- chopped chives for garnish (optional)
- Sauce
- 2 tablespoons milk
- 1 tablespoon butter
- 2 ounces sharp Cheddar cheese, grated
- 1 tablespoon sour cream

Directions:
1. Place potato cubes in large bowl and sprinkle with garlic, salt, and pepper. Add oil and stir to coat well.
2. Cook at 390°F (200°C) for 13 minutes or until potatoes are tender. Stir every 4 or 5minutes during cooking time.
3. While potatoes are cooking, combine milk and butter in a small saucepan. Warm over medium-low heat to melt butter. Add cheese and stir until it melts. The melted cheese will remain separated from the milk mixture. Remove from heat until potatoes are done.
4. When ready to serve, add sour cream to cheese mixture and stir over medium-low heat just until warmed. Place cooked potatoes in serving bowl. Pour sauce over potatoes and stir to combine.
5. Garnish with chives if desired.

Crispy, Cheesy Leeks

Servings: 4
Cooking Time: 15 Minutes
Ingredients:
- 2 Medium leek(s), about 9 ounces each
- Olive oil spray
- ¼ cup Seasoned Italian-style dried bread crumbs (gluten-free, if a concern)
- ¼ cup (about ¾ ounce) Finely grated Parmesan cheese
- 2 tablespoons Olive oil

Directions:
1. Preheat the air fryer to 350°F (175°C) .
2. Trim off the root end of the leek(s) as well as the dark green top(s), leaving about a 5-inch usable section. Split the leek section(s) in half lengthwise. Set the leek halves cut side up on your work surface. Pull out and remove in one piece the semicircles that make up the inner structure of the leek, about halfway down. Set the removed "inside" next to the outer leek "shells" on your cutting board. Generously coat them all on all sides (particularly the "bottoms") with olive oil spray.
3. Set the leeks and their insides cut side up in the basket with as much air space between them as possible. Air-fry undisturbed for 12 minutes.
4. Meanwhile, mix the bread crumbs, cheese, and olive oil in a small bowl until well combined.
5. After 12 minutes in the air fryer, sprinkle this mixture inside the leek shells and on top of the leek insides. Increase the machine's temperature to 375°F (190°C) (or 380°F (195°C) or 390°F (200°C), if one of these is the closest setting). Air-fry undisturbed for 3 minutes, or until the topping is lightly browned.
6. Use a nonstick-safe spatula to transfer the leeks to a serving platter. Cool for a few minutes before serving warm.

Roast Sweet Potatoes With Parmesan

Servings: 4
Cooking Time: 30 Minutes
Ingredients:
- 2 peeled sweet potatoes, sliced
- ¼ cup grated Parmesan
- 1 tsp olive oil
- 1 tbsp balsamic vinegar
- 1 tsp dried rosemary

Directions:
1. Preheat air fryer to 400°F (205°C). Place the sweet potatoes and some olive oil in a bowl and shake to coat. Spritz with balsamic vinegar and rosemary, then shake again. Put the potatoes in the frying basket and Roast for 18-25 minutes, shaking at least once until the potatoes are soft. Sprinkle with Parmesan cheese and serve warm.

Almond-crusted Zucchini Fries

Servings: 2

Cooking Time: 30 Minutes

Ingredients:

- ½ cup grated Pecorino cheese
- 1 zucchini, cut into fries
- 1 tsp salt
- 1 egg
- 1 tbsp almond milk
- ½ cup almond flour

Directions:

1. Preheat air fryer to 370ºF. Distribute zucchini fries evenly over a paper towel, sprinkle with salt, and let sit for 10 minutes to pull out moisture. Pat them dry with paper towels. In a bowl, beat egg and almond milk. In another bowl, combine almond flour and Pecorino cheese. Dip fries in egg mixture and then dredge them in flour mixture. Place zucchini fries in the lightly greased frying basket and Air Fry for 10 minutes, flipping once. Serve.

Smoked Avocado Wedges

Servings: 4

Cooking Time: 15 Minutes

Ingredients:

- ½ tsp smoked paprika
- 2 tsp olive oil
- ½ lime, juiced
- 8 peeled avocado wedges
- 1 tsp chipotle powder
- ¼ tsp salt

Directions:

1. Preheat air fryer to 400ºF. Drizzle the avocado wedges with olive oil and lime juice. In a bowl, combine chipotle powder, smoked paprika, and salt. Sprinkle over the avocado wedges. Place them in the frying basket and Air Fry for 7 minutes. Serve immediately.

Spicy Fried Green Beans

Servings: 2

Cooking Time: 8 Minutes

Ingredients:

- 12 ounces green beans, trimmed
- 2 small dried hot red chili peppers (like árbol)
- ¼ cup panko breadcrumbs
- 1 tablespoon olive oil
- ½ teaspoon salt
- ⅛ teaspoon crushed red pepper flakes
- 2 scallions, thinly sliced

Directions:

1. Preheat the air fryer to 400°F (205°C).
2. Toss the green beans, chili peppers and panko breadcrumbs with the olive oil, salt and crushed red pepper flakes.
3. Air-fry for 8 minutes (depending on the size of the beans), shaking the basket once during the cooking process. The crumbs will fall into the bottom drawer – don't worry.
4. Transfer the green beans to a serving dish, sprinkle the scallions and the toasted crumbs from the air fryer drawer on top and serve. The dried peppers are not to be eaten, but they do look nice with the green beans. You can leave them in, or take them out as you please.

Stuffed Avocados

Servings: 4

Cooking Time: 8 Minutes

Ingredients:

- 1 cup frozen shoepeg corn, thawed
- 1 cup cooked black beans
- ¼ cup diced onion
- ½ teaspoon cumin
- 2 teaspoons lime juice, plus extra for serving
- salt and pepper
- 2 large avocados, split in half, pit removed

Directions:

1. Mix together the corn, beans, onion, cumin, and lime juice. Season to taste with salt and pepper.
2. Scoop out some of the flesh from center of each avocado and set aside. Divide corn mixture evenly between the cavities.
3. Set avocado halves in air fryer basket and cook at 360°F (180°C) for 8 minutes, until corn mixture is hot.
4. Season the avocado flesh that you scooped out with a squirt of lime juice, salt, and pepper. Spoon it over the cooked halves.

Cheese Sage Cauliflower

Servings: 4

Cooking Time: 25 Minutes

Ingredients:

- 1 head cauliflower, cut into florets
- 3 tbsp butter, melted
- 2 tbsp grated asiago cheese
- 2 tsp dried sage
- ½ tsp garlic powder
- ¼ tsp salt

Directions:

1. Preheat air fryer to 350ºF. Mix all ingredients in a bowl. Add cauliflower mixture to the frying basket and Air Fry for 6 minutes, shaking once. Serve immediately.

Italian Breaded Eggplant Rounds

Servings: 4

Cooking Time: 30 Minutes

Ingredients:
- 1 eggplant, sliced into rounds
- 1 egg
- ½ cup bread crumbs
- 1 tsp onion powder
- ½ tsp Italian seasoning
- ½ tsp garlic salt
- ½ tsp paprika
- 1 tbsp olive oil

Directions:

1. Preheat air fryer to 360°F (180°C). Whisk the egg and 1 tbsp of water in a bowl until frothy. Mix the bread crumbs, onion powder, Italian seasoning, salt, and paprika in a separate bowl. Dip the eggplant slices into the egg mixture, then coat them into the bread crumb mixture. Put the slices in a single layer in the frying basket. Drizzle with olive oil. Air Fry for 23-25 minutes, turning once. Serve warm.

Pork Tenderloin Salad

Servings: 4

Cooking Time: 25 Minutes

Ingredients:
- Pork Tenderloin
- ½ teaspoon smoked paprika
- ¼ teaspoon salt
- ¼ teaspoon garlic powder
- ½ teaspoon onion powder
- ⅛ teaspoon ginger
- 1 teaspoon extra-light olive oil
- ¾ pound pork tenderloin
- Dressing
- 3 tablespoons extra-light olive oil
- 2 tablespoons red wine vinegar
- 2 tablespoons Dijon mustard
- 1 tablespoon honey
- Salad
- ¼ sweet red bell pepper
- 1 large Granny Smith apple
- 8 cups shredded Napa cabbage

Directions:

1. Mix the tenderloin seasonings together with oil and rub all over surface of meat.
2. Place pork tenderloin in the air fryer basket and cook at 390°F (200°C) for 25minutes, until meat registers 130°F (55°C) on a meat thermometer.
3. Allow meat to rest while preparing salad and dressing.
4. In a jar, shake all dressing ingredients together until well mixed.
5. Cut the bell pepper into slivers, then core, quarter, and slice the apple crosswise.
6. In a large bowl, toss together the cabbage, bell pepper, apple, and dressing.
7. Divide salad mixture among 4 plates.
8. Slice pork tenderloin into ½-inch slices and divide among the 4 salads.
9. Serve with sweet potato or other vegetable chips.

Smoky Roasted Veggie Chips

Servings: 4

Cooking Time: 40 Minutes

Ingredients:
- 2 tbsp butter
- 2 tsp smoked paprika
- 1 tsp dried dill
- Salt and pepper to taste
- 2 carrots, cut into rounds
- 1 parsnip, cut into rounds
- 1 tbsp chopped fresh dill

Directions:

1. Preheat the air fryer to 375°F (190°C). Combine the butter, paprika, dried dill, salt, and pepper in a small pan, over low heat until the butter melts. Put the carrots and parsnip in the frying basket, top with the butter mix, and toss. Air Fry for 20-25 minutes or until the veggies are tender and golden around the edges. Toss with fresh dill and serve.

Polenta

Servings: 4

Cooking Time: 15 Minutes

Ingredients:
- 1 pound polenta
- ¼ cup flour
- oil for misting or cooking spray

Directions:

1. Cut polenta into ½-inch slices.
2. Dip slices in flour to coat well. Spray both sides with oil or cooking spray.
3. Cook at 390°F (200°C) for 5minutes. Turn polenta and spray both sides again with oil.
4. Cook 10 more minutes or until brown and crispy.

Parsnip Fries With Romesco Sauce

Servings: 2

Cooking Time: 24 Minutes

Ingredients:

- Romesco Sauce:
- 1 red bell pepper, halved and seeded
- 1 (1-inch) thick slice of Italian bread, torn into pieces (about 1 to 1½ cups)
- 1 cup almonds, toasted
- olive oil
- ½ Jalapeño pepper, seeded
- 1 tablespoon fresh parsley leaves
- 1 clove garlic
- 2 Roma tomatoes, peeled and seeded (or ⅓ cup canned crushed tomatoes)
- 1 tablespoon red wine vinegar
- ¼ teaspoon smoked paprika
- ½ teaspoon salt
- ¾ cup olive oil
- 3 parsnips, peeled and cut into long strips
- 2 teaspoons olive oil
- salt and freshly ground black pepper

Directions:

1. Preheat the air fryer to 400°F (205°C).
2. Place the red pepper halves, cut side down, in the air fryer basket and air-fry for 10 minutes, or until the skin turns black all over. Remove the pepper from the air fryer and let it cool. When it is cool enough to handle, peel the pepper.
3. Toss the torn bread and almonds with a little olive oil and air-fry for 4 minutes, shaking the basket a couple times throughout the cooking time. When the bread and almonds are nicely toasted, remove them from the air fryer and let them cool for just a minute or two.
4. Combine the toasted bread, almonds, roasted red pepper, Jalapeño pepper, parsley, garlic, tomatoes, vinegar, smoked paprika and salt in a food processor or blender. Process until smooth. With the processor running, add the olive oil through the feed tube until the sauce comes together in a smooth paste that is barely pourable.
5. Toss the parsnip strips with the olive oil, salt and freshly ground black pepper and air-fry at 400°F (205°C) for 10 minutes, shaking the basket a couple times during the cooking process so they brown and cook evenly. Serve the parsnip fries warm with the Romesco sauce to dip into.

Yukon Gold Potato Purée

Servings: 4

Cooking Time: 25 Minutes

Ingredients:

- 1 lb Yukon Gold potatoes, scrubbed and cubed
- 2 tbsp butter, melted
- Salt and pepper to taste
- 1/8 cup whole milk
- ¼ cup cream cheese
- 1 tbsp butter, softened
- ¼ cup chopped dill

Directions:

1. Preheat air fryer at 350°F. Toss the potatoes and melted butter in a bowl, place them in the frying basket, and Air Fry for 13-15 minutes, tossing once. Transfer them into a bowl. Using a fork, mash the potatoes. Stir in salt, pepper, half of the milk, cream cheese, and 1 tbsp of butter until you reach your desired consistency. Garnish with dill to serve.

Vegetable Roast

Servings: 6

Cooking Time: 20 Minutes

Ingredients:

- 2 tbsp dill, chopped
- 2 zucchini, cubed
- 1 red bell pepper, diced
- 2 garlic cloves, sliced
- 2 tbsp olive oil
- ½ tsp salt
- ½ tsp red pepper flakes

Directions:

1. Preheat air fryer to 380°F (195°C). Combine the zucchini, bell pepper, red pepper flakes, dill and garlic with olive oil and salt in a bowl. Pour the mixture into the frying basket and Roast for 14-16 minutes, shaking once. Serve warm.

Herb Roasted Jicama

Servings: 6

Cooking Time: 25 Minutes

Ingredients:

- 1 lb jicama, cut into fries
- ¼ cup olive oil
- Salt and pepper to taste
- 1 garlic clove, minced
- 4 thyme sprigs

Directions:

1. Preheat air fryer to 360°F (180°C). Coat the jicamas with olive oil, salt, pepper, and garlic in a bowl. Pour the jicama fries into the frying basket and top with the thyme sprigs. Roast for 20 minutes, stirring twice. Remove the rosemary sprigs. Serve and enjoy!

Homemade Potato Puffs

Servings: 4
Cooking Time: 15 Minutes

Ingredients:
- 1¾ cups Water
- 4 tablespoons (¼ cup/½ stick) Butter
- 2 cups plus 2 tablespoons Instant mashed potato flakes
- 1½ teaspoons Table salt
- ¾ teaspoon Ground black pepper
- ¼ teaspoon Mild paprika
- ¼ teaspoon Dried thyme
- 1¼ cups Seasoned Italian-style dried bread crumbs (gluten-free, if a concern)
- Olive oil spray

Directions:
1. Heat the water with the butter in a medium saucepan set over medium-low heat just until the butter melts. Do not bring to a boil.
2. Remove the saucepan from the heat and stir in the potato flakes, salt, pepper, paprika, and thyme until smooth. Set aside to cool for 5 minutes.
3. Preheat the air fryer to 400°F (205°C). Spread the bread crumbs on a dinner plate.
4. Scrape up 2 tablespoons of the potato flake mixture and form it into a small, oblong puff, like a little cylinder about 1½ inches long. Gently roll the puff in the bread crumbs until coated on all sides. Set it aside and continue making more, about 12 for the small batch, 18 for the medium batch, or 24 for the large.
5. Coat the potato cylinders with olive oil spray on all sides, then arrange them in the basket in one layer with some air space between them. Air-fry undisturbed for 15 minutes, or until crisp and brown.
6. Gently dump the contents of the basket onto a wire rack. Cool for 5 minutes before serving.

Crispy Cauliflower Puffs

Servings: 12
Cooking Time: 9 Minutes

Ingredients:
- 1½ cups Riced cauliflower
- 1 cup (about 4 ounces) Shredded Monterey Jack cheese
- ¾ cup Seasoned Italian-style panko bread crumbs (gluten-free, if a concern)
- 2 tablespoons plus 1 teaspoon All-purpose flour or potato starch
- 2 tablespoons plus 1 teaspoon Vegetable oil
- 1 plus 1 large yolk Large egg(s)
- ¾ teaspoon Table salt
- Vegetable oil spray

Directions:
1. Preheat the air fryer to 375°F (190°C).
2. Stir the riced cauliflower, cheese, bread crumbs, flour or potato starch, oil, egg(s) and egg yolk (if necessary), and salt in a large bowl to make a thick batter.
3. Using 2 tablespoons of the batter, form a compact ball between your clean, dry palms. Set it aside and continue forming more balls: 7 more for a small batch, 11 more for a medium batch, or 15 more for a large batch.
4. Generously coat the balls on all sides with vegetable oil spray. Set them in the basket with as much air space between them as possible. Air-fry undisturbed for 7 minutes, or until golden brown and crisp. If the machine is at 360°F (180°C), you may need to add 2 minutes to the cooking time.
5. Gently pour the contents of the basket onto a wire rack. Cool the puffs for 5 minutes before serving.

Green Dip With Pine Nuts

Servings: 3
Cooking Time: 30 Minutes

Ingredients:
- 10 oz canned artichokes, chopped
- 2 tsp grated Parmesan cheese
- 10 oz spinach, chopped
- 2 scallions, finely chopped
- ½ cup pine nuts
- ½ cup milk
- 3 tbsp lemon juice
- 2 tsp tapioca flour
- 1 tsp allspice

Directions:
1. Preheat air fryer to 360°F (180°C). Arrange spinach, artichokes, and scallions in a pan. Set aside. In a food processor, blitz the pine nuts, milk, lemon juice, Parmesan cheese, flour, and allspice on high until smooth. Pour it over the veggies and Bake for 20 minutes, stirring every 5 minutes. Serve.

Five-spice Roasted Sweet Potatoes

Servings: 4
Cooking Time: 12 Minutes

Ingredients:
- ½ teaspoon ground cinnamon
- ¼ teaspoon ground cumin
- ¼ teaspoon paprika
- 1 teaspoon chile powder
- ⅛ teaspoon turmeric
- ½ teaspoon salt (optional)
- freshly ground black pepper
- 2 large sweet potatoes, peeled and cut into ¾-inch cubes (about 3 cups)

- 1 tablespoon olive oil

Directions:

1. In a large bowl, mix together cinnamon, cumin, paprika, chile powder, turmeric, salt, and pepper to taste.
2. Add potatoes and stir well.
3. Drizzle the seasoned potatoes with the olive oil and stir until evenly coated.
4. Place seasoned potatoes in the air fryer baking pan or an ovenproof dish that fits inside your air fryer basket.
5. Cook for 6minutes at 390°F (200°C), stop, and stir well.
6. Cook for an additional 6minutes.

Roman Artichokes

Servings: 4

Cooking Time: 12 Minutes

Ingredients:

- 2 9-ounce box(es) frozen artichoke heart quarters, thawed
- 1½ tablespoons Olive oil
- 2 teaspoons Minced garlic
- 1 teaspoon Table salt
- Up to ½ teaspoon Red pepper flakes

Directions:

1. Preheat the air fryer to 400°F (205°C).
2. Gently toss the artichoke heart quarters, oil, garlic, salt, and red pepper flakes in a bowl until the quarters are well coated.
3. When the machine is at temperature, scrape the contents of the bowl into the basket. Spread the artichoke heart quarters out into as close to one layer as possible. Air-fry undisturbed for 8 minutes. Gently toss and rearrange the quarters so that any covered or touching parts are now exposed to the air currents, then air-fry undisturbed for 4 minutes more, until very crisp.
4. Gently pour the contents of the basket onto a wire rack. Cool for a few minutes before serving.

The Ultimate Mac`n´cheese

Servings: 4

Cooking Time: 35 Minutes

Ingredients:

- ¼ cup shredded sharp cheddar cheese
- ¼ cup grated Swiss cheese
- ¼ cup grated Parmesan
- ½ lb cooked elbow macaroni
- 3 tbsp butter, divided
- 1 sweet onion, diced
- 2 tsp red chili
- 1 tbsp flour
- 4 oz mascarpone cheese
- ¼ cup whole milk
- ¼ cup bread crumbs

Directions:

1. Melt 2 tbsp of butter in a skillet over -high heat for 30 seconds. Add in onions and red chili and stir-fry for 3 minutes until they´re translucent. Stir in flour until the sauce thickens. Stir in all cheeses and milk, then mix in macaroni. Spoon macaroni mixture into a greased cake pan. Preheat air fryer at 375ºF. Mix the breadcrumbs and the remaining butter in a bowl. Scatter over pasta mixture. Place cake pan in the frying basket and Bake for 15 minutes. Let sit for 10 minutes before serving.

Lemony Green Bean Sautée

Servings: 6

Cooking Time: 15 Minutes

Ingredients:

- 1 tbsp cilantro, chopped
- 1 lb green beans, trimmed
- ½ red onion, sliced
- 2 tbsp olive oil
- Salt and pepper to taste
- 1 tbsp grapefruit juice
- 6 lemon wedges

Directions:

1. Preheat air fryer to 360°F (180°C). Coat the green beans, red onion, olive oil, salt, pepper, cilantro and grapefruit juice in a bowl. Pour the mixture into the air fryer and Bake for 5 minutes. Stir well and cook for 5 minutes more. Serve with lemon wedges. Enjoy!

Salt And Pepper Baked Potatoes

Cooking Time: 40 Minutes

Servings: 4

Ingredients:

- 1 to 2 tablespoons olive oil
- 4 medium russet potatoes (about 9 to 10 ounces each)
- salt and coarsely ground black pepper
- butter, sour cream, chopped fresh chives, scallions or bacon bits (optional)

Directions:

1. Preheat the air fryer to 400°F (180°C).
2. Rub the olive oil all over the potatoes and season them generously with salt and coarsely ground black pepper. Pierce all sides of the potatoes several times with the tines of a fork.
3. Air-fry for 40 minutes, turning the potatoes over halfway through the cooking time.
4. Serve the potatoes, split open with butter, sour cream, fresh chives, scallions or bacon bits.

Air-fried Potato Salad

Servings: 4

Cooking Time: 15 Minutes

Ingredients:

- 1⅓ pounds Yellow potatoes, such as Yukon Golds, cut into ½-inch chunks
- 1 large Sweet white onion(s), such as Vidalia, chopped into ½-inch pieces
- 1 tablespoon plus 2 teaspoons Olive oil
- ¾ cup Thinly sliced celery
- 6 tablespoons Regular or low-fat mayonnaise (gluten-free, if a concern)
- 2½ tablespoons Apple cider vinegar
- 1½ teaspoons Dijon mustard (gluten-free, if a concern)
- ¾ teaspoon Table salt
- ¼ teaspoon Ground black pepper

Directions:

1. Preheat the air fryer to 400°F (205°C).
2. Toss the potatoes, onion(s), and oil in a large bowl until the vegetables are glistening with oil.
3. When the machine is at temperature, transfer the vegetables to the basket, spreading them out into as even a layer as you can. Air-fry for 15 minutes, tossing and rearranging the vegetables every 3 minutes so that all surfaces get exposed to the air currents, until the vegetables are tender and even browned at the edges.
4. Pour the contents of the basket into a serving bowl. Cool for at least 5 minutes or up to 30 minutes. Add the celery, mayonnaise, vinegar, mustard, salt, and pepper. Stir well to coat. The potato salad can be made in advance; cover and refrigerate for up to 4 days.

Dauphinoise (potatoes Au Gratin)

Servings: 4

Cooking Time: 30 Minutes

Ingredients:

- ½ cup grated cheddar cheese
- 3 peeled potatoes, sliced
- ½ cup milk
- ½ cup heavy cream
- Salt and pepper to taste
- 1 tsp ground nutmeg

Directions:

1. Preheat air fryer to 350°F (175°C). Place the milk, heavy cream, salt, pepper, and nutmeg in a bowl and mix well. Dip in the potato slices and arrange on a baking dish. Spoon the remaining mixture over the potatoes. Scatter the grated cheddar cheese on top. Place the baking dish in the air fryer and Bake for 20 minutes. Serve warm and enjoy!

Stuffed Onions

Servings: 6

Cooking Time: 27 Minutes

Ingredients:

- 6 Small 3½- to 4-ounce yellow or white onions
- Olive oil spray
- 6 ounces Bulk sweet Italian sausage meat (gluten-free, if a concern)
- 9 Cherry tomatoes, chopped
- 3 tablespoons Seasoned Italian-style dried bread crumbs (gluten-free, if a concern)
- 3 tablespoons (about ½ ounce) Finely grated Parmesan cheese

Directions:

1. Preheat the air fryer to 325°F (160°C) (or 330°F (165°C), if that's the closest setting).
2. Cut just enough off the root ends of the onions so they will stand up on a cutting board when this end is turned down. Carefully peel off just the brown, papery skin. Now cut the top quarter off each and place the onion back on the cutting board with this end facing up. Use a flatware spoon (preferably a serrated grapefruit spoon) or a melon baller to scoop out the "insides" (interior layers) of the onion, leaving enough of the bottom and side walls so that the onion does not collapse. Depending on the thickness of the layers in the onion, this may be one or two of those layers—or even three, if they're very thin.
3. Coat the insides and outsides of the onions with olive oil spray. Set the onion "shells" in the basket and air-fry for 15 minutes.
4. Meanwhile, make the filling. Set a medium skillet over medium heat for a couple of minutes, then crumble in the sausage meat. Cook, stirring often, until browned, about 4 minutes. Transfer the contents of the skillet to a medium bowl (leave the fat behind in the skillet or add it to the bowl, depending on your cross-trainer regimen). Stir in the tomatoes, bread crumbs, and cheese until well combined.
5. When the onions are ready, use a nonstick-safe spatula to gently transfer them to a cutting board. Increase the air fryer's temperature to 350°F (175°C).
6. Pack the sausage mixture into the onion shells, gently compacting the filling and mounding it up at the top.
7. When the machine is at temperature, set the onions stuffing side up in the basket with at least ¼ inch between them. Air-fry for 12 minutes, or until lightly browned and sizzling hot.
8. Use a nonstick-safe spatula, and perhaps a flatware fork for balance, to transfer the onions to a cutting board or serving platter. Cool for 5 minutes before serving.

Baked Shishito Peppers

Servings: 2

Cooking Time: 15 Minutes

Ingredients:

- 6 oz shishito peppers
- 1 tsp olive oil
- 1 tsp salt
- ¼ cup soy sauce

Directions:

1. Preheat air fryer at 375ºF (190°C). Combine all ingredients in a bowl. Place peppers in the frying basket and Bake for 8 minutes until the peppers are blistered, shaking once. Serve with soy sauce for dipping.

Grilled Lime Scallions

Servings: 6

Cooking Time: 15 Minutes

Ingredients:

- 2 bunches of scallions
- 1 tbsp olive oil
- 2 tsp lime juice
- Salt and pepper to taste
- ¼ tsp Italian seasoning
- 2 tsp lime zest

Directions:

1. Preheat air fryer to 370ºF. Trim the scallions and cut them in half lengthwise. Place them in a bowl and add olive oil and lime juice. Toss to coat. Place the mix in the frying basket and Air Fry for 7 minutes, tossing once. Transfer to a serving dish and stir in salt, pepper, Italian seasoning and lime zest. Serve immediately.

Perfect Broccolini

Servings: 4

Cooking Time: 15 Minutes

Ingredients:

- 1 pound Broccolini
- Olive oil spray
- Coarse sea salt or kosher salt

Directions:

1. Preheat the air fryer to 375°F (190°C).
2. Place the broccolini on a cutting board. Generously coat it with olive oil spray, turning the vegetables and rearranging them before spraying a couple of times more, to make sure everything's well coated, even the flowery bits in their heads.
3. When the machine is at temperature, pile the broccolini in the basket, spreading it into as close to one layer as you can. Air-fry for 5 minutes, tossing once to get any covered or touching parts exposed to the air currents, until the leaves begin to get brown and even crisp. Watch carefully and use this visual cue to know the moment to stop the cooking.
4. Transfer the broccolini to a platter. Spread out the pieces and sprinkle them with salt to taste.

Tofu & Broccoli Salad

Servings: 4

Cooking Time: 17 Minutes

Ingredients:

- Broccoli Salad
- 4 cups fresh broccoli, cut into bite-size pieces
- ½ cup red onion, chopped
- ⅓ cup raisins or dried cherries
- ¾ cup sliced almonds
- ½ cup Asian-style salad dressing
- Tofu
- 4 ounces extra firm tofu
- 1 teaspoon smoked paprika
- 1 teaspoon onion powder
- ¼ teaspoon salt
- 2 tablespoons cornstarch
- 1 tablespoon extra virgin olive oil

Directions:

1. Place several folded paper towels on a plate and set tofu on top. Cover tofu with another folded paper towel, put another plate on top, and add heavy items such as canned goods to weigh it down. Press tofu for 30 minutes.
2. While tofu is draining, combine all salad ingredients in a large bowl. Toss together well, cover, and chill until ready to serve.
3. Cut the tofu into small cubes, about ¼-inch thick. Sprinkle the cubes top and bottom with the paprika, onion powder, and salt.
4. Place cornstarch in small plastic bag, add tofu, and shake until cubes are well coated.
5. Place olive oil in another small plastic bag, add coated tofu, and shake to coat well.
6. Cook at 330°F (165°C) for 17 minutes or until as crispy as you like.
7. To serve, stir chilled salad well, divide among 4 plates, and top with fried tofu.

Appetizers And Snacks

Muffuletta Sliders

Servings: 8
Cooking Time: 7 Minutes

Ingredients:

- ¼ pound thin-sliced deli ham
- ¼ pound thin-sliced pastrami
- 4 ounces low-fat mozzarella cheese, grated or sliced thin
- 8 slider buns
- olive oil for misting
- 1 tablespoon sesame seeds
- Olive Mix
- ¼ cup sliced black olives
- ½ cup sliced green olives with pimentos
- ¼ cup chopped kalamata olives
- 1 teaspoon red wine vinegar
- ¼ teaspoon basil
- ⅛ teaspoon garlic powder

Directions:

1. In a small bowl, stir together all the Olive Mix ingredients.
2. Divide the meats and cheese into 8 equal portions. To assemble sliders, stack in this order: bottom bun, ham, pastrami, 2 tablespoons olive mix, cheese, top bun.
3. Mist tops of sliders lightly with oil. Sprinkle with sesame seeds.
4. Cooking 4 at a time, place sliders in air fryer basket and cook at 360°F (1805°C) for 7 minutes to melt cheese and heat through.

Garlic Wings

Servings: 4
Cooking Time: 15 Minutes

Ingredients:

- 2 pounds chicken wings
- oil for misting
- cooking spray
- Marinade
- 1 cup buttermilk
- 2 cloves garlic, mashed flat
- 1 teaspoon Worcestershire sauce
- 1 bay leaf
- Coating
- 1½ cups grated Parmesan cheese
- ¾ cup breadcrumbs
- 1½ tablespoons garlic powder
- ½ teaspoon salt

Directions:

1. Mix all marinade ingredients together.
2. Remove wing tips (the third joint) and discard or freeze for stock. Cut the remaining wings at the joint and toss them into the marinade, stirring to coat well. Refrigerate for at least an hour but no more than 8 hours.
3. When ready to cook, combine all coating ingredients in a shallow dish.
4. Remove wings from marinade, shaking off excess, and roll in coating mixture. Press coating into wings so that it sticks well. Spray wings with oil.
5. Spray air fryer basket with cooking spray. Place wings in basket in single layer, close but not touching.
6. Cook at 360°F (180°C) for 15minutes or until chicken is done and juices run clear.
7. Repeat previous step to cook remaining wings.

Jalapeño & Mozzarella Stuffed Mushrooms

Servings: 4
Cooking Time: 30 Minutes

Ingredients:

- 16 button mushrooms
- 1/3 cup salsa
- 3 garlic cloves, minced
- 1 onion, finely chopped
- 1 jalapeño pepper, minced
- ⅛ tsp cayenne pepper
- 3 tbsp shredded mozzarella
- 2 tsp olive oil

Directions:

1. Preheat air fryer to 350°F (175°C). Cut the stem off the mushrooms, then slice them finely. Set the caps aside. Combine the salsa, garlic, onion, jalapeño, cayenne, and mozzarella cheese in a bowl, then add the stems. Fill the mushroom caps with the mixture, making sure to overfill so the mix is coming out of the top. Drizzle with olive oil. Place the caps in the air fryer and Bake for 8-12 minutes. The filling should be hot and the mushrooms soft. Serve warm.

Prosciutto Mozzarella Bites

Servings: 8

Cooking Time: 6 Minutes

Ingredients:

- 8 pieces full-fat mozzarella string cheese
- 8 thin slices prosciutto
- 16 basil leaves

Directions:

1. Preheat the air fryer to 360°F (180°C).
2. Cut the string cheese in half across the center, not lengthwise. Do the same with the prosciutto.
3. Place a piece of prosciutto onto a clean workspace. Top the prosciutto with a basil leaf and then a piece of string cheese. Roll up the string cheese inside the prosciutto and secure with a wooden toothpick. Repeat with the remaining cheese sticks.
4. Place the prosciutto mozzarella bites into the air fryer basket and cook for 6 minutes, checking for doneness at 4 minutes.

Avocado Fries

Servings: 8

Cooking Time: 8 Minutes

Ingredients:

- 2 medium avocados, firm but ripe
- 1 large egg
- ½ teaspoon garlic powder
- ¼ teaspoon cayenne pepper
- ¼ teaspoon salt
- ¾ cup almond flour
- ½ cup finely grated Parmesan cheese
- ½ cup gluten-free breadcrumbs

Directions:

1. Preheat the air fryer to 370°F (185°C).
2. Rinse the outside of the avocado with water. Slice the avocado in half, slice it in half again, and then slice it in half once more to get 8 slices. Remove the outer skin. Repeat for the other avocado. Set the avocado slices aside.
3. In a small bowl, whisk the egg, garlic powder, cayenne pepper, and salt in a small bowl. Set aside.
4. In a separate bowl, pour the almond flour.
5. In a third bowl, mix the Parmesan cheese and breadcrumbs.
6. Carefully roll the avocado slices in the almond flour, then dip them in the egg wash, and coat them in the cheese and breadcrumb topping. Repeat until all 16 fries are coated.
7. Liberally spray the air fryer basket with olive oil spray and place the avocado fries into the basket, leaving a little space around the sides between fries. Depending on the size of your air fryer, you may need to cook these in batches.
8. Cook fries for 8 minutes, or until the outer coating turns light brown.
9. Carefully remove, repeat with remaining slices, and then serve warm.

Buffalo Bites

Servings: 16

Cooking Time: 12 Minutes

Ingredients:

- 1 pound ground chicken
- 8 tablespoons buffalo wing sauce
- 2 ounces Gruyère cheese, cut into 16 cubes
- 1 tablespoon maple syrup

Directions:

1. Mix 4 tablespoons buffalo wing sauce into all the ground chicken.
2. Shape chicken into a log and divide into 16 equal portions.
3. With slightly damp hands, mold each chicken portion around a cube of cheese and shape into a firm ball. When you have shaped 8 meatballs, place them in air fryer basket.
4. Cook at 390°F (200°C) for approximately 5 minutes. Shake basket, reduce temperature to 360°F (180°C), and cook for 5 minutes longer.
5. While the first batch is cooking, shape remaining chicken and cheese into 8 more meatballs.
6. Repeat step 4 to cook second batch of meatballs.
7. In a medium bowl, mix the remaining 4 tablespoons of buffalo wing sauce with the maple syrup. Add all the cooked meatballs and toss to coat.
8. Place meatballs back into air fryer basket and cook at 390°F (200°C) for 2 minutes to set the glaze. Skewer each with a toothpick and serve.

Mouth-watering Vegetable Casserole

Servings: 3

Cooking Time: 45 Minutes

Ingredients:

- 1 red bell pepper, chopped
- ½ lb okra, trimmed
- 1 red onion, chopped
- 1 can diced tomatoes
- 2 tbsp balsamic vinegar
- 1 tbsp allspice
- 1 tsp ground cumin
- 1 cup baby spinach

Directions:

1. Preheat air fryer to 400°F (205°C). Combine the bell pepper, red onion, okra, tomatoes and juices, balsamic vinegar, allspice, and cumin in a baking pan and Roast for 25 minutes, stirring every 10 minutes. Stir in spinach and Roast for another 5 minutes. Serve warm.

Spicy Chicken And Pepper Jack Cheese Bites

Servings: 8
Cooking Time: 8 Minutes
Ingredients:
- 8 ounces cream cheese, softened
- 2 cups grated pepper jack cheese
- 1 Jalapeño pepper, diced
- 2 scallions, minced
- 1 teaspoon paprika
- 2 teaspoons salt, divided
- 3 cups shredded cooked chicken
- ¼ cup all-purpose flour*
- 2 eggs, lightly beaten
- 1 cup panko breadcrumbs*
- olive oil, in a spray bottle
- salsa

Directions:
1. Beat the cream cheese in a bowl until it is smooth and easy to stir. Add the pepper jack cheese, Jalapeño pepper, scallions, paprika and 1 teaspoon of salt. Fold in the shredded cooked chicken and combine well. Roll this mixture into 1-inch balls.
2. Set up a dredging station with three shallow dishes. Place the flour into one shallow dish. Place the eggs into a second shallow dish. Finally, combine the panko breadcrumbs and remaining teaspoon of salt in a third dish.
3. Coat the chicken cheese balls by rolling each ball in the flour first, then dip them into the eggs and finally roll them in the panko breadcrumbs to coat all sides. Refrigerate for at least 30 minutes.
4. Preheat the air fryer to 400°F (205°C).
5. Spray the chicken cheese balls with oil and air-fry in batches for 8 minutes. Shake the basket a few times throughout the cooking process to help the balls brown evenly.
6. Serve hot with salsa on the side.

Vegetarian Fritters With Green Dip

Servings: 6
Cooking Time: 40 Minutes
Ingredients:
- ½ cup grated carrots
- ½ cup grated zucchini
- ¼ cup minced yellow onion
- 1 garlic clove, minced
- 1 large egg
- ¼ cup flour
- ¼ cup bread crumbs
- Salt and pepper to taste
- ½ tsp ground cumin
- ½ avocado, peeled and pitted
- ½ cup plain Greek yogurt
- 1 tsp lime juice
- 1 tbsp white vinegar
- ¼ cup chopped cilantro

Directions:
1. Preheat air fryer to 375°F (190°C). Combine carrots, zucchini, onion, garlic, egg, flour, bread crumbs, salt, pepper, and cumin in a large bowl. Scoop out 12 equal portions of the vegetables and form them into patties. Arrange the patties on the greased basket. Air Fry for 5 minutes, then flip the patties. Air Fry for another 5 minutes. Check if the fritters are golden and cooked through. If more time is needed, cook for another 3-5 minutes.
2. While the fritters are cooking, prepare the avocado sauce. Mash the avocado in a small bowl to the desired texture. Stir in yogurt, white vinegar, chopped cilantro, lime juice, and salt. When the fritter is done, transfer to a serving plate along with the avocado sauce for dipping. Serve warm and enjoy.

Rich Egg-fried Cauliflower Rice

Servings: 4
Cooking Time: 45 Minutes
Ingredients:
- 2 ½ cups riced cauliflower
- 2 tsp sesame oil
- 1 green bell pepper, diced
- 1 cup peas
- 1 cup diced carrots
- 2 spring onions
- Salt and pepper to taste
- 1 tbsp tamari sauce
- 2 eggs, scrambled

Directions:
1. Preheat air fryer to 370°F (185°C). Combine riced cauliflower, bell pepper, peas, carrots, and spring onions in a large bowl. Stir in 1 tsp of sesame oil, salt, and pepper. Grease a baking pan with the remaining tsp of sesame oil. Transfer the rice mixture to the pan and place in the air fryer. Bake for 10 minutes. Remove the pan and drizzle with tamari sauce. Stir in scrambled eggs and serve warm.

Cheesy Spinach Dip(2)

Servings: 8
Cooking Time: 30 Minutes

Ingredients:

- 1 can refrigerated biscuit dough
- 4 oz cream cheese, softened
- ¼ cup mayonnaise
- 1 cup spinach
- 2 oz cooked bacon, crumbled
- 2 scallions, chopped
- 2 cups grated Fontina cheese
- 1 cup grated cheddar
- ½ tsp garlic powder

Directions:

1. Preheat the air fryer to 350°F (175°C). Divide the dough into 8 biscuits and press each one into and up the sides of the silicone muffin cup, then set aside. Combine the cream cheese and mayonnaise and beat until smooth. Stir in the spinach, bacon, scallions, 1 cup of cheddar cheese and garlic powder. Then divide the mixture between the muffin cups. Put them in the basket and top each with 1 tbsp of Fontina cheese. Bake for 8-13 minutes or until the dough is golden and the filling is hot and bubbling. Remove from the air fryer and cool on a wire rack. Serve.

Warm And Salty Edamame

Servings: 4
Cooking Time: 10 Minutes

Ingredients:

- 1 pound Unshelled edamame
- Vegetable oil spray
- ¾ teaspoon Coarse sea salt or kosher salt

Directions:

1. Preheat the air fryer to 400°F (205°C).
2. Place the edamame in a large bowl and lightly coat them with vegetable oil spray. Toss well, spray again, and toss until they are evenly coated.
3. When the machine is at temperature, pour the edamame into the basket and air-fry, tossing the basket quite often to rearrange the edamame, for 7 minutes, or until warm and aromatic. (Air-fry for 10 minutes if the edamame were frozen and not thawed.)
4. Pour the edamame into a bowl and sprinkle the salt on top. Toss well, then set aside for a couple of minutes before serving with an empty bowl on the side for the pods.

Barbecue Chicken Nachos

Servings: 3
Cooking Time: 5 Minutes

Ingredients:

- 3 heaping cups (a little more than 3 ounces) Corn tortilla chips (gluten-free, if a concern)
- ¾ cup Shredded deboned and skinned rotisserie chicken meat (gluten-free, if a concern)
- 3 tablespoons Canned black beans, drained and rinsed
- 9 rings Pickled jalapeño slices
- 4 Small pickled cocktail onions, halved
- 3 tablespoons Barbecue sauce (any sort)
- ¾ cup (about 3 ounces) Shredded Cheddar cheese

Directions:

1. Preheat the air fryer to 400°F (205°C).
2. Cut a circle of parchment paper to line a 6-inch round cake pan for a small air fryer, a 7-inch round cake pan for a medium air fryer, or an 8-inch round cake pan for a large machine.
3. Fill the pan with an even layer of about two-thirds of the chips. Sprinkle the chicken evenly over the chips. Set the pan in the basket and air-fry undisturbed for 2 minutes.
4. Remove the basket from the machine. Scatter the beans, jalapeño rings, and pickled onion halves over the chicken. Drizzle the barbecue sauce over everything, then sprinkle the cheese on top.
5. Return the basket to the machine and air-fry undisturbed for 3 minutes, or until the cheese has melted and is bubbly. Remove the pan from the machine and cool for a couple of minutes before serving.

Spicy Pearl Onion Dip

Servings: 4
Cooking Time: 20 Minutes+chilling Time

Ingredients:

- 2 cups peeled pearl onions
- 3 garlic cloves
- 3 tbsp olive oil
- Salt and pepper to taste
- 1 cup Greek yogurt
- ¼ tsp Worcestershire sauce
- 1 tbsp lemon juice
- ⅛ tsp red pepper flakes
- 1 tbsp chives, chopped

Directions:

1. Preheat air fryer to 360°F (180°C). Place the onions, garlic, and 2 tbsp of olive oil in a bowl and combine until the onions are well coated. Pour the mixture into the frying basket and Roast for 11-13 minutes. Transfer the garlic and onions to your food processor. Pulse the vegetables several times until the onions are minced but still have some chunks.
2. Combine the garlic and onions and the remaining olive oil, along with the salt, yogurt, Worcestershire sauce, lemon juice, black pepper, chives and red pepper flakes in a bowl. Cover and chill for at least 1 hour. Serve with toasted bread if desired.

Mozzarella Sticks

Servings: 4

Cooking Time: 5 Minutes

Ingredients:
- 1 egg
- 1 tablespoon water
- 8 eggroll wraps
- 8 mozzarella string cheese "sticks"
- sauce for dipping

Directions:

1. Beat together egg and water in a small bowl.
2. Lay out egg roll wraps and moisten edges with egg wash.
3. Place one piece of string cheese on each wrap near one end.
4. Fold in sides of egg roll wrap over ends of cheese, and then roll up.
5. Brush outside of wrap with egg wash and press gently to seal well.
6. Place in air fryer basket in single layer and cook 390°F (200°C) for 5 minutes. Cook an additional 1 or 2minutes, if necessary, until they are golden brown and crispy.
7. Serve with your favorite dipping sauce.

Balsamic Grape Dip

Servings: 6

Cooking Time: 25 Minutes

Ingredients:
- 2 cups seedless red grapes
- 1 tbsp balsamic vinegar
- 1 tbsp honey
- 1 cup Greek yogurt
- 2 tbsp milk
- 2 tbsp minced fresh basil

Directions:

1. Preheat air fryer to 380°F (195°C). Add the grapes and balsamic vinegar to the frying basket, then pour honey over and toss to coat. Roast for 8-12 minutes, shriveling the grapes, and take them out of the air fryer. Mix the milk and yogurt together, then gently stir in the grapes and basil. Serve and enjoy!

Basil Feta Crostini

Servings: 4

Cooking Time: 10 Minutes

Ingredients:
- 1 baguette, sliced
- ¼ cup olive oil
- 2 garlic cloves, minced
- 4 oz feta cheese
- 2 tbsp basil, minced

Directions:

1. Preheat air fryer to 380°F (195°C). Combine together the olive oil and garlic in a bowl. Brush it over one side of each slice of bread. Put the bread in a single layer in the frying basket and Bake for 5 minutes. In a small bowl, mix together the feta cheese and basil. Remove the toast from the air fryer, then spread a thin layer of the goat cheese mixture over the top of each piece. Serve.

Fried Apple Wedges

Servings: 4

Cooking Time: 9 Minutes

Ingredients:
- ¼ cup panko breadcrumbs
- ¼ cup pecans
- 1½ teaspoons cinnamon
- 1½ teaspoons brown sugar
- ¼ cup cornstarch
- 1 egg white
- 2 teaspoons water
- 1 medium apple
- oil for misting or cooking spray

Directions:

1. In a food processor, combine panko, pecans, cinnamon, and brown sugar. Process to make small crumbs.
2. Place cornstarch in a plastic bag or bowl with lid. In a shallow dish, beat together the egg white and water until slightly foamy.
3. Preheat air fryer to 390°F (200°C).
4. Cut apple into small wedges. The thickest edge should be no more than ⅜- to ½-inch thick. Cut away the core, but do not peel.
5. Place apple wedges in cornstarch, reseal bag or bowl, and shake to coat.
6. Dip wedges in egg wash, shake off excess, and roll in crumb mixture. Spray with oil.
7. Place apples in air fryer basket in single layer and cook for 5 minutes. Shake basket and break apart any apples that have stuck together. Mist lightly with oil and cook 4 minutes longer, until crispy.

Tasty Roasted Black Olives & Tomatoes

Servings: 6

Cooking Time: 25 Minutes

Ingredients:

- 2 cups grape tomatoes
- 4 garlic cloves, chopped
- ½ red onion, chopped
- 1 cup black olives
- 1 cup green olives
- 1 tbsp thyme, minced
- 1 tbsp oregano, minced
- 2 tbsp olive oil
- ½ tsp salt

Directions:

1. Preheat air fryer to 380°F (195°C). Add all ingredients to a bowl and toss well to coat. Pour the mixture into the frying basket and Roast for 10 minutes. Stir the mixture, then Roast for an additional 10 minutes. Serve and enjoy!

Honey-lemon Chicken Wings

Servings: 4

Cooking Time: 30 Minutes

Ingredients:

- 8 chicken wings
- Salt and pepper to taste
- 3 tbsp honey
- 1 tbsp lemon juice
- 1 tbsp chicken stock
- 2 cloves garlic, minced
- 2 thinly sliced green onions
- ¾ cup barbecue sauce
- 1 tbsp sesame seeds

Directions:

1. Preheat air fryer to 390°F (200°C). Season the wings with salt and pepper and place them in the frying basket. Air Fry for 20 minutes. Shake the basket a couple of times during cooking. In a bowl, mix the honey, lemon juice, chicken stock, and garlic. Take the wings out of the fryer and place them in a baking pan. Add the sauce and toss, coating completely. Put the pan in the air fryer and Air Fry for 4-5 minutes until golden and cooked through, with no pink showing. Top with green onions and sesame seeds, then serve with BBQ sauce.

Shrimp Egg Rolls

Servings: 8

Cooking Time: 10 Minutes

Ingredients:

- 1 tablespoon vegetable oil
- ½ head green or savoy cabbage, finely shredded
- 1 cup shredded carrots
- 1 cup canned bean sprouts, drained
- 1 tablespoon soy sauce
- ½ teaspoon sugar
- 1 teaspoon sesame oil
- ¼ cup hoisin sauce
- freshly ground black pepper
- 1 pound cooked shrimp, diced
- ¼ cup scallions
- 8 egg roll wrappers
- vegetable oil
- duck sauce

Directions:

1. Preheat a large sauté pan over medium-high heat. Add the oil and cook the cabbage, carrots and bean sprouts until they start to wilt – about 3 minutes. Add the soy sauce, sugar, sesame oil, hoisin sauce and black pepper. Sauté for a few more minutes. Stir in the shrimp and scallions and cook until the vegetables are just tender. Transfer the mixture to a colander in a bowl to cool. Press or squeeze out any excess water from the filling so that you don't end up with soggy egg rolls.

2. To make the egg rolls, place the egg roll wrappers on a flat surface with one of the points facing towards you so they look like diamonds. Dividing the filling evenly between the eight wrappers, spoon the mixture onto the center of the egg roll wrappers. Spread the filling across the center of the wrappers from the left corner to the right corner, but leave 2 inches from each corner empty. Brush the empty sides of the wrapper with a little water. Fold the bottom corner of the wrapper tightly up over the filling, trying to avoid making any air pockets. Fold the left corner in toward the center and then the right corner toward the center. It should now look like an envelope. Tightly roll the egg roll from the bottom to the top open corner. Press to seal the egg roll together, brushing with a little extra water if need be. Repeat this technique with all 8 egg rolls.

3. Preheat the air fryer to 370°F (185°C).

4. Spray or brush all sides of the egg rolls with vegetable oil. Air-fry four egg rolls at a time for 10 minutes, turning them over halfway through the cooking time.

5. Serve hot with duck sauce or your favorite dipping sauce.

Za'atar Garbanzo Beans

Servings: 6

Cooking Time: 12 Minutes

Ingredients:

- One 14.5-ounce can garbanzo beans, drained and rinsed
- 1 tablespoon extra-virgin olive oil
- 6 teaspoons za'atar seasoning mix
- 2 tablespoons chopped parsley
- Salt and pepper, to taste

Directions:

1. Preheat the air fryer to 390°F (200°C).
2. In a medium bowl, toss the garbanzo beans with olive oil and za'atar seasoning.
3. Pour the beans into the air fryer basket and cook for 12 minutes, or until toasted as you like. Stir every 3 minutes while roasting.
4. Remove the beans from the air fryer basket into a serving bowl, top with fresh chopped parsley, and season with salt and pepper.

Beef Steak Sliders

Servings: 8

Cooking Time: 22 Minutes

Ingredients:

- 1 pound top sirloin steaks, about ¾-inch thick
- salt and pepper
- 2 large onions, thinly sliced
- 1 tablespoon extra-light olive oil
- 8 slider buns
- Horseradish Mayonnaise
- 1 cup light mayonnaise
- 4 teaspoons prepared horseradish
- 2 teaspoons Worcestershire sauce
- 1 teaspoon coarse brown mustard

Directions:

1. Place steak in air fryer basket and cook at 390°F (200°C) for 6 minutes. Turn and cook 6 more minutes for medium rare. If you prefer your steak medium, continue cooking for 3 minutes.
2. While the steak is cooking, prepare the Horseradish Mayonnaise by mixing all ingredients together.
3. When steak is cooked, remove from air fryer, sprinkle with salt and pepper to taste, and set aside to rest.
4. Toss the onion slices with the oil and place in air fryer basket. Cook at 390°F (200°C) for 7 minutes, until onion rings are soft and browned.
5. Slice steak into very thin slices.
6. Spread slider buns with the horseradish mayo and pile on the meat and onions. Serve with remaining horseradish dressing for dipping.

Skinny Fries

Servings: 2

Cooking Time: 15 Minutes

Ingredients:

- 2 to 3 russet potatoes, peeled and cut into ¼-inch sticks
- 2 to 3 teaspoons olive or vegetable oil
- salt

Directions:

1. Cut the potatoes into ¼-inch strips. (A mandolin with a julienne blade is really helpful here.) Rinse the potatoes with cold water several times and let them soak in cold water for at least 10 minutes or as long as overnight.
2. Preheat the air fryer to 380°F (195°C).
3. Drain and dry the potato sticks really well, using a clean kitchen towel. Toss the fries with the oil in a bowl and then air-fry the fries in two batches at 380°F (195°C) for 15 minutes, shaking the basket a couple of times while they cook.
4. Add the first batch of French fries back into the air fryer basket with the finishing batch and let everything warm through for a few minutes. As soon as the fries are done, season them with salt and transfer to a plate or basket. Serve them warm with ketchup or your favorite dip.

Rich Clam Spread

Servings: 6

Cooking Time: 40 Minutes

Ingredients:

- 2 cans chopped clams in clam juice
- 1/3 cup panko bread crumbs
- 1 garlic clove, minced
- 1 tbsp olive oil
- 1 tbsp lemon juice
- ¼ tsp hot sauce
- 1 tsp Worcestershire sauce
- ½ tsp shallot powder
- ¼ tsp dried dill
- Salt and pepper to taste
- ½ tsp sweet paprika
- 4 tsp grated Parmesan cheese
- 2 celery stalks, chopped

Directions:

1. Completely drain one can of clams. Add them to a bowl along with the entire can of clams, breadcrumbs, garlic, olive oil, lemon juice, Worcestershire sauce, hot sauce,

shallot powder, dill, pepper, salt, paprika, and 2 tbsp Parmesan. Combine well and set aside for 10 minutes. After that time, put the mixture in a greased baking dish.

2. Preheat air fryer to 325°F (160°C). Put the dish in the air fryer and Bake for 10 minutes. Sprinkle the remaining paprika and Parmesan, and continue to cook until golden brown on top, 8-10 minutes. Serve hot along with celery sticks.

Cauliflower "tater" Tots

Servings: 6

Cooking Time: 10 Minutes

Ingredients:

- 1 head of cauliflower
- 2 eggs
- ¼ cup all-purpose flour*
- ½ cup grated Parmesan cheese
- 1 teaspoon salt
- freshly ground black pepper
- vegetable or olive oil, in a spray bottle

Directions:

1. Grate the head of cauliflower with a box grater or finely chop it in a food processor. You should have about 3½ cups. Place the chopped cauliflower in the center of a clean kitchen towel and twist the towel tightly to squeeze all the water out of the cauliflower. (This can be done in two batches to make it easier to drain all the water from the cauliflower.)

2. Place the squeezed cauliflower in a large bowl. Add the eggs, flour, Parmesan cheese, salt and freshly ground black pepper. Shape the cauliflower into small cylinders or "tater tot" shapes, rolling roughly one tablespoon of the mixture at a time. Place the tots on a cookie sheet lined with paper towel to absorb any residual moisture. Spray the cauliflower tots all over with oil.

3. Preheat the air fryer to 400°F (205°C).

4. Air-fry the tots at 400°F (205°C), one layer at a time for 10 minutes, turning them over for the last few minutes of the cooking process for even browning. Season with salt and black pepper. Serve hot with your favorite dipping sauce.

Brie-currant & Bacon Spread

Servings: 6

Cooking Time: 30 Minutes

Ingredients:

- 4 oz cream cheese, softened
- 3 tbsp mayonnaise
- 1 cup diced Brie cheese
- ½ tsp dried thyme
- 4 oz cooked bacon, crumbled
- 1/3 cup dried currants

Directions:

1. Preheat the air fryer to 350°F (175°C). Beat the cream cheese with the mayo until well blended. Stir in the Brie, thyme, bacon, and currants and pour the dip mix in a 6-inch round pan. Put the pan in the fryer and Air Fry for 10-12 minutes, stirring once until the dip is melting and bubbling. Serve warm.

Cayenne-spiced Roasted Pecans

Servings: 4

Cooking Time: 15 Minutes

Ingredients:

- ¼ tsp chili powder
- Salt and pepper to taste
- ⅛ tsp cayenne pepper
- 1 tsp cumin powder
- 1 tsp cinnamon powder
- ⅛ tsp garlic powder
- ⅛ tsp onion powder
- 1 cup raw pecans
- 2 tbsp butter, melted
- 1 tsp honey

Directions:

1. Preheat air fryer to 300°F (150°C). Whisk together black pepper, chili powder, salt, cayenne pepper, cumin, garlic powder, cinnamon, and onion powder. Set to the side. Toss pecans, butter, and honey in a medium bowl, then toss in the spice mixture. Pour pecans in the frying basket and toast for 3 minutes. Stir the pecans and toast for another 3 to 5 minutes until the nuts are crisp. Cool and serve.

Roasted Jalapeño Salsa Verde

Servings: 4

Cooking Time: 20 Minutes

Ingredients:

- ¾ lb fresh tomatillos, husked
- 1 jalapeño, stem removed
- 4 green onions, sliced
- 3 garlic cloves, peeled
- ½ tsp salt
- 1 tsp lime juice
- ¼ tsp apple cider vinegar
- ¼ cup cilantro leaves

Directions:

1. Preheat air fryer to 400°F. Add tomatillos and jalapeño to the frying basket and Bake for 5 minutes. Put in green onions and garlic and Bake for 5 more minutes. Transfer it into a food processor along with salt, lime juice, vinegar and cilantro and blend until the sauce is finely chopped. Pour it into a small sealable container and refrigerate it until ready to use up to five days.

Bbq Chips

Servings: 2

Cooking Time: 30 Minutes

Ingredients:

- 1 scrubbed russet potato, sliced
- ½ tsp smoked paprika
- ¼ tsp chili powder
- ¼ tsp garlic powder
- 1/8 tsp onion powder
- ¼ tbsp smoked paprika
- 1/8 tsp light brown sugar
- Salt and pepper to taste
- 2 tsp olive oil

Directions:

1. Preheat air fryer at 400ºF. Combine all seasoning in a bowl. Set aside. In another bowl, mix potato chips, olive oil, black pepper, and salt until coated. Place potato chips in the frying basket and Air Fry for 17 minutes, shaking 3 times. Transfer it into a bowl. Sprinkle with the bbq mixture and let sit for 15 minutes. Serve immediately.

Roasted Red Pepper Dip

Servings: 2

Cooking Time: 15 Minutes

Ingredients:

- 2 Medium-size red bell pepper(s)
- 1¾ cups (one 15-ounce can) Canned white beans, drained and rinsed
- 1 tablespoon Fresh oregano leaves, packed
- 3 tablespoons Olive oil
- 1 tablespoon Lemon juice
- ½ teaspoon Table salt
- ½ teaspoon Ground black pepper

Directions:

1. Preheat the air fryer to 400°F (205°C).
2. Set the pepper(s) in the basket and air-fry undisturbed for 15 minutes, until blistered and even blackened.
3. Use kitchen tongs to transfer the pepper(s) to a zip-closed plastic bag or small bowl. Seal the bag or cover the bowl with plastic wrap. Set aside for 20 minutes.
4. Peel each pepper, then stem it, cut it in half, and remove all its seeds and their white membranes.
5. Set the pieces of the pepper in a food processor. Add the beans, oregano, olive oil, lemon juice, salt, and pepper. Cover and process until smooth, stopping the machine at least once to scrape down the inside of the canister. Scrape the dip into a bowl and serve warm, or cover and refrigerate for up to 3 days (although the dip tastes best if it's allowed to come back to room temperature).

Crunchy Spicy Chickpeas

Servings: 6

Cooking Time: 12 Minutes

Ingredients:

- 2½ cups Canned chickpeas, drained and rinsed
- 2½ tablespoons Vegetable or canola oil
- up to 1 tablespoon Cajun or jerk dried seasoning blend (see here for a Cajun blend, here for a jerk blend)
- up to ¾ teaspoon Table salt (optional)

Directions:

1. Preheat the air fryer to 400°F (205°C).
2. Toss the chickpeas, oil, seasoning blend, and salt (if using) in a large bowl until the chickpeas are evenly coated.
3. When the machine is at temperature, pour the chickpeas into the basket. Air-fry for 12 minutes, removing the basket at the 4- and 8-minute marks to toss and rearrange the chickpeas, until very aromatic and perhaps sizzling but not burned.
4. Pour the chickpeas into a large serving bowl. Cool for a couple of minutes, gently stirring once, before you dive in.

Plantain Chips

Servings: 2

Cooking Time: 14 Minutes

Ingredients:

- 1 large green plantain
- 2½ cups filtered water, divided
- 2 teaspoons sea salt, divided

Directions:

1. Slice the plantain into 1-inch pieces. Place the plantains into a large bowl, cover with 2 cups water and 1 teaspoon salt. Soak the plantains for 30 minutes; then remove and pat dry.
2. Preheat the air fryer to 390°F (200°C).
3. Place the plantain pieces into the air fryer basket, leaving space between the plantain rounds. Cook the plantains for 5 minutes, and carefully remove them from the air fryer basket.
4. Add the remaining water to a small bowl.
5. Using a small drinking glass, dip the bottom of the glass into the water and mash the warm plantains until they're ¼-inch thick. Return the plantains to the air fryer basket, sprinkle with the remaining sea salt, and spray lightly with cooking spray.
6. Cook for another 6 to 8 minutes, or until lightly golden brown edges appear.

Artichoke Samosas

Servings: 6

Cooking Time: 25 Minutes

Ingredients:

- ½ cup minced artichoke hearts
- ¼ cup ricotta cheese
- 1 egg white
- 3 tbsp grated mozzarella
- ½ tsp dried thyme
- 6 phyllo dough sheets
- 2 tbsp melted butter
- 1 cup mango chutney

Directions:

1. Preheat air fryer to 400°F (205°C). Mix together ricotta cheese, egg white, artichoke hearts, mozzarella cheese, and thyme in a small bowl until well blended. When you bring out the phyllo dough, cover it with a damp kitchen towel so that it doesn't dry out while you are working with it. Take one sheet of phyllo and place it on the work surface.
2. Cut it into thirds lengthwise. At the base of each strip, place about 1 ½ tsp of filling. Fold the bottom right-hand tip of the strip over to the left-hand side to make a triangle. Continue flipping and folding triangles along the strip. Brush the triangle with butter to seal the edges. Place triangles in the greased frying basket and Bake until golden and crisp, 4 minutes. Serve with mango chutney.

Onion Ring Nachos

Servings: 3

Cooking Time: 8 Minutes

Ingredients:

- ¾ pound Frozen breaded (not battered) onion rings (do not thaw)
- 1½ cups (about 6 ounces) Shredded Cheddar, Monterey Jack, or Swiss cheese, or a purchased Tex-Mex blend
- Up to 12 Pickled jalapeño rings

Directions:

1. Preheat the air fryer to 400°F (205°C).
2. When the machine is at temperature, spread the onion rings in the basket in a fairly even layer. Air-fry undisturbed for 6 minutes, or until crisp. Remove the basket from the machine.
3. Cut a circle of parchment paper to line a 6-inch round cake pan for a small air fryer, a 7-inch round cake pan for a medium air fryer, or an 8-inch round cake pan for a large machine.
4. Pour the onion rings into a fairly even layer in the cake pan, then sprinkle the cheese evenly over them. Dot with the jalapeño rings.
5. Set the pan in the basket and air-fry undisturbed for 2 minutes, until the cheese has melted and is bubbling.
6. Remove the pan from the basket. Cool for 5 minutes before serving.

Sandwiches And Burgers Recipes

Inside Out Cheeseburgers

Servings: 2

Cooking Time: 20 Minutes

Ingredients:

- ¾ pound lean ground beef
- 3 tablespoons minced onion
- 4 teaspoons ketchup
- 2 teaspoons yellow mustard
- salt and freshly ground black pepper
- 4 slices of Cheddar cheese, broken into smaller pieces
- 8 hamburger dill pickle chips

Directions:

1. Combine the ground beef, minced onion, ketchup, mustard, salt and pepper in a large bowl. Mix well to thoroughly combine the ingredients. Divide the meat into four equal portions.
2. To make the stuffed burgers, flatten each portion of meat into a thin patty. Place 4 pickle chips and half of the cheese onto the center of two of the patties, leaving a rim around the edge of the patty exposed. Place the remaining two patties on top of the first and press the meat together firmly, sealing the edges tightly. With the burgers on a flat surface, press the sides of the burger with the palm of your hand to create a straight edge. This will help keep the stuffing inside the burger while it cooks.
3. Preheat the air fryer to 370°F (185°C).
4. Place the burgers inside the air fryer basket and air-fry for 20 minutes, flipping the burgers over halfway through the cooking time.
5. Serve the cheeseburgers on buns with lettuce and tomato.

White Bean Veggie Burgers

Servings: 3

Cooking Time: 13 Minutes

Ingredients:

- 1⅓ cups Drained and rinsed canned white beans
- 3 tablespoons Rolled oats (not quick-cooking or steel-cut; gluten-free, if a concern)
- 3 tablespoons Chopped walnuts
- 2 teaspoons Olive oil
- 2 teaspoons Lemon juice
- 1½ teaspoons Dijon mustard (gluten-free, if a concern)
- ¾ teaspoon Dried sage leaves
- ¼ teaspoon Table salt
- Olive oil spray
- 3 Whole-wheat buns or gluten-free whole-grain buns (if a concern), split open

Directions:

1. Preheat the air fryer to 400°F (205°C).
2. Place the beans, oats, walnuts, oil, lemon juice, mustard, sage, and salt in a food processor. Cover and process to make a coarse paste that will hold its shape, about like wet sugar-cookie dough, stopping the machine to scrape down the inside of the canister at least once.
3. Scrape down and remove the blade. With clean and wet hands, form the bean paste into two 4-inch patties for the small batch, three 4-inch patties for the medium, or four 4-inch patties for the large batch. Generously coat the patties on both sides with olive oil spray.
4. Set them in the basket with some space between them and air-fry undisturbed for 12 minutes, or until lightly brown and crisp at the edges. The tops of the burgers will feel firm to the touch.
5. Use a nonstick-safe spatula, and perhaps a flatware fork for balance, to transfer the burgers to a cutting board. Set the buns cut side down in the basket in one layer (working in batches as necessary) and air-fry undisturbed for 1 minute, to toast a bit and warm up. Serve the burgers warm in the buns.

Philly Cheesesteak Sandwiches

Servings: 3

Cooking Time: 9 Minutes

Ingredients:

- ¾ pound Shaved beef
- 1 tablespoon Worcestershire sauce (gluten-free, if a concern)
- ¼ teaspoon Garlic powder
- ¼ teaspoon Mild paprika
- 6 tablespoons (1½ ounces) Frozen bell pepper strips (do not thaw)
- 2 slices, broken into rings Very thin yellow or white medium onion slice(s)
- 6 ounces (6 to 8 slices) Provolone cheese slices
- 3 Long soft rolls such as hero, hoagie, or Italian sub rolls, or hot dog buns (gluten-free, if a concern), split open lengthwise

Directions:

1. Preheat the air fryer to 400°F (205°C).
2. When the machine is at temperature, spread the shaved beef in the basket, leaving a ½-inch perimeter around the

meat for good air flow. Sprinkle the meat with the Worcestershire sauce, paprika, and garlic powder. Spread the peppers and onions on top of the meat.

3. Air-fry undisturbed for 6 minutes, or until cooked through. Set the cheese on top of the meat. Continue air-frying undisturbed for 3 minutes, or until the cheese has melted.

4. Use kitchen tongs to divide the meat and cheese layers in the basket between the rolls or buns. Serve hot.

Chili Cheese Dogs

Servings: 3

Cooking Time: 12 Minutes

Ingredients:

- ¾ pound Lean ground beef
- 1½ tablespoons Chile powder
- 1 cup plus 2 tablespoons Jarred sofrito
- 3 Hot dogs (gluten-free, if a concern)
- 3 Hot dog buns (gluten-free, if a concern), split open lengthwise
- 3 tablespoons Finely chopped scallion
- 9 tablespoons (a little more than 2 ounces) Shredded Cheddar cheese

Directions:

1. Crumble the ground beef into a medium or large saucepan set over medium heat. Brown well, stirring often to break up the clumps. Add the chile powder and cook for 30 seconds, stirring the whole time. Stir in the sofrito and bring to a simmer. Reduce the heat to low and simmer, stirring occasionally, for 5 minutes. Keep warm.

2. Preheat the air fryer to 400°F (205°C).

3. When the machine is at temperature, put the hot dogs in the basket and air-fry undisturbed for 10 minutes, or until the hot dogs are bubbling and blistered, even a little crisp.

4. Use kitchen tongs to put the hot dogs in the buns. Top each with a ½ cup of the ground beef mixture, 1 tablespoon of the minced scallion, and 3 tablespoons of the cheese. (The scallion should go under the cheese so it superheats and wilts a bit.) Set the filled hot dog buns in the basket and air-fry undisturbed for 2 minutes, or until the cheese has melted.

5. Remove the basket from the machine. Cool the chili cheese dogs in the basket for 5 minutes before serving.

Chicken Club Sandwiches

Servings: 3

Cooking Time: 15 Minutes

Ingredients:

- 3 5- to 6-ounce boneless skinless chicken breasts
- 6 Thick-cut bacon strips (gluten-free, if a concern)
- 3 Long soft rolls, such as hero, hoagie, or Italian sub rolls (gluten-free, if a concern)
- 3 tablespoons Regular, low-fat, or fat-free mayonnaise (gluten-free, if a concern)
- 3 Lettuce leaves, preferably romaine or iceberg
- 6 ¼-inch-thick tomato slices

Directions:

1. Preheat the air fryer to 375°F (190°C).

2. Wrap each chicken breast with 2 strips of bacon, spiraling the bacon around the meat, slightly overlapping the strips on each revolution. Start the second strip of bacon farther down the breast but on a line with the start of the first strip so they both end at a lined-up point on the chicken breast.

3. When the machine is at temperature, set the wrapped breasts bacon-seam side down in the basket with space between them. Air-fry undisturbed for 12 minutes, until the bacon is browned, crisp, and cooked through and an instant-read meat thermometer inserted into the center of a breast registers 165°F (75°C). You may need to add 2 minutes in the air fryer if the temperature is at 360°F (180°C).

4. Use kitchen tongs to transfer the breasts to a wire rack. Split the rolls open lengthwise and set them cut side down in the basket. Air-fry for 1 minute, or until warmed through.

5. Use kitchen tongs to transfer the rolls to a cutting board. Spread 1 tablespoon mayonnaise on the cut side of one half of each roll. Top with a chicken breast, lettuce leaf, and tomato slice. Serve warm.

Perfect Burgers

Servings: 3

Cooking Time: 13 Minutes

Ingredients:

- 1 pound 2 ounces 90% lean ground beef
- 1½ tablespoons Worcestershire sauce (gluten-free, if a concern)
- ½ teaspoon Ground black pepper
- 3 Hamburger buns (gluten-free if a concern), split open

Directions:

1. Preheat the air fryer to 375°F (190°C).

2. Gently mix the ground beef, Worcestershire sauce, and pepper in a bowl until well combined but preserving as much of the meat's fibers as possible. Divide this mixture into two 5-inch patties for the small batch, three 5-inch patties for the medium, or four 5-inch patties for the large. Make a thumbprint indentation in the center of each patty, about halfway through the meat.

3. Set the patties in the basket in one layer with some space between them. Air-fry undisturbed for 10 minutes, or until an instant-read meat thermometer inserted into the

center of a burger registers 160°F (70°C) (a medium-well burger). You may need to add 2 minutes cooking time if the air fryer is at 360°F (180°C).

4. Use a nonstick-safe spatula, and perhaps a flatware fork for balance, to transfer the burgers to a cutting board. Set the buns cut side down in the basket in one layer (working in batches as necessary) and air-fry undisturbed for 1 minute, to toast a bit and warm up. Serve the burgers in the warm buns.

Sausage And Pepper Heros

Servings: 3

Cooking Time: 11 Minutes

Ingredients:

- 3 links (about 9 ounces total) Sweet Italian sausages (gluten-free, if a concern)
- 1½ Medium red or green bell pepper(s), stemmed, cored, and cut into ½-inch-wide strips
- 1 medium Yellow or white onion(s), peeled, halved, and sliced into thin half-moons
- 3 Long soft rolls, such as hero, hoagie, or Italian sub rolls (gluten-free, if a concern), split open lengthwise
- For garnishing Balsamic vinegar
- For garnishing Fresh basil leaves

Directions:

1. Preheat the air fryer to 400°F (205°C).
2. When the machine is at temperature, set the sausage links in the basket in one layer and air-fry undisturbed for 5 minutes.
3. Add the pepper strips and onions. Continue air-frying, tossing and rearranging everything about once every minute, for 5 minutes, or until the sausages are browned and an instant-read meat thermometer inserted into one of the links registers 160°F (70°C).
4. Use a nonstick-safe spatula and kitchen tongs to transfer the sausages and vegetables to a cutting board. Set the rolls cut side down in the basket in one layer (working in batches as necessary) and air-fry undisturbed for 1 minute, to toast the rolls a bit and warm them up. Set 1 sausage with some pepper strips and onions in each warm roll, sprinkle balsamic vinegar over the sandwich fillings, and garnish with basil leaves.

Chicken Gyros

Servings: 4

Cooking Time: 14 Minutes

Ingredients:

- 4 4- to 5-ounce boneless skinless chicken thighs, trimmed of any fat blobs
- 2 tablespoons Lemon juice
- 2 tablespoons Red wine vinegar
- 2 tablespoons Olive oil
- 2 teaspoons Dried oregano
- 2 teaspoons Minced garlic
- 1 teaspoon Table salt
- 1 teaspoon Ground black pepper
- 4 Pita pockets (gluten-free, if a concern)
- ½ cup Chopped tomatoes
- ½ cup Bottled regular, low-fat, or fat-free ranch dressing (gluten-free, if a concern)

Directions:

1. Mix the thighs, lemon juice, vinegar, oil, oregano, garlic, salt, and pepper in a zip-closed bag. Seal, gently massage the marinade into the meat through the plastic, and refrigerate for at least 2 hours or up to 6 hours. (Longer than that and the meat can turn rubbery.)
2. Set the plastic bag out on the counter (to make the contents a little less frigid). Preheat the air fryer to 375°F (190°C).
3. When the machine is at temperature, use kitchen tongs to place the thighs in the basket in one layer. Discard the marinade. Air-fry the chicken thighs undisturbed for 12 minutes, or until browned and an instant-read meat thermometer inserted into the thickest part of one thigh registers 165°F (75°C). You may need to air-fry the chicken 2 minutes longer if the machine's temperature is 360°F (180°C).
4. Use kitchen tongs to transfer the thighs to a cutting board. Cool for 5 minutes, then set one thigh in each of the pita pockets. Top each with 2 tablespoons chopped tomatoes and 2 tablespoons dressing. Serve warm.

Thanksgiving Turkey Sandwiches

Servings: 3

Cooking Time: 10 Minutes

Ingredients:

- 1½ cups Herb-seasoned stuffing mix (not cornbread-style; gluten-free, if a concern)
- 1 Large egg white(s)
- 2 tablespoons Water
- 3 5- to 6-ounce turkey breast cutlets
- Vegetable oil spray
- 4½ tablespoons Purchased cranberry sauce, preferably whole berry
- ⅛ teaspoon Ground cinnamon
- ⅛ teaspoon Ground dried ginger
- 4½ tablespoons Regular, low-fat, or fat-free mayonnaise (gluten-free, if a concern)
- 6 tablespoons Shredded Brussels sprouts
- 3 Kaiser rolls (gluten-free, if a concern), split open

Directions:
1. Preheat the air fryer to 375°F (190°C).
2. Put the stuffing mix in a heavy zip-closed bag, seal it, lay it flat on your counter, and roll a rolling pin over the bag to crush the stuffing mix to the consistency of rough sand. (Or you can pulse the stuffing mix to the desired consistency in a food processor.)
3. Set up and fill two shallow soup plates or small pie plates on your counter: one for the egg white(s), whisked with the water until foamy; and one for the ground stuffing mix.
4. Dip a cutlet in the egg white mixture, coating both sides and letting any excess egg white slip back into the rest. Set the cutlet in the ground stuffing mix and coat it evenly on both sides, pressing gently to coat well on both sides. Lightly coat the cutlet on both sides with vegetable oil spray, set it aside, and continue dipping and coating the remaining cutlets in the same way.
5. Set the cutlets in the basket and air-fry undisturbed for 10 minutes, or until crisp and brown. Use kitchen tongs to transfer the cutlets to a wire rack to cool for a few minutes.
6. Meanwhile, stir the cranberry sauce with the cinnamon and ginger in a small bowl. Mix the shredded Brussels sprouts and mayonnaise in a second bowl until the vegetable is evenly coated.
7. Build the sandwiches by spreading about 1½ tablespoons of the cranberry mixture on the cut side of the bottom half of each roll. Set a cutlet on top, then spread about 3 tablespoons of the Brussels sprouts mixture evenly over the cutlet. Set the other half of the roll on top and serve warm.

Mexican Cheeseburgers

Servings: 4
Cooking Time: 22 Minutes
Ingredients:
- 1¼ pounds ground beef
- ¼ cup finely chopped onion
- ½ cup crushed yellow corn tortilla chips
- 1 (1.25-ounce) packet taco seasoning
- ¼ cup canned diced green chilies
- 1 egg, lightly beaten
- 4 ounces pepper jack cheese, grated
- 4 (12-inch) flour tortillas
- shredded lettuce, sour cream, guacamole, salsa (for topping)

Directions:
1. Combine the ground beef, minced onion, crushed tortilla chips, taco seasoning, green chilies, and egg in a large bowl. Mix thoroughly until combined – your hands are good tools for this. Divide the meat into four equal portions and shape each portion into an oval-shaped burger.
2. Preheat the air fryer to 370°F (185°C).
3. Air-fry the burgers for 18 minutes, turning them over halfway through the cooking time. Divide the cheese between the burgers, lower fryer to 340°F (170°C) and air-fry for an additional 4 minutes to melt the cheese. (This will give you a burger that is medium-well. If you prefer your cheeseburger medium-rare, shorten the cooking time to about 15 minutes and then add the cheese and proceed with the recipe.)
4. While the burgers are cooking, warm the tortillas wrapped in aluminum foil in a 350°F (175°C) oven, or in a skillet with a little oil over medium-high heat for a couple of minutes. Keep the tortillas warm until the burgers are ready.
5. To assemble the burgers, spread sour cream over three quarters of the tortillas and top each with some shredded lettuce and salsa. Place the Mexican cheeseburgers on the lettuce and top with guacamole. Fold the tortillas around the burger, starting with the bottom and then folding the sides in over the top. (A little sour cream can help hold the seam of the tortilla together.) Serve immediately.

Salmon Burgers

Servings: 3
Cooking Time: 8 Minutes
Ingredients:
- 1 pound 2 ounces Skinless salmon fillet, preferably fattier Atlantic salmon
- 1½ tablespoons Minced chives or the green part of a scallion
- ½ cup Plain panko bread crumbs (gluten-free, if a concern)
- 1½ teaspoons Dijon mustard (gluten-free, if a concern)
- 1½ teaspoons Drained and rinsed capers, minced
- 1½ teaspoons Lemon juice
- ¼ teaspoon Table salt
- ¼ teaspoon Ground black pepper
- Vegetable oil spray

Directions:
1. Preheat the air fryer to 375°F (190°C).
2. Cut the salmon into pieces that will fit in a food processor. Cover and pulse until coarsely chopped. Add the chives and pulse to combine, until the fish is ground but not a paste. Scrape down and remove the blade. Scrape the salmon mixture into a bowl. Add the bread crumbs, mustard, capers, lemon juice, salt, and pepper. Stir gently until well combined.
3. Use clean and dry hands to form the mixture into two 5-inch patties for a small batch, three 5-inch patties for a medium batch, or four 5-inch patties for a large one.

4. Coat both sides of each patty with vegetable oil spray. Set them in the basket in one layer and air-fry undisturbed for 8 minutes, or until browned and an instant-read meat thermometer inserted into the center of a burger registers 145°F (60°C).

5. Use a nonstick-safe spatula, and perhaps a flatware fork for balance, to transfer the burgers to a wire rack. Cool for 2 or 3 minutes before serving.

Dijon Thyme Burgers

Servings: 3

Cooking Time: 18 Minutes

Ingredients:

- 1 pound lean ground beef
- ⅓ cup panko breadcrumbs
- ¼ cup finely chopped onion
- 3 tablespoons Dijon mustard
- 1 tablespoon chopped fresh thyme
- 4 teaspoons Worcestershire sauce
- 1 teaspoon salt
- freshly ground black pepper
- Topping (optional):
- 2 tablespoons Dijon mustard
- 1 tablespoon dark brown sugar
- 1 teaspoon Worcestershire sauce
- 4 ounces sliced Swiss cheese, optional

Directions:

1. Combine all the burger ingredients together in a large bowl and mix well. Divide the meat into 4 equal portions and then form the burgers, being careful not to over-handle the meat. One good way to do this is to throw the meat back and forth from one hand to another, packing the meat each time you catch it. Flatten the balls into patties, making an indentation in the center of each patty with your thumb (this will help it stay flat as it cooks) and flattening the sides of the burgers so that they will fit nicely into the air fryer basket.

2. Preheat the air fryer to 370°F (185°C).

3. If you don't have room for all four burgers, air-fry two or three burgers at a time for 8 minutes. Flip the burgers over and air-fry for another 6 minutes.

4. While the burgers are cooking combine the Dijon mustard, dark brown sugar, and Worcestershire sauce in a small bowl and mix well. This optional topping to the burgers really adds a boost of flavor at the end. Spread the Dijon topping evenly on each burger. If you cooked the burgers in batches, return the first batch to the cooker at this time – it's ok to place the fourth burger on top of the others in the center of the basket. Air-fry the burgers for another 3 minutes.

5. Finally, if desired, top each burger with a slice of Swiss cheese. Lower the air fryer temperature to 330°F (165°C) and air-fry for another minute to melt the cheese. Serve the burgers on toasted brioche buns, dressed the way you like them.

Chicken Spiedies

Servings: 3

Cooking Time: 12 Minutes

Ingredients:

- 1¼ pounds Boneless skinless chicken thighs, trimmed of any fat blobs and cut into 2-inch pieces
- 3 tablespoons Red wine vinegar
- 2 tablespoons Olive oil
- 2 tablespoons Minced fresh mint leaves
- 2 tablespoons Minced fresh parsley leaves
- 2 teaspoons Minced fresh dill fronds
- ¾ teaspoon Fennel seeds
- ¾ teaspoon Table salt
- Up to a ¼ teaspoon Red pepper flakes
- 3 Long soft rolls, such as hero, hoagie, or Italian sub rolls (gluten-free, if a concern), split open lengthwise
- 4½ tablespoons Regular or low-fat mayonnaise (not fat-free; gluten-free, if a concern)
- 1½ tablespoons Distilled white vinegar
- 1½ teaspoons Ground black pepper

Directions:

1. Mix the chicken, vinegar, oil, mint, parsley, dill, fennel seeds, salt, and red pepper flakes in a zip-closed plastic bag. Seal, gently massage the marinade ingredients into the meat, and refrigerate for at least 2 hours or up to 6 hours. (Longer than that and the meat can turn rubbery.)

2. Set the plastic bag out on the counter (to make the contents a little less frigid). Preheat the air fryer to 400°F (205°C).

3. When the machine is at temperature, use kitchen tongs to set the chicken thighs in the basket (discard any remaining marinade) and air-fry undisturbed for 6 minutes. Turn the thighs over and continue air-frying undisturbed for 6 minutes more, until well browned, cooked through, and even a little crunchy.

4. Dump the contents of the basket onto a wire rack and cool for 2 or 3 minutes. Divide the chicken evenly between the rolls. Whisk the mayonnaise, vinegar, and black pepper in a small bowl until smooth. Drizzle this sauce over the chicken pieces in the rolls.

Inside-out Cheeseburgers

Servings: 3

Cooking Time: 9-11 Minutes

Ingredients:

- 1 pound 2 ounces 90% lean ground beef
- ¾ teaspoon Dried oregano
- ¾ teaspoon Table salt
- ¾ teaspoon Ground black pepper
- ¼ teaspoon Garlic powder
- 6 tablespoons (about 1½ ounces) Shredded Cheddar, Swiss, or other semi-firm cheese, or a purchased blend of shredded cheeses
- 3 Hamburger buns (gluten-free, if a concern), split open

Directions:

1. Preheat the air fryer to 375°F (190°C).
2. Gently mix the ground beef, oregano, salt, pepper, and garlic powder in a bowl until well combined without turning the mixture to mush. Form it into two 6-inch patties for the small batch, three for the medium, or four for the large.
3. Place 2 tablespoons of the shredded cheese in the center of each patty. With clean hands, fold the sides of the patty up to cover the cheese, then pick it up and roll it gently into a ball to seal the cheese inside. Gently press it back into a 5-inch burger without letting any cheese squish out. Continue filling and preparing more burgers, as needed.
4. Place the burgers in the basket in one layer and air-fry undisturbed for 8 minutes for medium or 10 minutes for well-done. (An instant-read meat thermometer won't work for these burgers because it will hit the mostly melted cheese inside and offer a hotter temperature than the surrounding meat.)
5. Use a nonstick-safe spatula, and perhaps a flatware fork for balance, to transfer the burgers to a cutting board. Set the buns cut side down in the basket in one layer (working in batches as necessary) and air-fry undisturbed for 1 minute, to toast a bit and warm up. Cool the burgers a few minutes more, then serve them warm in the buns.

Black Bean Veggie Burgers

Servings: 3

Cooking Time: 10 Minutes

Ingredients:

- 1 cup Drained and rinsed canned black beans
- ⅓ cup Pecan pieces
- ⅓ cup Rolled oats (not quick-cooking or steel-cut; gluten-free, if a concern)
- 2 tablespoons (or 1 small egg) Pasteurized egg substitute, such as Egg Beaters (gluten-free, if a concern)
- 2 teaspoons Red ketchup-like chili sauce, such as Heinz
- ¼ teaspoon Ground cumin
- ¼ teaspoon Dried oregano
- ¼ teaspoon Table salt
- ¼ teaspoon Ground black pepper
- Olive oil
- Olive oil spray

Directions:

1. Preheat the air fryer to 400°F (205°C).
2. Put the beans, pecans, oats, egg substitute or egg, chili sauce, cumin, oregano, salt, and pepper in a food processor. Cover and process to a coarse paste that will hold its shape like sugar-cookie dough, adding olive oil in 1-teaspoon increments to get the mixture to blend smoothly. The amount of olive oil is actually dependent on the internal moisture content of the beans and the oats. Figure on about 1 tablespoon (three 1-teaspoon additions) for the smaller batch, with proportional increases for the other batches. A little too much olive oil can't hurt, but a dry paste will fall apart as it cooks and a far-too-wet paste will stick to the basket.
3. Scrape down and remove the blade. Using clean, wet hands, form the paste into two 4-inch patties for the small batch, three 4-inch patties for the medium, or four 4-inch patties for the large batch, setting them one by one on a cutting board. Generously coat both sides of the patties with olive oil spray.
4. Set them in the basket in one layer. Air-fry undisturbed for 10 minutes, or until lightly browned and crisp at the edges.
5. Use a nonstick-safe spatula, and perhaps a flatware fork for balance, to transfer the burgers to a wire rack. Cool for 5 minutes before serving.

Desserts And Sweets

Sweet Potato Donut Holes

Servings: 18
Cooking Time: 4 Minutes Per Batch

Ingredients:
- 1 cup flour
- ⅓ cup sugar
- ¼ teaspoon baking soda
- 1 teaspoon baking powder
- ⅛ teaspoon salt
- ½ cup cooked mashed purple sweet potatoes
- 1 egg, beaten
- 2 tablespoons butter, melted
- 1 teaspoon pure vanilla extract
- oil for misting or cooking spray

Directions:
1. Preheat air fryer to 390°F (200°C).
2. In a large bowl, stir together the flour, sugar, baking soda, baking powder, and salt.
3. In a separate bowl, combine the potatoes, egg, butter, and vanilla and mix well.
4. Add potato mixture to dry ingredients and stir into a soft dough.
5. Shape dough into 1½-inch balls. Mist lightly with oil or cooking spray.
6. Place 9 donut holes in air fryer basket, leaving a little space in between. Cook for 4 minutes, until done in center and lightly browned outside.
7. Repeat step 6 to cook remaining donut holes.

Oatmeal Blackberry Crisp

Servings: 6
Cooking Time: 20 Minutes

Ingredients:
- 1 cup rolled oats
- ½ cup flour
- ¼ cup olive oil
- ¼ tsp salt
- 1 tsp cinnamon
- 1/3 cup honey
- 4 cups blackberries

Directions:
1. Preheat air fryer to 350°F (175°C). Combine rolled oats, flour, olive oil, salt, cinnamon, and honey in a large bowl. Mix well. Spread blackberries on the bottom of a greased cooking pan. Cover them with the oat mixture. Place pan in air fryer and Bake for 15 minutes. Cool for a few minutes. Serve and enjoy.

Cheese Blintzes

Servings: 6
Cooking Time: 10 Minutes

Ingredients:
- 1½ 7½-ounce package(s) farmer cheese
- 3 tablespoons Regular or low-fat cream cheese (not fat-free)
- 3 tablespoons Granulated white sugar
- ¼ teaspoon Vanilla extract
- 6 Egg roll wrappers
- 3 tablespoons Butter, melted and cooled

Directions:
1. Preheat the air fryer to 375°F (190°C).
2. Use a flatware fork to mash the farmer cheese, cream cheese, sugar, and vanilla in a small bowl until smooth.
3. Set one egg roll wrapper on a clean, dry work surface. Place ¼ cup of the filling at the edge closest to you, leaving a ½-inch gap before the edge of the wrapper. Dip your clean finger in water and wet the edges of the wrapper. Fold the perpendicular sides over the filling, then roll the wrapper closed with the filling inside. Set it aside seam side down and continue filling the remainder of the wrappers.
4. Brush the wrappers on all sides with the melted butter. Be generous. Set them seam side down in the basket with as much space between them as possible. Air-fry undisturbed for 10 minutes, or until lightly browned.
5. Use a nonstick-safe spatula to transfer the blintzes to a wire rack. Cool for at least 5 minutes or up to 20 minutes before serving.

Fall Pumpkin Cake

Servings: 6
Cooking Time: 50 Minutes

Ingredients:
- 1/3 cup pecan pieces
- 5 gingersnap cookies
- 1/3 cup light brown sugar
- 6 tbsp butter, melted
- 3 eggs
- ½ tsp vanilla extract
- 1 cup pumpkin purée

- 2 tbsp sour cream
- ½ cup flour
- ¼ cup tapioca flour
- ½ tsp cornstarch
- ½ cup granulated sugar
- ½ tsp baking soda
- 1 tsp baking powder
- 1 tsp pumpkin pie spice
- 6 oz mascarpone cheese
- 1 1/3 cups powdered sugar
- 1 tsp cinnamon
- 2 tbsp butter, softened
- 1 tbsp milk
- 1 tbsp flaked almonds

Directions:

1. Blitz the pecans, gingersnap cookies, brown sugar, and 3 tbsp of melted butter in a food processor until combined. Press mixture into the bottom of a lightly greased cake pan. Preheat air fryer at 350ºF. In a bowl, whisk the eggs, remaining melted butter, ½ tsp of vanilla extract, pumpkin purée, and sour cream. In another bowl, combine the flour, tapioca flour, cornstarch, granulated sugar, baking soda, baking powder, and pumpkin pie spice. Add wet ingredients to dry ingredients and combine. Do not overmix. Pour the batter into a cake pan and cover it with aluminum foil. Place cake pan in the frying basket and Bake for 30 minutes. Remove the foil and cook for another 5 minutes. Let cool onto a cooling rack for 10 minutes. Then, turn cake onto a large serving platter. In a small bowl, whisk the mascarpone cheese, powdered sugar, remaining vanilla extract, cinnamon, softened butter, and milk. Spread over cooled cake and cut into slices. Serve sprinkled with almonds and enjoy!

Oreo-coated Peanut Butter Cups

Servings:8

Cooking Time: 4 Minutes

Ingredients:

- 8 Standard ¾-ounce peanut butter cups, frozen
- 1/3 cup All-purpose flour
- 2 Large egg white(s), beaten until foamy
- 16 Oreos or other creme-filled chocolate sandwich cookies, ground to crumbs in a food processor
- Vegetable oil spray

Directions:

1. Set up and fill three shallow soup plates or small pie plates on your counter: one for the flour, one for the beaten egg white(s), and one for the cookie crumbs.
2. Dip a frozen peanut butter cup in the flour, turning it to coat all sides. Shake off any excess, then set it in the beaten egg white(s). Turn it to coat all sides, then let any excess egg white slip back into the rest. Set the candy bar in the cookie crumbs. Turn to coat on all parts, even the sides. Dip the peanut butter cup back in the egg white(s) as before, then into the cookie crumbs as before, making sure you have a solid, even coating all around the cup. Set aside while you dip and coat the remaining cups.
3. When all the peanut butter cups are dipped and coated, lightly coat them on all sides with the vegetable oil spray. Set them on a plate and freeze while the air fryer heats.
4. Preheat the air fryer to 400°F (205°C).
5. Set the dipped cups wider side up in the basket with as much air space between them as possible. Air-fry undisturbed for 4 minutes, or until they feel soft but the coating is set.
6. Turn off the machine and remove the basket from it. Set aside the basket with the fried cups for 10 minutes. Use a nonstick-safe spatula to transfer the fried cups to a wire rack. Cool for at least another 5 minutes before serving.

Fried Twinkies

Servings:6

Cooking Time: 5 Minutes

Ingredients:

- 2 Large egg white(s)
- 2 tablespoons Water
- 1½ cups (about 9 ounces) Ground gingersnap cookie crumbs
- 6 Twinkies
- Vegetable oil spray

Directions:

1. Preheat the air fryer to 400°F (205°C).
2. Set up and fill two shallow soup plates or small pie plates on your counter: one for the egg white(s), whisked with the water until foamy; and one for the gingersnap crumbs.
3. Dip a Twinkie in the egg white(s), turning it to coat on all sides, even the ends. Let the excess egg white mixture slip back into the rest, then set the Twinkie in the crumbs. Roll it to coat on all sides, even the ends, pressing gently to get an even coating. Then repeat this process: egg white(s), followed by crumbs. Lightly coat the prepared Twinkie on all sides with vegetable oil spray. Set aside and coat each of the remaining Twinkies with the same double-dipping technique, followed by spraying.
4. Set the Twinkies flat side up in the basket with as much air space between them as possible. Air-fry for 5 minutes, or until browned and crunchy.
5. Use a nonstick-safe spatula to gently transfer the Twinkies to a wire rack. Cool for at least 10 minutes before serving.

Mixed Berry Pie

Servings: 4

Cooking Time: 25 Minutes

Ingredients:
- 2/3 cup blackberries, cut into thirds
- ¼ cup sugar
- 2 tbsp cornstarch
- ¼ tsp vanilla extract
- ¼ tsp peppermint extract
- ½ tsp lemon zest
- 1 cup sliced strawberries
- 1 cup raspberries
- 1 refrigerated piecrust
- 1 large egg

Directions:

1. Mix the sugar, cornstarch, vanilla, peppermint extract, and lemon zest in a bowl. Toss in all berries gently until combined. Pour into a greased dish. On a clean workspace, lay out the dough and cut into a 7-inch diameter round. Cover the baking dish with the round and crimp the edges. With a knife, cut 4 slits in the top to vent.
2. Beat 1 egg and 1 tbsp of water to make an egg wash. Brush the egg wash over the crust. Preheat air fryer to 350°F (175°C). Put the baking dish into the frying basket. Bake for 15 minutes or until the crust is golden and the berries are bubbling through the vents. Remove from the air fryer and let cool for 15 minutes. Serve warm.

Coconut Cream Roll-ups

Servings: 4

Cooking Time: 20 Minutes

Ingredients:
- ½ cup cream cheese, softened
- 1 cup fresh raspberries
- ¼ cup brown sugar
- ¼ cup coconut cream
- 1 egg
- 1 tsp corn starch
- 6 spring roll wrappers

Directions:

1. Preheat air fryer to 350°F (175°C). Add the cream cheese, brown sugar, coconut cream, cornstarch, and egg to a bowl and whisk until all ingredients are completely mixed and fluffy, thick and stiff. Spoon even amounts of the creamy filling into each spring roll wrapper, then top each dollop of filling with several raspberries. Roll up the wraps around the creamy raspberry filling, and seal the seams with a few dabs of water.
2. Place each roll on the foil-lined frying basket, seams facing down. Bake for 10 minutes, flipping them once until golden brown and perfect on the outside, while the raspberries and cream filling will have cooked together in a glorious fusion. Remove with tongs and serve hot or cold. Serve and enjoy!

Blueberry Crisp

Servings: 6

Cooking Time: 13 Minutes

Ingredients:
- 3 cups Fresh or thawed frozen blueberries
- ⅓ cup Granulated white sugar
- 1 tablespoon Instant tapioca
- ⅓ cup All-purpose flour
- ⅓ cup Rolled oats (not quick-cooking or steel-cut)
- ⅓ cup Chopped walnuts or pecans
- ⅓ cup Packed light brown sugar
- 5 tablespoons plus 1 teaspoon (⅔ stick) Butter, melted and cooled
- ¾ teaspoon Ground cinnamon
- ¼ teaspoon Table salt

Directions:

1. Preheat the air fryer to 400°F (205°C).
2. Mix the blueberries, granulated white sugar, and instant tapioca in a 6-inch round cake pan for a small batch, a 7-inch round cake pan for a medium batch, or an 8-inch round cake pan for a large batch.
3. When the machine is at temperature, set the cake pan in the basket and air-fry undisturbed for 5 minutes, or just until the blueberries begin to bubble.
4. Meanwhile, mix the flour, oats, nuts, brown sugar, butter, cinnamon, and salt in a medium bowl until well combined.
5. When the blueberries have begun to bubble, crumble this flour mixture evenly on top. Continue air-frying undisturbed for 8 minutes, or until the topping has browned a bit and the filling is bubbling.
6. Use two hot pads or silicone baking mitts to transfer the cake pan to a wire rack. Cool for at least 10 minutes or to room temperature before serving.

Nutty Cookies

Servings: 6

Cooking Time: 25 Minutes

Ingredients:
- ¼ cup pistachios
- ¼ cup evaporated cane sugar
- ¼ cup raw almonds
- ½ cup almond flour

- 1 tsp pure vanilla extract
- 1 egg white

Directions:

1. Preheat air fryer to 375°F (190°C). Add ¼ cup of pistachios and almonds into a food processor. Pulse until they resemble crumbles. Roughly chop the rest of the pistachios with a sharp knife. Combine all ingredients in a large bowl until completely incorporated. Form 6 equally-sized balls and transfer to the parchment-lined frying basket. Allow for 1 inch between each portion. Bake for 7 minutes. Cool on a wire rack for 5 minutes. Serve and enjoy.

Pumpkin Brownies

Servings: 4

Cooking Time: 30 Minutes

Ingredients:

- ¼ cup canned pumpkin
- ½ cup maple syrup
- 2 eggs, beaten
- 1 tbsp vanilla extract
- ¼ cup tapioca flour
- ¼ cup flour
- ½ tsp baking powder

Directions:

1. Preheat air fryer to 320°F (160°C). Mix the pumpkin, maple syrup, eggs, and vanilla extract in a bowl. Toss in tapioca flour, flour, and baking powder until smooth. Pour the batter into a small round cake pan and Bake for 20 minutes until a toothpick comes out clean. Let cool completely before slicing into 4 brownies. Serve and enjoy!

Fast Brownies

Servings: 4

Cooking Time: 25 Minutes

Ingredients:

- ½ cup flour
- 2 tbsp cocoa
- 1/3 cup granulated sugar
- ¼ tsp baking soda
- 3 tbsp butter, melted
- 1 egg
- ¼ tsp salt
- ½ cup chocolate chips
- ¼ cup chopped hazelnuts
- 1 tbsp powdered sugar
- 1 tsp vanilla extract

Directions:

1. Preheat air fryer at 350ºF. Combine all ingredients, except chocolate chips, hazelnuts, and powdered sugar, in a bowl. Fold in chocolate chips and pecans. Press mixture into a greased cake pan. Place cake pan in the frying basket and Bake for 12 minutes. Let cool for 10 minutes before slicing into 9 brownies. Scatter with powdered sugar and serve.

Apple Crisp

Servings: 4

Cooking Time: 16 Minutes

Ingredients:

- Filling
- 3 Granny Smith apples, thinly sliced (about 4 cups)
- ¼ teaspoon ground cinnamon
- ⅛ teaspoon salt
- 1½ teaspoons lemon juice
- 2 tablespoons honey
- 1 tablespoon brown sugar
- cooking spray
- Crumb Topping
- 2 tablespoons oats
- 2 tablespoons oat bran
- 2 tablespoons cooked quinoa
- 2 tablespoons chopped walnuts
- 2 tablespoons brown sugar
- 2 teaspoons coconut oil

Directions:

1. Combine all filling ingredients and stir well so that apples are evenly coated.

2. Spray air fryer baking pan with nonstick cooking spray and spoon in the apple mixture.

3. Cook at 360°F (180°C) for 5minutes. Stir well, scooping up from the bottom to mix apples and sauce.

4. At this point, the apples should be crisp-tender. Continue cooking in 3-minute intervals until apples are as soft as you like.

5. While apples are cooking, combine all topping ingredients in a small bowl. Stir until coconut oil mixes in well and distributes evenly. If your coconut oil is cold, it may be easier to mix in by hand.

6. When apples are cooked to your liking, sprinkle crumb mixture on top. Cook at 360°F (180°C) for 8 minutes or until crumb topping is golden brown and crispy.

Wild Blueberry Sweet Empanadas

Servings: 12

Cooking Time: 8 Minutes

Ingredients:
- 2 cups frozen wild blueberries
- 5 tablespoons chia seeds
- ¼ cup honey
- 1 tablespoon lemon or lime juice
- ¼ cup water
- 1½ cups all-purpose flour
- 1 cup whole-wheat flour
- ½ teaspoon salt
- 1 tablespoon sugar
- ½ cup cold unsalted butter
- 1 egg
- ½ cup plus 2 tablespoons milk, divided
- 1 cup powdered sugar
- 1 teaspoon vanilla extract

Directions:

1. To make the wild blueberry chia jam, place the blueberries, chia seeds, honey, lemon or lime juice, and water into a blender and pulse for 2 minutes. Pour the chia jam into a glass jar or bowl and cover. Store in the refrigerator at least 4 to 8 hours or until the jam is thickened.
2. In a food processor, place the all-purpose flour, whole-wheat flour, salt, sugar, and butter and process for 2 minutes, scraping down the sides of the food processor every 30 seconds. Add in the egg and blend for 30 seconds. Using the pulse button, add in ½ cup of the milk 1 tablespoon at a time or until the dough is moist enough to handle and be rolled into a ball. Let the dough rest at room temperature for 30 minutes.
3. On a floured surface, cut the dough in half; then form a ball and cut each ball into 6 equal pieces, totaling 12 equal pieces. Work with one piece at a time, and cover the remaining dough with a towel. Roll out the dough into a 6-inch round, much like a tortilla, with ¼ inch thickness. Place 4 tablespoons of filling in the center of round, fold over to form a half-circle. Using a fork, crimp the edges together and pierce the top with a fork for air holes. Repeat with the remaining dough and filling.
4. Preheat the air fryer to 350°F (175°C).
5. Working in batches, place 3 to 4 empanadas in the air fryer basket and spray with cooking spray. Cook for 8 minutes. Repeat in batches, as needed. Allow the sweet empanadas to cool for 15 minutes. Meanwhile, in a small bowl, whisk together the powdered sugar, the remaining 2 tablespoons of milk, and the vanilla extract. Then drizzle the glaze over the surface and serve.

Sugared Pizza Dough Dippers With Raspberry Cream Cheese Dip

Servings: 10

Cooking Time: 8 Minutes

Ingredients:
- 1 pound pizza dough*
- ½ cup butter, melted
- ¾ to 1 cup sugar
- Raspberry Cream Cheese Dip
- 4 ounces cream cheese, softened
- 2 tablespoons powdered sugar
- ½ teaspoon almond extract or almond paste
- 1½ tablespoons milk
- ¼ cup raspberry preserves
- fresh raspberries

Directions:

1. Cut the ingredients in half or save half of the dough for another recipe.
2. When you're ready to make your sugared dough dippers, remove your pizza dough from the refrigerator at least 1 hour prior to baking and let it sit on the counter, covered gently with plastic wrap.
3. Roll the dough into two 15-inch logs. Cut each log into 20 slices and roll each slice so that it is 3- to 3½-inches long. Cut each slice in half and twist the dough halves together 3 to 4 times. Place the twisted dough on a cookie sheet, brush with melted butter and sprinkle sugar over the dough twists.
4. Preheat the air fryer to 350°F (175°C).
5. Brush the bottom of the air fryer basket with a little melted butter. Air-fry the dough twists in batches. Place 8 to 12 (depending on the size of your air fryer) in the air fryer basket.
6. Air-fry for 6 minutes. Turn the dough strips over and brush the other side with butter. Air-fry for an additional 2 minutes.
7. While the dough twists are cooking, make the cream cheese and raspberry dip. Whip the cream cheese with a hand mixer until fluffy. Add the powdered sugar, almond extract and milk, and beat until smooth. Fold in the raspberry preserves and transfer to a serving dish.
8. As the batches of dough twists are complete, place them into a shallow dish. Brush with more melted butter and generously coat with sugar, shaking the dish to cover both sides. Serve the sugared dough dippers warm with the raspberry cream cheese dip on the side. Garnish with fresh raspberries.

Baked Caramelized Peaches

Servings: 6

Cooking Time: 25 Minutes

Ingredients:

- 3 pitted peaches, halved
- 2 tbsp brown sugar
- 1 cup heavy cream
- 1 tsp vanilla extract
- ¼ tsp ground cinnamon
- 1 cup fresh blueberries

Directions:

1. Preheat air fryer to 380°F (195°C). Lay the peaches in the frying basket with the cut side up, then top them with brown sugar. Bake for 7-11 minutes, allowing the peaches to brown around the edges. In a mixing bowl, whisk heavy cream, vanilla, and cinnamon until stiff peaks form. Fold the peaches into a plate. Spoon the cream mixture into the peach cups, top with blueberries, and serve.

Strawberry Pastry Rolls

Servings: 4

Cooking Time: 6 Minutes

Ingredients:

- 3 ounces low-fat cream cheese
- 2 tablespoons plain yogurt
- 2 teaspoons sugar
- ¼ teaspoon pure vanilla extract
- 8 ounces fresh strawberries
- 8 sheets phyllo dough
- butter-flavored cooking spray
- ¼–½ cup dark chocolate chips (optional)

Directions:

1. In a medium bowl, combine the cream cheese, yogurt, sugar, and vanilla. Beat with hand mixer at high speed until smooth, about 1 minute.
2. Wash strawberries and destem. Chop enough of them to measure ½ cup. Stir into cheese mixture.
3. Preheat air fryer to 330°F (165°C).
4. Phyllo dough dries out quickly, so cover your stack of phyllo sheets with waxed paper and then place a damp dish towel on top of that. Remove only one sheet at a time as you work.
5. To create one pastry roll, lay out a single sheet of phyllo. Spray lightly with butter-flavored spray, top with a second sheet of phyllo, and spray the second sheet lightly.
6. Place a quarter of the filling (about 3 tablespoons) about ½ inch from the edge of one short side. Fold the end of the phyllo over the filling and keep rolling a turn or two. Fold in both the left and right sides so that the edges meet in the middle of your roll. Then roll up completely. Spray outside of pastry roll with butter spray.
7. When you have 4 rolls, place them in the air fryer basket, seam side down, leaving some space in between each. Cook at 330°F (165°C) for 6 minutes, until they turn a delicate golden brown.
8. Repeat step 7 for remaining rolls.
9. Allow pastries to cool to room temperature.
10. When ready to serve, slice the remaining strawberries. If desired, melt the chocolate chips in microwave or double boiler. Place 1 pastry on each dessert plate, and top with sliced strawberries. Drizzle melted chocolate over strawberries and onto plate.

Vanilla Butter Cake

Servings: 6

Cooking Time: 20-24 Minutes

Ingredients:

- ¾ cup plus 1 tablespoon All-purpose flour
- 1 teaspoon Baking powder
- ¼ teaspoon Table salt
- 8 tablespoons (½ cup/1 stick) Butter, at room temperature
- ½ cup Granulated white sugar
- 2 Large egg(s)
- 2 tablespoons Whole or low-fat milk (not fat-free)
- ¾ teaspoon Vanilla extract
- Baking spray (see here)

Directions:

1. Preheat the air fryer to 160°C (or 165°C, if that's the closest setting).
2. Mix the flour, baking powder, and salt in a small bowl until well combined.
3. Using an electric hand mixer at medium speed, beat the butter and sugar in a medium bowl until creamy and smooth, about 3 minutes, occasionally scraping down the inside of the bowl.
4. Beat in the egg or eggs, as well as the white or a yolk as necessary. Beat in the milk and vanilla until smooth. Turn off the beaters and add the flour mixture. Beat at low speed until thick and smooth.
5. Use the baking spray to generously coat the inside of a 6-inch round cake pan for a small batch, a 7-inch round cake pan for a medium batch, or an 8-inch round cake pan for a large batch. Scrape and spread the batter into the pan, smoothing the batter out to an even layer.
6. Set the pan in the basket and air-fry undisturbed for 20 minutes for a 6-inch layer, 22 minutes for a 7-inch layer, or 24 minutes for an 8-inch layer, or until a toothpick or cake tester inserted into the center of the cake comes out clean.

Start checking it at the 15-minute mark to know where you are.

7. Use hot pads or silicone baking mitts to transfer the cake pan to a wire rack. Cool for 5 minutes. To unmold, set a cutting board over the baking pan and invert both the board and the pan. Lift the still-warm pan off the cake layer. Set the wire rack on top of the cake layer and invert all of it with the cutting board so that the cake layer is now right side up on the wire rack. Remove the cutting board and continue cooling the cake for at least 10 minutes or to room temperature, about 30 minutes, before slicing into wedges.

Fruit Turnovers

Servings: 6

Cooking Time: 25 Minutes

Ingredients:

- 1 sheet puff pastry dough
- 6 tsp peach preserves
- 3 kiwi, sliced
- 1 large egg, beaten
- 1 tbsp icing sugar

Directions:

1. Prepare puff pastry by cutting it into 6 rectangles. Roll out the pastry with a rolling pin into 5-inch squares. On your workspace, position one square so that it looks like a diamond with points to the top and bottom. Spoon 1 tsp of the preserves on the bottom half and spread it, leaving a ½-inch border from the edge. Place half of one kiwi on top of the preserves. Brush the clean edges with the egg, then fold the top corner over the filling to make a triangle. Crimp with a fork to seal the pastry. Brush the top of the pastry with egg. Preheat air fryer to 350°F (175°C). Put the pastries in the greased frying basket. Air Fry for 10 minutes, flipping once until golden and puffy. Remove from the fryer, let cool and dush with icing sugar. Serve.

Roasted Pears

Servings: 4

Cooking Time: 10 Minutes

Ingredients:

- 2 Ripe pears, preferably Anjou, stemmed, peeled, halved lengthwise, and cored
- 2 tablespoons Butter, melted
- 2 teaspoons Granulated white sugar
- Grated nutmeg
- ¼ cup Honey
- ½ cup (about 1½ ounces) Shaved Parmesan cheese

Directions:

1. Preheat the air fryer to 400°F (205°C).

2. Brush each pear half with about 1½ teaspoons of the melted butter, then sprinkle their cut sides with ½ teaspoon sugar. Grate a pinch of nutmeg over each pear.

3. When the machine is at temperature, set the pear halves cut side up in the basket with as much air space between them as possible. Air-fry undisturbed for 10 minutes, or until hot and softened.

4. Use a nonstick-safe spatula, and perhaps a flatware tablespoon for balance, to transfer the pear halves to a serving platter or plates. Cool for a minute or two, then drizzle each pear half with 1 tablespoon of the honey. Lay about 2 tablespoons of shaved Parmesan over each half just before serving.

Famous Chocolate Lava Cake

Servings: 4

Cooking Time: 15 Minutes

Ingredients:

- ¼ cup flour
- 1 tbsp cocoa powder
- ⅛ tsp salt
- ½ tsp baking powder
- 1 tsp vanilla extract
- ¼ cup raw honey
- 1 egg, beaten
- 2 tbsp olive oil
- 2 tbsp icing sugar, to dust

Directions:

1. Preheat air fryer to 380°F (195°C). Sift the flour, cocoa powder, salt, vanilla, and baking powder in a bowl. Add in honey, egg, and olive oil and stir to combine. Divide the batter evenly among greased ramekins. Put the filled ramekins inside the air fryer and Bake for 10 minutes. Remove the lava cakes from the fryer and slide a knife around the outside edge of each cake. Turn each ramekin upside down on a saucer and serve dusted with icing sugar.

Donut Holes

Servings: 13

Cooking Time: 12 Minutes

Ingredients:

- 6 tablespoons Granulated white sugar
- 1½ tablespoons Butter, melted and cooled
- 2 tablespoons (or 1 small egg, well beaten) Pasteurized egg substitute, such as Egg Beaters
- 6 tablespoons Regular or low-fat sour cream (not fat-free)
- ¾ teaspoon Vanilla extract
- 1⅔ cups All-purpose flour

- ¾ teaspoon Baking powder
- ¼ teaspoon Table salt
- Vegetable oil spray

Directions:

1. Preheat the air fryer to 350°F (175°C).
2. Whisk the sugar and melted butter in a medium bowl until well combined. Whisk in the egg substitute or egg, then the sour cream and vanilla until smooth. Remove the whisk and stir in the flour, baking powder, and salt with a wooden spoon just until a soft dough forms.
3. Use 2 tablespoons of this dough to create a ball between your clean palms. Set it aside and continue making balls: 8 more for the small batch, 12 more for the medium batch, or 17 more for the large one.
4. Coat the balls in the vegetable oil spray, then set them in the basket with as much air space between them as possible. Even a fraction of an inch will be enough, but they should not touch. Air-fry undisturbed for 12 minutes, or until browned and cooked through. A toothpick inserted into the center of a ball should come out clean.
5. Pour the contents of the basket onto a wire rack. Cool for at least 5 minutes before serving.

Fried Pineapple Chunks

Servings: 3

Cooking Time: 10 Minutes

Ingredients:

- 3 tablespoons Cornstarch
- 1 Large egg white, beaten until foamy
- 1 cup (4 ounces) Ground vanilla wafer cookies (not low-fat cookies)
- ¼ teaspoon Ground dried ginger
- 18 (about 2¼ cups) Fresh 1-inch chunks peeled and cored pineapple

Directions:

1. Preheat the air fryer to 400°F (205°C).
2. Put the cornstarch in a medium or large bowl. Put the beaten egg white in a small bowl. Pour the cookie crumbs and ground dried ginger into a large zip-closed plastic bag, shaking it a bit to combine them.
3. Dump the pineapple chunks into the bowl with the cornstarch. Toss and stir until well coated. Use your cleaned fingers or a large fork like a shovel to pick up a few pineapple chunks, shake off any excess cornstarch, and put them in the bowl with the egg white. Stir gently, then pick them up and let any excess egg white slip back into the rest. Put them in the bag with the crumb mixture. Repeat the cornstarch-then-egg process until all the pineapple chunks are in the bag. Seal the bag and shake gently, turning the bag this way and that, to coat the pieces well.
4. Set the coated pineapple chunks in the basket with as much air space between them as possible. Even a fraction of an inch will work, but they should not touch. Air-fry undisturbed for 10 minutes, or until golden brown and crisp.
5. Gently dump the contents of the basket onto a wire rack. Cool for at least 5 minutes or up to 15 minutes before serving.

Spiced Fruit Skewers

Servings: 4

Cooking Time: 15 Minutes

Ingredients:

- 2 peeled peaches, thickly sliced
- 3 plums, halved and pitted
- 3 peeled kiwi, quartered
- 1 tbsp honey
- ½ tsp ground cinnamon
- ¼ tsp ground allspice
- ¼ tsp cayenne pepper

Directions:

1. Preheat air fryer to 400°F (205°C). Combine the honey, cinnamon, allspice, and cayenne and set aside. Alternate fruits on 8 bamboo skewers, then brush the fruit with the honey mix. Lay the skewers in the air fryer and Air Fry for 3-5 minutes. Allow to chill for 5 minutes before serving.

Holiday Peppermint Cake

Servings: 4

Cooking Time: 20 Minutes

Ingredients:

- 1 ½ cups flour
- 3 eggs
- 1/3 cup molasses
- ½ cup olive oil
- ½ cup almond milk
- ½ tsp vanilla extract
- ½ tsp peppermint extract
- 1 tsp baking powder
- ½ tsp salt

Directions:

1. Preheat air fryer to 380°F (195°C). Whisk the eggs and molasses in a bowl until smooth. Slowly mix in the olive oil, almond milk, and vanilla and peppermint extracts until combined. Sift the flour, baking powder, and salt in another bowl. Gradually incorporate the dry ingredients into the wet ingredients until combined. Pour the batter into a greased baking pan and place in the fryer. Bake for 12-15 minutes until a toothpick inserted in the center comes out clean. Serve and enjoy!

Black And Blue Clafoutis

Servings: 2

Cooking Time: 15minutes

Ingredients:

- 6-inch pie pan
- 3 large eggs
- ½ cup sugar
- 1 teaspoon vanilla extract
- 2 tablespoons butter, melted 1 cup milk
- ½ cup all-purpose flour*
- 1 cup blackberries
- 1 cup blueberries
- 2 tablespoons confectioners' sugar

Directions:

1. Preheat the air fryer to 320°F (160°C).
2. Combine the eggs and sugar in a bowl and whisk vigorously until smooth, lighter in color and well combined. Add the vanilla extract, butter and milk and whisk together well. Add the flour and whisk just until no lumps or streaks of white remain.
3. Scatter half the blueberries and blackberries in a greased (6-inch) pie pan or cake pan. Pour half of the batter (about 1¼ cups) on top of the berries and transfer the tart pan to the air fryer basket. You can use an aluminum foil sling to help with this by taking a long piece of aluminum foil, folding it in half lengthwise twice until it is roughly 26-inches by 3-inches. Place this under the pie dish and hold the ends of the foil to move the pie dish in and out of the air fryer basket. Tuck the ends of the foil beside the pie dish while it cooks in the air fryer.
4. Air-fry at 320°F (160°C) for 15 minutes or until the clafoutis has puffed up and is still a little jiggly in the center. Remove the clafoutis from the air fryer, invert it onto a plate and let it cool while you bake the second batch. Serve the clafoutis warm, dusted with confectioners' sugar on top.

Coconut-custard Pie

Servings: 4

Cooking Time: 20 Minutes

Ingredients:

- 1 cup milk
- ¼ cup plus 2 tablespoons sugar
- ¼ cup biscuit baking mix
- 1 teaspoon vanilla
- 2 eggs
- 2 tablespoons melted butter
- cooking spray
- ½ cup shredded, sweetened coconut

Directions:

1. Place all ingredients except coconut in a medium bowl.
2. Using a hand mixer, beat on high speed for 3minutes.
3. Let sit for 5minutes.
4. Preheat air fryer to 330°F (165°C).
5. Spray a 6-inch round or 6 x 6-inch square baking pan with cooking spray and place pan in air fryer basket.
6. Pour filling into pan and sprinkle coconut over top.
7. Cook pie at 330°F (165°C) for 20 minutes or until center sets.

Spanish Churro Bites

Servings: 5

Cooking Time: 35 Minutes

Ingredients:

- ¼ tsp salt
- 2 tbsp vegetable oil
- 3 tbsp white sugar
- 1 cup flour
- ½ tsp ground cinnamon
- 2 tbsp granulated sugar

Directions:

1. On the stovetop, add 1 cup of water, salt, 1 tbsp of vegetable oil and 1 tbsp sugar in a pot. Bring to a boil over high heat. Remove from the heat and add flour. Stir with a wooden spoon until the flour is combined and a ball of dough forms. Cool for 5 minutes. Put the ball of dough in a plastic pastry bag with a star tip. Squeeze the dough to the tip and twist the top of the bag. Squeeze 10 strips of dough, about 5-inches long each, onto a workspace. Spray with cooking oil.
2. Preheat air fryer to 340°F (170°C). Place the churros in the greased frying basket and Air Fry for 22-25 minutes, flipping once halfway through until golden. Meanwhile, heat the remaining vegetable oil in a small bowl. In another shallow bowl, mix the remaining 2 tbsp sugar and cinnamon. Roll the cooked churros in cinnamon sugar. Top with granulated sugar and serve immediately.

Guilty Chocolate Cookies

Servings: 6

Cooking Time: 25 Minutes

Ingredients:

- 3 eggs, beaten
- 1 tsp vanilla extract
- 1 tsp apple cider vinegar
- 1/3 cup butter, softened
- 1/3 cup sugar
- ¼ cup cacao powder
- ¼ tsp baking soda

Directions:

1. Preheat air fryer to 300°F (150°C). Combine eggs, vanilla extract, and apple vinegar in a bowl until well combined. Refrigerate for 5 minutes. Whisk in butter and sugar until smooth, finally toss in cacao powder and baking soda until smooth. Make balls out of the mixture. Place the balls onto the parchment-lined frying basket. Bake for 13 minutes until brown. Using a fork, flatten each cookie. Let cool completely before serving.

Struffoli

Servings: X
Cooking Time: 20 Minutes

Ingredients:

- ¼ cup butter, softened
- ⅔ cup sugar
- 5 eggs
- 2 teaspoons vanilla extract
- zest of 1 lemon
- 4 cups all-purpose flour
- 2 teaspoons baking soda
- ¼ teaspoon salt
- 16 ounces honey
- 1 teaspoon ground cinnamon
- zest of 1 orange
- 2 tablespoons water
- nonpareils candy sprinkles

Directions:

1. Cream the butter and sugar together in a bowl until light and fluffy using a hand mixer (or a stand mixer). Add the eggs, vanilla and lemon zest and mix. In a separate bowl, combine the flour, baking soda and salt. Add the dry ingredients to the wet ingredients and mix until you have a soft dough. Shape the dough into a ball, wrap it in plastic and let it rest for 30 minutes.
2. Divide the dough ball into four pieces. Roll each piece into a long rope. Cut each rope into about 25 (½-inch) pieces. Roll each piece into a tight ball. You should have 100 little balls when finished.
3. Preheat the air fryer to 370°F (185°C).
4. In batches of about 20, transfer the dough balls to the air fryer basket, leaving a small space in between them. Air-fry the dough balls at 370°F (185°C) for 3 to 4 minutes, shaking the basket when one minute of cooking time remains.
5. After all the dough balls are air-fried, make the honey topping. Melt the honey in a small saucepan on the stovetop. Add the cinnamon, orange zest, and water. Simmer for one minute. Place the air-fried dough balls in a large bowl and drizzle the honey mixture over top. Gently toss to coat all the dough balls evenly. Transfer the coated struffoli to a platter and sprinkle the nonpareil candy sprinkles over top. You can dress the presentation up by piling the balls into the shape of a wreath or pile them high in a cone shape to resemble a Christmas tree.
6. Struffoli can be made ahead. Store covered tightly.

Vegetarians Recipes

Honey Pear Chips

Servings: 4
Cooking Time: 30 Minutes

Ingredients:

- 2 firm pears, thinly sliced
- 1 tbsp lemon juice
- ½ tsp ground cinnamon
- 1 tsp honey

Directions:

1. Preheat air fryer to 380°F (195°C). Arrange the pear slices on the parchment-lined cooking basket. Drizzle with lemon juice and honey and sprinkle with cinnamon. Air Fry for 6-8 minutes, shaking the basket once, until golden. Leave to cool. Serve immediately or save for later in an airtight container. Good for 2 days.

Pizza Portobello Mushrooms

Servings: 2
Cooking Time: 18 Minutes

Ingredients:

- 2 portobello mushroom caps, gills removed (see Figure 13-1)
- 1 teaspoon extra-virgin olive oil
- ¼ cup diced onion
- 1 teaspoon minced garlic

- 1 medium zucchini, shredded
- 1 teaspoon dried oregano
- ½ teaspoon black pepper
- ¼ teaspoon salt
- ⅓ cup marinara sauce
- ¼ cup shredded part-skim mozzarella cheese
- ¼ teaspoon red pepper flakes
- 2 tablespoons Parmesan cheese
- 2 tablespoons chopped basil

Directions:
1. Preheat the air fryer to 370°F (185°C).
2. Lightly spray the mushrooms with an olive oil mist and place into the air fryer to cook for 10 minutes, cap side up.
3. Add the olive oil to a pan and sauté the onion and garlic together for about 2 to 4 minutes. Stir in the zucchini, oregano, pepper, and salt, and continue to cook. When the zucchini has cooked down (usually about 4 to 6 minutes), add in the marinara sauce. Remove from the heat and stir in the mozzarella cheese.
4. Remove the mushrooms from the air fryer basket when cooking completes. Reset the temperature to 350°F (17°C).
5. Using a spoon, carefully stuff the mushrooms with the zucchini marinara mixture.
6. Return the stuffed mushrooms to the air fryer basket and cook for 5 to 8 minutes, or until the cheese is lightly browned. You should be able to easily insert a fork into the mushrooms when they're cooked.
7. Remove the mushrooms and sprinkle the red pepper flakes, Parmesan cheese, and fresh basil over the top.
8. Serve warm.

Green Bean Sautée

Servings: 4
Cooking Time: 25 Minutes

Ingredients:
- 1 ½ lb green beans, trimmed
- 1 tbsp olive oil
- ½ tsp garlic powder
- Salt and pepper to taste
- 4 garlic cloves, thinly sliced
- 1 tbsp fresh basil, chopped

Directions:
1. Preheat the air fryer to 375°F (190°C). Toss the beans with the olive oil, garlic powder, salt, and pepper in a bowl, then add to the frying basket. Air Fry for 6 minutes, shaking the basket halfway through the cooking time. Add garlic to the air fryer and cook for 3-6 minutes or until the green beans are tender and the garlic slices start to brown. Sprinkle with basil and serve warm.

Tropical Salsa

Servings: 4
Cooking Time: 15 Minutes

Ingredients:
- 1 cup pineapple cubes
- ½ apple, cubed
- Salt to taste
- ¼ tsp olive oil
- 2 tomatoes, diced
- 1 avocado, diced
- 3-4 strawberries, diced
- ¼ cup diced red onion
- 1 tbsp chopped cilantro
- 1 tbsp chopped parsley
- 2 cloves garlic, minced
- ½ tsp granulated sugar
- ½ lime, juiced

Directions:
1. Preheat air fryer at 400ºF. Combine pineapple cubes, apples, olive oil, and salt in a bowl. Place pineapple in the greased frying basket, and Air Fry for 8 minutes, shaking once. Transfer it to a bowl. Toss in tomatoes, avocado, strawberries, onion, cilantro, parsley, garlic, sugar, lime juice, and salt. Let chill in the fridge before using.

Veggie Burgers

Servings: 4
Cooking Time: 15 Minutes

Ingredients:
- 2 cans black beans, rinsed and drained
- ½ cup cooked quinoa
- ½ cup shredded raw sweet potato
- ¼ cup diced red onion
- 2 teaspoons ground cumin
- 1 teaspoon coriander powder
- ½ teaspoon salt
- oil for misting or cooking spray
- 8 slices bread
- suggested toppings: lettuce, tomato, red onion, Pepper Jack cheese, guacamole

Directions:
1. In a medium bowl, mash the beans with a fork.
2. Add the quinoa, sweet potato, onion, cumin, coriander, and salt and mix well with the fork.
3. Shape into 4 patties, each ¾-inch thick.
4. Mist both sides with oil or cooking spray and also mist the basket.
5. Cook at 390°F (200°C) for 15minutes.
6. Follow the recipe for Toast, Plain & Simple.
7. Pop the veggie burgers back in the air fryer for a minute or two to reheat if necessary.
8. Serve on the toast with your favorite burger toppings.

Cheesy Eggplant Rounds

Servings: 4

Cooking Time: 35 Minutes

Ingredients:

- 1 eggplant, peeled
- 2 eggs
- ½ cup all-purpose flour
- ¾ cup bread crumbs
- 2 tbsp grated Swiss cheese
- Salt and pepper to taste
- ¾ cup tomato passata
- ½ cup shredded Parmesan
- ½ cup shredded mozzarella

Directions:

1. Preheat air fryer to 400°F (205°C). Slice the eggplant into ½-inch rounds. Set aside. Set out three small bowls. In the first bowl, add flour. In the second bowl, beat the eggs. In the third bowl, mix the crumbs, 2 tbsp of grated Swiss cheese, salt, and pepper. Dip each eggplant in the flour, then dredge in egg, then coat with bread crumb mixture. Arrange the eggplant rounds on the greased frying basket and spray with cooking oil. Bake for 7 minutes. Top each eggplant round with 1 tsp passata and ½ tbsp each of shredded Parmesan and mozzarella. Cook until the cheese melts, 2-3 minutes. Serve warm and enjoy!

Rigatoni With Roasted Onions, Fennel, Spinach And Lemon Pepper Ricotta

Servings: 2

Cooking Time: 13 Minutes

Ingredients:

- 1 red onion, rough chopped into large chunks
- 2 teaspoons olive oil, divided
- 1 bulb fennel, sliced ¼-inch thick
- ¾ cup ricotta cheese
- 1½ teaspoons finely chopped lemon zest, plus more for garnish
- 1 teaspoon lemon juice
- salt and freshly ground black pepper
- 8 ounces (½ pound) dried rigatoni pasta
- 3 cups baby spinach leaves

Directions:

1. Bring a large stockpot of salted water to a boil on the stovetop and Preheat the air fryer to 400°F (205°C).
2. While the water is coming to a boil, toss the chopped onion in 1 teaspoon of olive oil and transfer to the air fryer basket. Air-fry at 400°F (205°C) for 5 minutes. Toss the sliced fennel with 1 teaspoon of olive oil and add this to the air fryer basket with the onions. Continue to air-fry at 400°F (205°C) for 8 minutes, shaking the basket a few times during the cooking process.
3. Combine the ricotta cheese, lemon zest and juice, ¼ teaspoon of salt and freshly ground black pepper in a bowl and stir until smooth.
4. Add the dried rigatoni to the boiling water and cook according to the package directions. When the pasta is cooked al dente, reserve one cup of the pasta water and drain the pasta into a colander.
5. Place the spinach in a serving bowl and immediately transfer the hot pasta to the bowl, wilting the spinach. Add the roasted onions and fennel and toss together. Add a little pasta water to the dish if it needs moistening. Then, dollop the lemon pepper ricotta cheese on top and nestle it into the hot pasta. Garnish with more lemon zest if desired.

Home-style Cinnamon Rolls

Servings: 4

Cooking Time: 40 Minutes

Ingredients:

- ½ pizza dough
- 1/3 cup dark brown sugar
- ¼ cup butter, softened
- ½ tsp ground cinnamon

Directions:

1. Preheat air fryer to 360°F (180°C). Roll out the dough into a rectangle. Using a knife, spread the brown sugar and butter, covering all the edges, and sprinkle with cinnamon.Fold the long side of the dough into a log, then cut it into 8 equal pieces, avoiding compression. Place the rolls, spiral-side up, onto a parchment-lined sheet. Let rise for 20 minutes. Grease the rolls with cooking spray and Bake for 8 minutes until golden brown. Serve right away.

Tortilla Pizza Margherita

Servings: 1

Cooking Time: 15 Minutes

Ingredients:

- 1 flour tortilla
- ¼ cup tomato sauce
- 1/3 cup grated mozzarella
- 3 basil leaves

Directions:

1. Preheat air fryer to 350°F (175°C). Put the tortilla in the greased basket and pour the sauce in the center. Spread across the whole tortilla. Sprinkle with cheese and Bake for 8-10 minutes or until crisp. Remove carefully and top with basil leaves. Serve hot.

Vegetarian Paella

Servings: 3
Cooking Time: 50 Minutes

Ingredients:

- ½ cup chopped artichoke hearts
- ½ sliced red bell peppers
- 4 mushrooms, thinly sliced
- ½ cup canned diced tomatoes
- ½ cup canned chickpeas
- 3 tbsp hot sauce
- 2 tbsp lemon juice
- 1 tbsp allspice
- 1 cup rice

Directions:

1. Preheat air fryer to 400°F (205°C). Combine the artichokes, peppers, mushrooms, tomatoes and their juices, chickpeas, hot sauce, lemon juice, and allspice in a baking pan. Roast for 10 minutes. Pour in rice and 2 cups of boiling water, cover with aluminum foil, and Roast for 22 minutes. Discard the foil and Roast for 3 minutes until the top is crisp. Let cool slightly before stirring. Serve.

Colorful Vegetable Medley

Servings: 4
Cooking Time: 20 Minutes

Ingredients:

- 1 lb green beans, chopped
- 2 carrots, cubed
- Salt and pepper to taste
- 1 zucchini, cut into chunks
- 1 red bell pepper, sliced

Directions:

1. Preheat air fryer to 390°F (200°C). Combine green beans, carrots, salt and pepper in a large bowl. Spray with cooking oil and transfer to the frying basket. Roast for 6 minutes.
2. Combine zucchini and red pepper in a bowl. Season to taste and spray with cooking oil; set aside. When the cooking time is up, add the zucchini and red pepper to the basket. Cook for another 6 minutes. Serve and enjoy.

Spaghetti Squash And Kale Fritters With Pomodoro Sauce

Servings: 3
Cooking Time: 45 Minutes

Ingredients:

- 1½-pound spaghetti squash (about half a large or a whole small squash)
- olive oil
- ½ onion, diced
- ½ red bell pepper, diced
- 2 cloves garlic, minced
- 4 cups coarsely chopped kale
- salt and freshly ground black pepper
- 1 egg
- ⅓ cup breadcrumbs, divided*
- ⅓ cup grated Parmesan cheese
- ½ teaspoon dried rubbed sage
- pinch nutmeg
- Pomodoro Sauce:
- 2 tablespoons olive oil
- ½ onion, chopped
- 1 to 2 cloves garlic, minced
- 1 (28-ounce) can peeled tomatoes
- ¼ cup red wine
- 1 teaspoon Italian seasoning
- 2 tablespoons chopped fresh basil, plus more for garnish
- salt and freshly ground black pepper
- ½ teaspoon sugar (optional)

Directions:

1. Preheat the air fryer to 370°F (185°C).
2. Cut the spaghetti squash in half lengthwise and remove the seeds. Rub the inside of the squash with olive oil and season with salt and pepper. Place the squash, cut side up, into the air fryer basket and air-fry for 30 minutes, flipping the squash over halfway through the cooking process.
3. While the squash is cooking, Preheat a large sauté pan over medium heat on the stovetop. Add a little olive oil and sauté the onions for 3 minutes, until they start to soften. Add the red pepper and garlic and continue to sauté for an additional 4 minutes. Add the kale and season with salt and pepper. Cook for 2 more minutes, or until the kale is soft. Transfer the mixture to a large bowl and let it cool.
4. While the squash continues to cook, make the Pomodoro sauce. Preheat the large sauté pan again over medium heat on the stovetop. Add the olive oil and sauté the onion and garlic for 2 to 3 minutes, until the onion begins to soften. Crush the canned tomatoes with your hands and add them to the pan along with the red wine and Italian seasoning and simmer for 20 minutes. Add the basil and season to taste with salt, pepper and sugar (if using).
5. When the spaghetti squash has finished cooking, use a fork to scrape the inside flesh of the squash onto a sheet pan. Spread the squash out and let it cool.
6. Once cool, add the spaghetti squash to the kale mixture, along with the egg, breadcrumbs, Parmesan cheese, sage,

nutmeg, salt and freshly ground black pepper. Stir to combine well and then divide the mixture into 6 thick portions. You can shape the portions into patties, but I prefer to keep them a little random and unique in shape. Spray or brush the fritters with olive oil.
7. Preheat the air fryer to 370°F (185°C).
8. Brush the air fryer basket with a little olive oil and transfer the fritters to the basket. Air-fry the squash and kale fritters at 370°F (185°C) for 15 minutes, flipping them over halfway through the cooking process.
9. Serve the fritters warm with the Pomodoro sauce spooned over the top or pooled on your plate. Garnish with the fresh basil leaves.

Egg Rolls

Servings: 4
Cooking Time: 8 Minutes
Ingredients:
- 1 clove garlic, minced
- 1 teaspoon sesame oil
- 1 teaspoon olive oil
- ½ cup chopped celery
- ½ cup grated carrots
- 2 green onions, chopped
- 2 ounces mushrooms, chopped
- 2 cups shredded Napa cabbage
- 1 teaspoon low-sodium soy sauce
- 1 teaspoon cornstarch
- salt
- 1 egg
- 1 tablespoon water
- 4 egg roll wraps
- olive oil for misting or cooking spray

Directions:
1. In a large skillet, sauté garlic in sesame and olive oils over medium heat for 1 minute.
2. Add celery, carrots, onions, and mushrooms to skillet. Cook 1 minute, stirring.
3. Stir in cabbage, cover, and cook for 1 minute or just until cabbage slightly wilts.
4. In a small bowl, mix soy sauce and cornstarch. Stir into vegetables to thicken. Remove from heat. Salt to taste if needed.
5. Beat together egg and water in a small bowl.
6. Divide filling into 4 portions and roll up in egg roll wraps. Brush all over with egg wash to seal.
7. Mist egg rolls very lightly with olive oil or cooking spray and place in air fryer basket.
8. Cook at 390°F (200°C) for 4 minutes. Turn over and cook 4 more minutes, until golden brown and crispy.

Golden Breaded Mushrooms

Servings: 2
Cooking Time: 20 Minutes
Ingredients:
- 2 cups crispy rice cereal
- 1 tsp nutritional yeast
- 2 tsp garlic powder
- 1tsp dried oregano
- 1 tsp dried basil
- Salt to taste
- 1 tbsp Dijon mustard
- 1 tbsp mayonnaise
- ¼ cup milk
- 8 oz whole mushrooms
- 4 tbsp chili sauce
- 3 tbsp mayonnaise

Directions:
1. Preheat air fryer at 350ºF. Blend rice cereal, garlic powder, oregano, basil, nutritional yeast, and salt in a food processor until it gets a breadcrumb consistency. Set aside in a bowl. Mix the mustard, mayonnaise, and milk in a bowl. Dip mushrooms in the mustard mixture; shake off any excess. Then, dredge them in the breadcrumbs; shake off any excess. Places mushrooms in the greased frying basket and Air Fry for 7 minutes, shaking once. Mix the mayonnaise with chili sauce in a small bowl. Serve the mushrooms with the dipping sauce on the side.

Meatless Kimchi Bowls

Servings:4
Cooking Time: 20 Minutes
Ingredients:
- 2 cups canned chickpeas
- 1 carrot, julienned
- 6 scallions, sliced
- 1 zucchini, diced
- 2 tbsp coconut aminos
- 2 tsp sesame oil
- 1 tsp rice vinegar
- 2 tsp granulated sugar
- 1 tbsp gochujang
- ¼ tsp salt
- ½ cup kimchi
- 2 tsp roasted sesame seeds

Directions:
1. Preheat air fryer to 350ºF. Combine all ingredients, except for the kimchi, 2 scallions, and sesame seeds, in a baking pan. Place the pan in the frying basket and Air Fry for 6 minutes. Toss in kimchi and cook for 2 more minutes. Divide between 2 bowls and garnish with the remaining scallions and sesame seeds. Serve immediately.

Farfalle With White Sauce

Servings: 4

Cooking Time: 30 Minutes

Ingredients:

- 4 cups cauliflower florets
- 1 medium onion, chopped
- 8 oz farfalle pasta
- 2 tbsp chives, minced
- ½ cup cashew pieces
- 1 tbsp nutritional yeast
- 2 large garlic cloves, peeled
- 2 tbsp fresh lemon juice
- Salt and pepper to taste

Directions:

1. Preheat air fryer to 390°F (200°C). Put the cauliflower in the fryer, spray with oil, and Bake for 8 minutes. Remove the basket, stir, and add the onion. Roast for 10 minutes or until the cauliflower is golden and the onions soft. Cook the farfalle pasta according to the package directions. Set aside. Put the roasted cauliflower and onions along with the cashews, 1 ½ of cups water, yeast, garlic, lemon, salt, and pepper in a blender. Blend until creamy. Pour a large portion of the sauce on top of the warm pasta and add the minced scallions. Serve.

Sushi-style Deviled Eggs

Servings: 4

Cooking Time: 20 Minutes

Ingredients:

- ¼ cup crabmeat, shells discarded
- 4 eggs
- 2 tbsp mayonnaise
- ½ tsp soy sauce
- ¼ avocado, diced
- ¼ tsp wasabi powder
- 2 tbsp diced cucumber
- 1 sheet nori, sliced
- 8 jarred pickled ginger slices
- 1 tsp toasted sesame seeds
- 2 spring onions, sliced

Directions:

1. Preheat air fryer to 260°F. Place the eggs in muffin cups to avoid bumping around and cracking during the cooking process. Add silicone cups to the frying basket and Air Fry for 15 minutes. Remove and plunge the eggs immediately into an ice bath to cool, about 5 minutes. Carefully peel and slice them in half lengthwise. Spoon yolks into a separate medium bowl and arrange white halves on a large plate. Mash the yolks with a fork. Stir in mayonnaise, soy sauce, avocado, and wasabi powder until smooth. Mix in cucumber and spoon into white halves. Scatter eggs with crabmeat, nori, pickled ginger, spring onions and sesame seeds to serve.

Quick-to-make Quesadillas

Servings: 4

Cooking Time: 30 Minutes

Ingredients:

- 12 oz goat cheese
- 2 tbsp vinegar
- 1 tbsp Taco seasoning
- 1 ripe avocado, pitted
- 4 scallions, finely sliced
- 2 tbsp lemon juice
- 4 flour tortillas
- ¼ cup hot sauce
- ½ cup Alfredo sauce
- 16 cherry tomatoes, halved

Directions:

1. Preheat air fryer to 400°F (205°C). Slice goat cheese into 4 pieces. Set aside. In a bowl, whisk vinegar and taco seasoning until combined. Submerge each slice into the vinegar and Air Fry for 12 minutes until crisp, turning once. Let cool slightly before cutting into 1/2-inch thick strips.

2. Using a fork, mash the avocado in a bowl. Stir in scallions and lemon juice and set aside. Lay one tortilla on a flat surface, cut from one edge to the center, then spread ¼ of the avocado mixture on one quadrant, 1 tbsp of hot sauce on the next quadrant, and finally 2 tbsp of Alfredo sauce on the other half. Top the non-sauce half with ¼ of cherry tomatoes and ¼ of goat cheese strips.

3. To fold, start with the avocado quadrant, folding each over the next one until you create a stacked triangle. Repeat the process with the remaining tortillas. Air Fry for 5 minutes until crispy, turning once. Serve warm.

Spicy Bean Patties

Servings: 4

Cooking Time: 20 Minutes

Ingredients:

- 1 cup canned black beans
- 1 bread slice, torn
- 2 tbsp spicy brown mustard
- 1 tbsp chili powder
- 1 egg white
- 2 tbsp grated carrots
- ¼ diced green bell pepper
- 1-2 jalapeño peppers, diced

- ¼ tsp ground cumin
- ¼ tsp smoked paprika
- 2 tbsp cream cheese
- 1 tbsp olive oil

Directions:

1. Preheat air fryer at 350°F. Using a fork, mash beans until smooth. Stir in the remaining ingredients, except olive oil. Form mixture into 4 patties. Place bean patties in the greased frying basket and Air Fry for 6 minutes, turning once, and brush with olive oil. Serve immediately.

Pineapple & Veggie Souvlaki

Servings: 4

Cooking Time: 35 Minutes

Ingredients:

- 1 can pineapple rings in pineapple juice
- 1 red bell pepper, stemmed and seeded
- 1/3 cup butter
- 2 tbsp apple cider vinegar
- 2 tbsp hot sauce
- 1 tbsp allspice
- 1 tsp ground nutmeg
- 16 oz feta cheese
- 1 red onion, peeled
- 8 mushrooms, quartered

Directions:

1. Preheat air fryer to 400°F (205°C). Whisk the butter, pineapple juice, apple vinegar, hot sauce, allspice, and nutmeg until smooth. Set aside. Slice feta cheese into 16 cubes, then the bell pepper into 16 chunks, and finally red onion into 8 wedges, separating each wedge into 2 pieces.

2. Cut pineapple ring into quarters. Place veggie cubes and feta into the butter bowl and toss to coat. Thread the veggies, tofu, and pineapple onto 8 skewers, alternating 16 pieces on each skewer. Grill for 15 minutes until golden brown and cooked. Serve warm.

Vegetarian Eggplant "pizzas"

Servings: 4

Cooking Time: 25 Minutes

Ingredients:

- ½ cup diced baby bella mushrooms
- 3 tbsp olive oil
- ¼ cup diced onions
- ½ cup pizza sauce
- 1 eggplant, sliced
- 1 tsp salt
- 1 cup shredded mozzarella
- ¼ cup chopped oregano

Directions:

1. Warm 2 tsp of olive oil in a skillet over medium heat. Add in onion and mushrooms and stir-fry for 4 minutes until tender. Stir in pizza sauce. Turn the heat off.

2. Preheat air fryer to 375°F. Brush the eggplant slices with the remaining olive oil on both sides. Lay out slices on a large plate and season with salt. Then, top with the sauce mixture and shredded mozzarella. Place the eggplant pizzas in the frying basket and Air Fry for 5 minutes. Garnish with oregano to serve.

Authentic Mexican Esquites

Servings: 4

Cooking Time: 25 Minutes

Ingredients:

- 4 ears of corn, husk and silk removed
- 1 tbsp ground coriander
- 1 tbsp smoked paprika
- 1 tsp sea salt
- 1 tsp garlic powder
- 1 tsp onion powder
- 1 tsp dried lime peel
- 1 tsp cayenne pepper
- 3 tbsp mayonnaise
- 3 tbsp grated Cotija cheese
- 1 tbsp butter, melted
- 1 tsp epazote seasoning

Directions:

1. Preheat the air fryer to 400°F (205°C). Combine the coriander, paprika, salt, garlic powder, onion powder, lime peel, epazote and cayenne pepper in a small bowl and mix well. Pour into a small glass jar. Put the corn in the greased frying basket and Bake for 6-8 minutes or until the corn is crispy but tender. Make sure to rearrange the ears halfway through cooking.

2. While the corn is frying, combine the mayonnaise, cheese, and melted butter in a small bowl. Spread the mixture over the cooked corn, return to the fryer, and Bake for 3-5 minutes more or until the corn has brown spots. Remove from the fryer and sprinkle each cob with about ½ tsp of the spice mix.

Bell Pepper & Lentil Tacos

Servings: 2

Cooking Time: 40 Minutes

Ingredients:

- 2 corn tortilla shells
- ½ cup cooked lentils
- ½ white onion, sliced

- ½ red pepper, sliced
- ½ green pepper, sliced
- ½ yellow pepper, sliced
- ½ cup shredded mozzarella
- ½ tsp Tabasco sauce

Directions:
1. Preheat air fryer to 320°F (160°C). Sprinkle half of the mozzarella cheese over one of the tortillas, then top with lentils, Tabasco sauce, onion, and peppers. Scatter the remaining mozzarella cheese, cover with the other tortilla and place in the frying basket. Bake for 6 minutes, flipping halfway through cooking. Serve and enjoy!

Spinach And Cheese Calzone

Servings: 2
Cooking Time: 10 Minutes

Ingredients:
- ⅔ cup frozen chopped spinach, thawed
- 1 cup grated mozzarella cheese
- 1 cup ricotta cheese
- ½ teaspoon Italian seasoning
- ½ teaspoon salt
- freshly ground black pepper
- 1 store-bought or homemade pizza dough* (about 12 to 16 ounces)
- 2 tablespoons olive oil
- pizza or marinara sauce (optional)

Directions:
1. Drain and squeeze all the water out of the thawed spinach and set it aside. Mix the mozzarella cheese, ricotta cheese, Italian seasoning, salt and freshly ground black pepper together in a bowl. Stir in the chopped spinach.
2. Divide the dough in half. With floured hands or on a floured surface, stretch or roll one half of the dough into a 10-inch circle. Spread half of the cheese and spinach mixture on half of the dough, leaving about one inch of dough empty around the edge.
3. Fold the other half of the dough over the cheese mixture, almost to the edge of the bottom dough to form a half moon. Fold the bottom edge of dough up over the top edge and crimp the dough around the edges in order to make the crust and seal the calzone. Brush the dough with olive oil. Repeat with the second half of dough to make the second calzone.
4. Preheat the air fryer to 360°F (180°C).
5. Brush or spray the air fryer basket with olive oil. Air-fry the calzones one at a time for 10 minutes, flipping the calzone over half way through. Serve with warm pizza or marinara sauce if desired.

Tomato & Squash Stuffed Mushrooms

Servings: 2
Cooking Time: 15 Minutes

Ingredients:
- 12 whole white button mushrooms
- 3 tsp olive oil
- 2 tbsp diced zucchini
- 1 tsp soy sauce
- ¼ tsp salt
- 2 tbsp tomato paste
- 1 tbsp chopped parsley

Directions:
1. Preheat air fryer to 350ºF. Remove the stems from the mushrooms. Chop the stems finely and set in a bowl. Brush 1 tsp of olive oil around the top ridge of mushroom caps. To the bowl of the stem, add all ingredients, except for parsley, and mix. Divide and press mixture into tops of mushroom caps. Place the mushrooms in the frying basket and Air Fry for 5 minutes. Top with parsley. Serve.

Effortless Mac `n´ Cheese

Servings: 4
Cooking Time: 15 Minutes

Ingredients:
- 1 cup heavy cream
- 1 cup milk
- ½ cup mozzarella cheese
- 2 tsp grated Parmesan cheese
- 16 oz cooked elbow macaroni

Directions:
1. Preheat air fryer to 400°F (205°C). Whisk the heavy cream, milk, mozzarella cheese, and Parmesan cheese until smooth in a bowl. Stir in the macaroni and pour into a baking dish. Cover with foil and Bake in the air fryer for 6 minutes. Remove foil and Bake until cooked through and bubbly, 3-5 minutes. Serve warm.

Curried Potato, Cauliflower And Pea Turnovers

Servings: 4
Cooking Time: 40 Minutes

Ingredients:
- Dough:
- 2 cups all-purpose flour
- ½ teaspoon baking powder
- 1 teaspoon salt

- freshly ground black pepper
- ¼ teaspoon dried thyme
- ¼ cup canola oil
- ½ to ⅔ cup water
- Turnover Filling:
- 1 tablespoon canola or vegetable oil
- 1 onion, finely chopped
- 1 clove garlic, minced
- 1 tablespoon grated fresh ginger
- ½ teaspoon cumin seeds
- ½ teaspoon fennel seeds
- 1 teaspoon curry powder
- 2 russet potatoes, diced
- 2 cups cauliflower florets
- ½ cup frozen peas
- 2 tablespoons chopped fresh cilantro
- salt and freshly ground black pepper
- 2 tablespoons butter, melted
- mango chutney, for serving

Directions:

1. Start by making the dough. Combine the flour, baking powder, salt, pepper and dried thyme in a mixing bowl or the bowl of a stand mixer. Drizzle in the canola oil and pinch it together with your fingers to turn the flour into a crumby mixture. Stir in the water (enough to bring the dough together). Knead the dough for 5 minutes or so until it is smooth. Add a little more water or flour as needed. Let the dough rest while you make the turnover filling.

2. Preheat a large skillet on the stovetop over medium-high heat. Add the oil and sauté the onion until it starts to become tender – about 4 minutes. Add the garlic and ginger and continue to cook for another minute. Add the dried spices and toss everything to coat. Add the potatoes and cauliflower to the skillet and pour in 1½ cups of water. Simmer everything together for 20 to 25 minutes, or until the potatoes are soft and most of the water has evaporated. If the water has evaporated and the vegetables still need more time, just add a little water and continue to simmer until everything is tender. Stir well, crushing the potatoes and cauliflower a little as you do so. Stir in the peas and cilantro, season to taste with salt and freshly ground black pepper and set aside to cool.

3. Divide the dough into 4 balls. Roll the dough balls out into ¼-inch thick circles. Divide the cooled potato filling between the dough circles, placing a mound of the filling on one side of each piece of dough, leaving an empty border around the edge of the dough. Brush the edges of the dough with a little water and fold one edge of circle over the filling to meet the other edge of the circle, creating a half moon. Pinch the edges together with your fingers and then press the edge with the tines of a fork to decorate and seal.

4. Preheat the air fryer to 380°F (195°C).

5. Spray or brush the air fryer basket with oil. Brush the turnovers with the melted butter and place 2 turnovers into the air fryer basket. Air-fry for 15 minutes. Flip the turnovers over and air-fry for another 5 minutes. Repeat with the remaining 2 turnovers.

6. These will be very hot when they come out of the air fryer. Let them cool for at least 20 minutes before serving warm with mango chutney.

Fennel Tofu Bites

Servings: 4

Cooking Time: 35 Minutes

Ingredients:

- 1/3 cup vegetable broth
- 2 tbsp tomato sauce
- 2 tsp soy sauce
- 1 tbsp nutritional yeast
- 1 tsp Italian seasoning
- 1 tsp granulated sugar
- 1 tsp ginger grated
- ½ tsp fennel seeds
- ½ tsp garlic powder
- Salt and pepper to taste
- 14 oz firm tofu, cubed
- 2/3 cup bread crumbs
- 1 tsp Italian seasoning
- 2 tsp toasted sesame seeds
- 1 cup marinara sauce, warm

Directions:

1. In a large bowl, whisk the vegetable broth, soy sauce, ginger, tomato sauce, nutritional yeast, Italian seasoning, sugar, fennel seeds, garlic powder, salt and black pepper. Toss in tofu to coat. Let marinate covered in the fridge for 30 minutes, tossing once.

2. Preheat air fryer at 350ºF. Mix the breadcrumbs, Italian seasoning, and salt in a bowl. Strain marinade from tofu cubes and dredge them in the breadcrumb mixture. Place tofu cubes in the greased frying basket and Air Fry for 10 minutes, turning once. Serve sprinkled with sesame seeds and marinara sauce on the side.

Tex-mex Stuffed Sweet Potatoes

Servings: 2

Cooking Time: 40 Minutes

Ingredients:

- 2 medium sweet potatoes
- 1 can black beans
- 2 scallions, finely sliced

- 1 tbsp hot sauce
- 1 tsp taco seasoning
- 2 tbsp lime juice
- ¼ cup Ranch dressing

Directions:

1. Preheat air fryer to 400°F (205°C). Add in sweet potatoes and Roast for 30 minutes. Toss the beans, scallions, hot sauce, taco seasoning, and lime juice. Set aside. Once the potatoes are ready, cut them lengthwise, 2/3 through. Spoon 1/4 of the bean mixture into each half and drizzle Ranch dressing before serving.

Easy Cheese & Spinach Lasagna

Servings: 6
Cooking Time: 50 Minutes

Ingredients:

- 1 zucchini, cut into strips
- 1 tbsp butter
- 4 garlic cloves, minced
- ½ yellow onion, diced
- 1 tsp dried oregano
- ¼ tsp red pepper flakes
- 1 can diced tomatoes
- 4 oz ricotta
- 3 tbsp grated mozzarella
- ½ cup grated cheddar
- 3 tsp grated Parmesan cheese
- ⅛ cup chopped basil
- 2 tbsp chopped parsley
- Salt and pepper to taste
- ¼ tsp ground nutmeg

Directions:

1. Preheat air fryer to 375°F (190°C). Melt butter in a medium skillet over medium heat. Stir in half of the garlic and onion and cook for 2 minutes. Stir in oregano and red pepper flakes and cook for 1 minute. Reduce the heat to medium-low and pour in crushed tomatoes and their juices. Cover the skillet and simmer for 5 minutes.
2. Mix ricotta, mozzarella, cheddar cheese, rest of the garlic, basil, black pepper, and nutmeg in a large bowl. Arrange a layer of zucchini strips in the baking dish. Scoop 1/3 of the cheese mixture and spread evenly over the zucchini. Spread 1/3 of the tomato sauce over the cheese. Repeat the steps two more times, then top the lasagna with Parmesan cheese. Bake in the frying basket for 25 minutes until the mixture is bubbling and the mozzarella is melted. Allow sitting for 10 minutes before cutting. Serve warm sprinkled with parsley and enjoy!

Mushroom Bolognese Casserole

Servings: 4
Cooking Time: 20 Minutes

Ingredients:

- 1 cup canned diced tomatoes
- 2 garlic cloves, minced
- 1 tsp onion powder
- ¾ tsp dried basil
- ¾ tsp dried oregano
- 1 cup chopped mushrooms
- 16 oz cooked spaghetti

Directions:

1. Preheat air fryer to 400°F (205°C). Whisk the tomatoes and their juices, garlic, onion powder, basil, oregano, and mushrooms in a baking pan. Cover with aluminum foil and Bake for 6 minutes. Slide out the pan and add the cooked spaghetti; stir to coat. Cover with aluminum foil and Bake for 3 minutes until and bubbly. Serve and enjoy!

Cauliflower Steaks Gratin

Servings: 2
Cooking Time: 13 Minutes

Ingredients:

- 1 head cauliflower
- 1 tablespoon olive oil
- salt and freshly ground black pepper
- ½ teaspoon chopped fresh thyme leaves
- 3 tablespoons grated Parmigiano-Reggiano cheese
- 2 tablespoons panko breadcrumbs

Directions:

1. Preheat the air-fryer to 370°F (190°C).
2. Cut two steaks out of the center of the cauliflower. To do this, cut the cauliflower in half and then cut one slice about 1-inch thick off each half. The rest of the cauliflower will fall apart into florets, which you can roast on their own or save for another meal.
3. Brush both sides of the cauliflower steaks with olive oil and season with salt, freshly ground black pepper and fresh thyme. Place the cauliflower steaks into the air fryer basket and air-fry for 6 minutes. Turn the steaks over and air-fry for another 4 minutes. Combine the Parmesan cheese and panko breadcrumbs and sprinkle the mixture over the tops of both steaks and air-fry for another 3 minutes until the cheese has melted and the breadcrumbs have browned. Serve this with some sautéed bitter greens and air-fried blistered tomatoes.

Bite-sized Blooming Onions

Servings: 4

Cooking Time: 35 Minutes + Cooling Time

Ingredients:

- 1 lb cipollini onions
- 1 cup flour
- 1 tsp salt
- ½ tsp paprika
- 1 tsp cayenne pepper
- 2 eggs
- 2 tbsp milk

Directions:

1. Preheat the air fryer to 375°F (190°C). Carefully peel the onions and cut a ½ inch off the stem ends and trim the root ends. Place them root-side down on the cutting surface and cut the onions into quarters. Be careful not to cut al the way to the bottom. Cut each quarter into 2 sections and pull the wedges apart without breaking them.

2. In a shallow bowl, add the flour, salt, paprika, and cayenne, and in a separate shallow bowl, beat the eggs with the milk. Dip the onions in the flour, then dip in the egg mix, coating evenly, and then in the flour mix again. Shake off excess flour. Put the onions in the frying basket, cut-side up, and spray with cooking oil. Air Fry for 10-15 minutes until the onions are crispy on the outside, tender on the inside. Let cool for 10 minutes, then serve.

Spring Veggie Empanadas

Servings: 4

Cooking Time: 75 Minutes

Ingredients:

- 10 empanada pastry discs
- 1 tbsp olive oil
- 1 shallot, minced
- 1 garlic clove, minced
- ½ cup whole milk
- 1 cup chopped broccoli
- ½ cup chopped cauliflower
- ½ cup diced carrots
- ¼ cup diced celery
- ⅛ tsp ground nutmeg
- 1 tsp cumin powder
- 1 tsp minced ginger
- 1 egg

Directions:

1. Melt the olive oil in a pot over medium heat. Stir in shallot and garlic and cook through for 1 minute. Next, add 1 tablespoon of flour and continue stirring. Whisk in milk, then lower the heat. After that, add broccoli, cauliflower, carrots, celery, cumin powder, pepper, ginger, and nutmeg. Cook for 2 minutes then remove from the heat. Allow to cool for 5 minutes.

2. Preheat air fryer to 350°F (175°C). Lightly flour a flat work surface and turn out the pastry discs. Scoop ¼ of the vegetables in the center of each circle. Whisk the egg and 1 teaspoon of water in a small bowl and brush the entire edge of the circle with the egg wash and fold the dough over the filling into a half-moon shape. Crimp the edge with a fork to seal. Arrange the patties in a single layer in the frying basket and bake for 12 minutes. Flip the patties and bake for another 10 to 12 minutes until the outside crust is golden. Serve immediately and enjoy.

Tex-mex Potatoes With Avocado Dressing

Servings: 2

Cooking Time: 60 Minutes

Ingredients:

- ¼ cup chopped parsley, dill, cilantro, chives
- ¼ cup yogurt
- ½ avocado, diced
- 2 tbsp milk
- 2 tsp lemon juice
- ½ tsp lemon zest
- 1 green onion, chopped
- 2 cloves garlic, quartered
- Salt and pepper to taste
- 2 tsp olive oil
- 2 russet potatoes, scrubbed and perforated with a fork
- 1 cup steamed broccoli florets
- ½ cup canned white beans

Directions:

1. In a food processor, blend the yogurt, avocado, milk, lemon juice, lemon zest, green onion, garlic, parsley, dill, cilantro, chives, salt and pepper until smooth. Transfer it to a small bowl and let chill the dressing covered in the fridge until ready to use.

2. Preheat air fryer at 400°F. Rub olive oil over both potatoes and sprinkle with salt and pepper. Place them in the frying basket and Bake for 45 minutes, flipping at 30 minutes mark. Let cool onto a cutting board for 5 minutes until cool enough to handle. Cut each potato lengthwise into slices and pinch ends together to open up each slice. Stuff broccoli and beans into potatoes and put them back into the basket, and cook for 3 more minutes. Drizzle avocado dressing over and serve.

Roasted Veggie Bowls

Servings: 4

Cooking Time: 30 Minutes

Ingredients:

- 1 cup Brussels sprouts, trimmed and quartered
- ½ onion, cut into half-moons
- ½ cup green beans, chopped
- 1 cup broccoli florets
- 1 red bell pepper, sliced
- 1 yellow bell pepper, sliced
- 1 tbsp olive oil
- ½ tsp chili powder
- ¼ tsp ground cumin
- ¼ tsp ground coriander

Directions:

1. Preheat air fryer to 350°F. Combine all ingredients in a bowl. Place veggie mixture in the frying basket and Air Fry for 15 minutes, tossing every 5 minutes. Divide between 4 medium bowls and serve.

Cheddar Bean Taquitos

Servings: 4

Cooking Time: 25 Minutes

Ingredients:

- 1 cup refried beans
- 2 cups cheddar shreds
- ½ jalapeño pepper, minced
- ¼ chopped white onion
- 1 tsp oregano
- 15 soft corn tortillas

Directions:

1. Preheat air fryer at 350°F. Spread refried beans, jalapeño pepper, white onion, oregano and cheddar shreds down the center of each corn tortilla. Roll each tortilla tightly. Place tacos, seam side down, in the frying basket, and Air Fry for 4 minutes. Serve immediately.

Spicy Vegetable And Tofu Shake Fry

Servings: 4

Cooking Time: 17 Minutes

Ingredients:

- 4 teaspoons canola oil, divided
- 2 tablespoons rice wine vinegar
- 1 tablespoon sriracha chili sauce
- ¼ cup soy sauce*
- ½ teaspoon toasted sesame oil
- 1 teaspoon minced garlic
- 1 tablespoon minced fresh ginger
- 8 ounces extra firm tofu
- ½ cup vegetable stock or water
- 1 tablespoon honey
- 1 tablespoon cornstarch
- ½ red onion, chopped
- 1 red or yellow bell pepper, chopped
- 1 cup green beans, cut into 2-inch lengths
- 4 ounces mushrooms, sliced
- 2 scallions, sliced
- 2 tablespoons fresh cilantro leaves
- 2 teaspoons toasted sesame seeds

Directions:

1. Combine 1 tablespoon of the oil, vinegar, sriracha sauce, soy sauce, sesame oil, garlic and ginger in a small bowl. Cut the tofu into bite-sized cubes and toss the tofu in with the marinade while you prepare the other vegetables. When you are ready to start cooking, remove the tofu from the marinade and set it aside. Add the water, honey and cornstarch to the marinade and bring to a simmer on the stovetop, just until the sauce thickens. Set the sauce aside.
2. Preheat the air fryer to 400°F (205°C).
3. Toss the onion, pepper, green beans and mushrooms in a bowl with a little canola oil and season with salt. Air-fry at 400°F (205°C) for 11 minutes, shaking the basket and tossing the vegetables every few minutes. When the vegetables are cooked to your preferred doneness, remove them from the air fryer and set aside.
4. Add the tofu to the air fryer basket and air-fry at 400°F (205°C) for 6 minutes, shaking the basket a few times during the cooking process. Add the vegetables back to the basket and air-fry for another minute. Transfer the vegetables and tofu to a large bowl, add the scallions and cilantro leaves and toss with the sauce. Serve over rice with sesame seeds sprinkled on top.

Quinoa & Black Bean Stuffed Peppers

Servings: 4

Cooking Time: 30 Minutes

Ingredients:

- ½ cup vegetable broth
- ½ cup quinoa
- 1 can black beans
- ½ cup diced red onion
- 1 garlic clove, minced
- ½ tsp salt
- ½ tsp ground cumin
- ¼ tsp paprika

- ¼ tsp ancho chili powder
- 4 bell peppers, any color
- ½ cup grated cheddar
- ¼ cup chopped cilantro
- ½ cup red enchilada sauce

Directions:

1. Add vegetable broth and quinoa to a small saucepan over medium heat. Bring to a boil, then cover and let it simmer for 5 minutes. Turn off the heat.

2. Preheat air fryer to 350°F (175°C). Transfer quinoa to a medium bowl and stir in black beans, onion, red enchilada sauce, ancho chili powder, garlic, salt, cumin, and paprika. Cut the top ¼-inch off the bell peppers. Remove seeds and membranes. Scoop quinoa filling into each pepper and top with cheddar cheese. Transfer peppers to the frying basket and bake for 10 minutes until peppers are soft and filling is heated through. Garnish with cilantro. Serve warm along with salsa. Enjoy!

Sicilian-style Vegetarian Pizza

Servings: 2

Cooking Time: 20 Minutes

Ingredients:

- 1 pizza pie crust
- ¼ cup ricotta cheese
- ½ tbsp tomato paste
- ½ white onion, sliced
- ½ tsp dried oregano
- ¼ cup Sicilian olives, sliced
- ¼ cup grated mozzarella

Directions:

1. Preheat air fryer to 350°F (175°C). Lay the pizza dough on a parchment paper sheet. Spread the tomato paste evenly over the pie crust, allowing at least ½ inch border. Sprinkle with oregano and scatter the ricotta cheese on top. Cover with onion and Sicilian olive slices and finish with a layer of mozzarella cheese. Bake for 10 minutes until the cheese has melted and lightly crisped, and the crust is golden brown. Serve sliced and enjoy!

Veggie-stuffed Bell Peppers

Servings: 4

Cooking Time: 40 Minutes

Ingredients:

- ½ cup canned fire-roasted diced tomatoes, including juice
- 2 red bell peppers
- 4 tsp olive oil
- ½ yellow onion, diced
- 1 zucchini, diced
- ¾ cup chopped mushrooms
- ¼ cup tomato sauce
- 2 tsp Italian seasoning
- ¼ tsp smoked paprika
- Salt and pepper to taste

Directions:

1. Cut bell peppers in half from top to bottom and discard the seeds. Brush inside and tops of the bell peppers with some olive oil. Set aside. Warm the remaining olive oil in a skillet over medium heat. Stir-fry the onion, zucchini, and mushrooms for 5 minutes until the onions are tender. Combine tomatoes and their juice, tomato sauce, Italian seasoning, paprika, salt, and pepper in a bowl.

2. Preheat air fryer to 350ºF. Divide both mixtures between bell pepper halves. Place bell pepper halves in the frying basket and Air Fry for 8 minutes. Serve immediately.

Sweet Roasted Carrots

Servings: 4

Cooking Time: 25 Minutes

Ingredients:

- 6 carrots, cut into ½-inch pieces
- 2 tbsp butter, melted
- 2 tbsp parsley, chopped
- 1 tsp honey

Directions:

1. Preheat air fryer to 390°F (200°C). Add carrots to a baking pan and pour over butter, honey, and 2-3 tbsp of water. Mix well. Transfer the carrots to the greased frying basket and Roast for 12 minutes, shaking the basket once. Sprinkle with parsley and serve warm.

Italian-style Fried Cauliflower

Servings: 4

Cooking Time: 35 Minutes

Ingredients:

- 2 eggs
- 1/3 cup all-purpose flour
- ½ tsp Italian seasoning
- ½ cup bread crumbs
- 1 tsp garlic powder
- 3 tsp grated Parmesan cheese
- Salt and pepper to taste
- 1 head cauliflower, cut into florets
- ½ tsp ground coriander

Directions:

1. Preheat air fryer to 370°F (185°C). Set out 3 small bowls. In the first, mix the flour with Italian seasoning. In the second, beat the eggs. In the third bowl, combine the crumbs, garlic, Parmesan, ground coriander, salt, and pepper.
2. Dip the cauliflower in the flour, then dredge in egg, and finally in the bread crumb mixture. Place a batch of cauliflower in the greased frying basket and spray with cooking oil. Bake for 10-12 minutes, shaking once until golden. Serve warm and enjoy!

Crispy Apple Fries With Caramel Sauce

Servings: 4
Cooking Time: 15 Minutes

Ingredients:
- 4 medium apples, cored
- ¼ tsp cinnamon
- ¼ tsp nutmeg
- 1 cup caramel sauce

Directions:
1. Preheat air fryer to 350°F (175°C). Slice the apples to a 1/3-inch thickness for a crunchy chip. Place in a large bowl and sprinkle with cinnamon and nutmeg. Place the slices in the air fryer basket. Bake for 6 minutes. Shake the basket, then cook for another 4 minutes or until crunchy. Serve drizzled with caramel sauce and enjoy!

Roasted Vegetable, Brown Rice And Black Bean Burrito

Servings: 2
Cooking Time: 20 Minutes

Ingredients:
- ½ zucchini, sliced ¼-inch thick
- ½ red onion, sliced
- 1 yellow bell pepper, sliced
- 2 teaspoons olive oil
- salt and freshly ground black pepper
- 2 burrito size flour tortillas
- 1 cup grated pepper jack cheese
- ½ cup cooked brown rice
- ½ cup canned black beans, drained and rinsed
- ¼ teaspoon ground cumin
- 1 tablespoon chopped fresh cilantro
- fresh salsa, guacamole and sour cream, for serving

Directions:
1. Preheat the air fryer to 400°F (205°C).
2. Toss the vegetables in a bowl with the olive oil, salt and freshly ground black pepper. Air-fry at 400°F (205°C) for 12 to 15 minutes, shaking the basket a few times during the cooking process. The vegetables are done when they are cooked to your liking.
3. In the meantime, start building the burritos. Lay the tortillas out on the counter. Sprinkle half of the cheese in the center of the tortillas. Combine the rice, beans, cumin and cilantro in a bowl, season to taste with salt and freshly ground black pepper and then divide the mixture between the two tortillas. When the vegetables have finished cooking, transfer them to the two tortillas, placing the vegetables on top of the rice and beans. Sprinkle the remaining cheese on top and then roll the burritos up, tucking in the sides of the tortillas as you roll. Brush or spray the outside of the burritos with olive oil and transfer them to the air fryer.
4. Air-fry at 360°F (180°C) for 8 minutes, turning them over when there are about 2 minutes left. The burritos will have slightly brown spots, but will still be pliable.
5. Serve with some fresh salsa, guacamole and sour cream.

Bread And Breakfast

Egg Muffins

Servings: 4

Cooking Time: 11 Minutes

Ingredients:
- 4 eggs
- salt and pepper
- olive oil
- 4 English muffins, split
- 1 cup shredded Colby Jack cheese
- 4 slices ham or Canadian bacon

Directions:

1. Preheat air fryer to 390°F (200°C).
2. Beat together eggs and add salt and pepper to taste. Spray air fryer baking pan lightly with oil and add eggs. Cook for 2minutes, stir, and continue cooking for 4minutes, stirring every minute, until eggs are scrambled to your preference. Remove pan from air fryer.
3. Place bottom halves of English muffins in air fryer basket. Take half of the shredded cheese and divide it among the muffins. Top each with a slice of ham and one-quarter of the eggs. Sprinkle remaining cheese on top of the eggs. Use a fork to press the cheese into the egg a little so it doesn't slip off before it melts.
4. Cook at 360°F (180°C) for 1 minute. Add English muffin tops and cook for 4minutes to heat through and toast the muffins.

English Scones

Servings: 8

Cooking Time: 8 Minutes

Ingredients:
- 2 cups all-purpose flour
- 1 tablespoon baking powder
- ½ teaspoon salt
- 2 tablespoons sugar
- ¼ cup unsalted butter
- ⅔ cup plus 1 tablespoon whole milk, divided

Directions:

1. Preheat the air fryer to 380°F (195°C).
2. In a large bowl, whisk together the flour, baking powder, salt, and sugar. Using a pastry blender or your fingers, cut in the butter until pea-size crumbles appear. Make a well in the center and pour in ⅔ cup of the milk. Quickly mix the batter until a ball forms. Knead the dough 3 times.
3. Place the dough onto a floured surface and, using your hands or a rolling pin, flatten the dough until it's ¾ inch thick. Using a biscuit cutter or drinking glass, cut out 10 circles, reforming the dough and flattening as needed to use up the batter.
4. Brush the tops lightly with the remaining 1 tablespoon of milk.
5. Place the scones into the air fryer basket. Cook for 8 minutes or until golden brown and cooked in the center.

Oat & Nut Granola

Servings: 6

Cooking Time: 25 Minutes

Ingredients:
- 2 cups rolled oats
- ¼ cup pistachios
- ¼ cup chopped almonds
- ¼ cup chopped cashews
- ¼ cup honey
- 2 tbsp light brown sugar
- 3 tbsp butter
- ½ tsp ground cinnamon
- ½ cup dried figs

Directions:

1. Preheat the air fryer to 325°F (160°C). Combine the oats, pistachios, almonds, and cashews in a bowl and toss, then set aside. In a saucepan, cook the honey, brown sugar, butter, and cinnamon and over low heat, stirring frequently, 4 minutes. Melt the butter completely and make sure the mixture is smooth, then pour over the oat mix and stir.
2. Scoop the granola mixture in a greased baking pan. Put the pan in the frying basket and Bake for 7 minutes, then remove the pan and stir. Cook for another 6-9 minutes or until the granola is golden, then add the dried figs and stir. Remove the pan and let cool. Store in a covered container at room temperature for up to 3 days.

Peppered Maple Bacon Knots

Servings: 6

Cooking Time: 8 Minutes

Ingredients:
- 1 pound maple smoked center-cut bacon
- ¼ cup maple syrup
- ¼ cup brown sugar
- coarsely cracked black peppercorns

Directions:

1. Tie each bacon strip in a loose knot and place them on a baking sheet.

2. Combine the maple syrup and brown sugar in a bowl. Brush each knot generously with this mixture and sprinkle with coarsely cracked black pepper.
3. Preheat the air fryer to 390°F (200°C).
4. Air-fry the bacon knots in batches. Place one layer of knots in the air fryer basket and air-fry for 5 minutes. Turn the bacon knots over and air-fry for an additional 3 minutes.
5. Serve warm.

Favorite Blueberry Muffins

Servings: 8

Cooking Time: 25 Minutes

Ingredients:
- 1 cup all-purpose flour
- ½ tsp baking soda
- 1/3 cup granulated sugar
- ¼ tsp salt
- 1 tbsp lemon juice
- 1 tsp lemon zest
- ¼ cup milk
- ½ tsp vanilla extract
- 1 egg
- 1 tbsp vegetable oil
- ¼ cup halved blueberries
- 1 tbsp powdered sugar

Directions:

1. Preheat air fryer at 375°F. Combine dry ingredients in a bowl. Mix ¼ cup of fresh milk with 1 tsp of lemon juice and leave for 10 minutes. Put it in another bowl with the wet ingredients. Pour wet ingredients into dry ingredients and gently toss to combine. Fold in blueberries. Spoon mixture into 8 greased silicone cupcake liners and Bake them in the fryer for 6-8 minutes. Let cool onto a cooling rack. Serve right away sprinkled with powdered sugar.

Smoked Salmon Croissant Sandwich

Servings: 1

Cooking Time: 30 Minutes

Ingredients:
- 1 croissant, halved
- 2 eggs
- 1 tbsp guacamole
- 1 smoked salmon slice
- Salt and pepper to taste

Directions:

1. Preheat air fryer to 360°F (180°C). Place the croissant, crusty side up, in the frying basket side by side. Whisk the eggs in a small ceramic dish until fluffy. Place in the air fryer. Bake for 10 minutes. Gently scramble the half-cooked egg in the baking dish with a fork. Flip the croissant and cook for another 10 minutes until the scrambled eggs are cooked, but still fluffy, and the croissant is toasted.
2. Place one croissant on a serving plate, then spread the guacamole on top. Scoop the scrambled eggs onto guacamole, then top with smoked salmon. Sprinkle with salt and pepper. Top with the second slice of toasted croissant, close sandwich, and serve hot.

Peach Fritters

Servings: 8

Cooking Time: 6 Minutes

Ingredients:
- 1½ cups bread flour
- 1 teaspoon active dry yeast
- ¼ cup sugar
- ¼ teaspoon salt
- ½ cup warm milk
- ½ teaspoon vanilla extract
- 2 egg yolks
- 2 tablespoons melted butter
- 2 cups small diced peaches (fresh or frozen)
- 1 tablespoon butter
- 1 teaspoon ground cinnamon
- 1 to 2 tablespoons sugar
- Glaze
- ¾ cup powdered sugar
- 4 teaspoons milk

Directions:

1. Combine the flour, yeast, sugar and salt in a bowl. Add the milk, vanilla, egg yolks and melted butter and combine until the dough starts to come together. Transfer the dough to a floured surface and knead it by hand for 2 minutes. Shape the dough into a ball, place it in a large oiled bowl, cover with a clean kitchen towel and let the dough rise in a warm place for 1 to 1½ hours, or until the dough has doubled in size.

2. While the dough is rising, melt one tablespoon of butter in a medium saucepan on the stovetop. Add the diced peaches, cinnamon and sugar to taste. Cook the peaches for about 5 minutes, or until they soften. Set the peaches aside to cool.

3. When the dough has risen, transfer it to a floured surface and shape it into a 12-inch circle. Spread the peaches over half of the circle and fold the other half of the dough over the top. With a knife or a board scraper, score the dough by making slits in the dough in a diamond shape. Push the knife straight down into the dough and peaches, rather than slicing through. You should cut through the top layer of dough, but not the bottom. Roll the dough up into a log from one short end to the other. It should be roughly 8 inches long. Some of the peaches will be sticking out of the

dough – don't worry, these are supposed to be a little random. Cut the log into 8 equal slices. Place the dough disks on a floured cookie sheet, cover with a clean kitchen towel and let rise in a warm place for 30 minutes.
4. Preheat the air fryer to 370°F (185°C).
5. Air-fry 2 or 3 fritters at a time at 370°F (185°C), for 3 minutes. Flip them over and continue to air-fry for another 2 to 3 minutes, until they are golden brown.
6. Combine the powdered sugar and milk together in a small bowl. Whisk vigorously until smooth. Allow the fritters to cool for at least 10 minutes and then brush the glaze over both the bottom and top of each one. Serve warm or at room temperature.

Chorizo Sausage & Cheese Balls

Servings: 4
Cooking Time: 25 Minutes

Ingredients:

- 1 egg white
- 1 lb chorizo ground sausage
- ¼ tsp smoked paprika
- 2 tbsp canned green chiles
- ¼ cup bread crumbs
- ¼ cup grated cheddar

Directions:

1. Preheat air fryer to 400°F (205°C). Mix all ingredients in a large bowl. Form into 16 balls. Put the sausage balls in the frying basket and Air Fry for 6 minutes. When done, shake the basket and cook for an additional 6 minutes. Transfer to a serving plate and serve.

Orange-glazed Cinnamon Rolls

Servings:
Cooking Time: 30 Minutes

Ingredients:

- ½ cup + 1 tbsp evaporated cane sugar
- 1 cup Greek yogurt
- 2 cups flour
- 2 tsp baking powder
- ½ tsp salt
- 4 tbsp butter, softened
- 2 tsp ground cinnamon
- 4 oz cream cheese
- ¼ cup orange juice
- 1 tbsp orange zest
- 1 tbsp lemon juice

Directions:

1. Preheat air fryer to 350°F (175°C). Grease a baking dish. Combine yogurt, 1 ¾ cups flour, baking powder, salt, and ¼ cup sugar in a large bowl until dough forms. Dust the rest of the flour onto a flat work surface. Transfer the dough on the flour and roll into a ¼-inch thick rectangle. If the dough continues to stick to the rolling pin, add 1 tablespoon of flour and continue to roll.
2. Mix the butter, cinnamon, orange zest and 1 tbsp of sugar in a bowl. Spread the butter mixture evenly over the dough. Roll the dough into a log, starting with the long side. Tuck in the end. Cut the log into 6 equal pieces. Place in the baking dish swirl-side up. The rolls can touch each other. Bake in the air fryer for 10-12 minutes until the rolls are cooked through, and the tops are golden. Let cool for 10 minutes. While the rolls are cooling, combine cream cheese, the rest of the sugar, lemon juice, and orange juice in a small bowl. When the rolls are cool enough, top with glaze and serve.

Shakshuka-style Pepper Cups

Servings: 4
Cooking Time: 35 Minutes

Ingredients:

- 2 tbsp ricotta cheese crumbles
- 1 tbsp olive oil
- ½ yellow onion, diced
- 2 cloves garlic, minced
- ¼ tsp turmeric
- 1 can diced tomatoes
- 1 tbsp tomato paste
- ½ tsp smoked paprika
- ½ tsp salt
- ½ tsp granular sugar
- ¼ tsp ground cumin
- ¼ tsp ground coriander
- ⅛ tsp cayenne pepper
- 4 bell peppers
- 4 eggs
- 2 tbsp chopped basil

Directions:

1. Warm the olive oil in a saucepan over medium heat. Stir-fry the onion for 10 minutes or until softened. Stir in the garlic and turmeric for another 1 minute. Add diced tomatoes, tomato paste, paprika, salt, sugar, cumin, coriander, and cayenne. Remove from heat and stir.
2. Preheat air fryer to 350°F (175°C). Slice the tops off the peppers, and carefully remove the core and seeds. Put the bell peppers in the frying basket. Divide the tomato mixture among bell peppers. Crack 1 egg into tomato mixture in each pepper. Bake for 8-10 minutes. Sprinkle with ricotta cheese and cook for 1 more minute. Let rest 5 minutes. Garnish with fresh basil and serve immediately.

Bread Boat Eggs

Servings: 4
Cooking Time: 10 Minutes

Ingredients:
- 4 pistolette rolls
- 1 teaspoon butter
- ¼ cup diced fresh mushrooms
- ½ teaspoon dried onion flakes
- 4 eggs
- ½ teaspoon salt
- ¼ teaspoon dried dill weed
- ¼ teaspoon dried parsley
- 1 tablespoon milk

Directions:
1. Cut a rectangle in the top of each roll and scoop out center, leaving ½-inch shell on the sides and bottom.
2. Place butter, mushrooms, and dried onion in air fryer baking pan and cook for 1 minute. Stir and cook 3 moreminutes.
3. In a medium bowl, beat together the eggs, salt, dill, parsley, and milk. Pour mixture into pan with mushrooms.
4. Cook at 390°F (200°C) for 2minutes. Stir. Continue cooking for 3 or 4minutes, stirring every minute, until eggs are scrambled to your liking.
5. Remove baking pan from air fryer and fill rolls with scrambled egg mixture.
6. Place filled rolls in air fryer basket and cook at 390°F (200°C) for 2 to 3minutes or until rolls are lightly browned.

Spring Vegetable Omelet

Servings: 4
Cooking Time: 20 Minutes

Ingredients:
- ¼ cup chopped broccoli, lightly steamed
- ½ cup grated cheddar cheese
- 6 eggs
- ¼ cup steamed kale
- 1 green onion, chopped
- Salt and pepper to taste

Directions:
1. Preheat air fryer to 360°F (180°C). In a bowl, beat the eggs. Stir in kale, broccoli, green onion, and cheddar cheese. Transfer the mixture to a greased baking dish and Bake in the fryer for 15 minutes until golden and crisp. Season to taste and serve immediately.

Breakfast Sausage Bites

Servings: 4
Cooking Time: 30 Minutes

Ingredients:
- 1 lb ground pork sausages
- ¼ cup diced onions
- 1 tsp rubbed sage
- ¼ tsp ground nutmeg
- ½ tsp fennel
- ¼ tsp garlic powder
- 2 tbsp parsley, chopped
- Salt and pepper to taste

Directions:
1. Preheat air fryer at 350°F. Combine all ingredients, except the parsley, in a bowl. Form mixture into balls. Place them in the greased frying basket and Air Fry for 10 minutes, flipping once. Sprinkle with parsley and serve immediately.

Morning Potato Cakes

Servings: 6
Cooking Time: 50 Minutes

Ingredients:
- 4 Yukon Gold potatoes
- 2 cups kale, chopped
- 1 cup rice flour
- ¼ cup cornstarch
- ¾ cup milk
- 2 tbsp lemon juice
- 2 tsp dried rosemary
- 2 tsp shallot powder
- Salt and pepper to taste
- ½ tsp turmeric powder

Directions:
1. Preheat air fryer to 390°F (200°C). Scrub the potatoes and put them in the air fryer. Bake for 30 minutes or until soft. When cool, chop them into small pieces and place them in a bowl. Mash with a potato masher or fork. Add kale, rice flour, cornstarch, milk, lemon juice, rosemary, shallot powder, salt, pepper, and turmeric. Stir well.
2. Make 12 balls out of the mixture and smash them lightly with your hands to make patties. Place them in the greased frying basket, and Air Fry for 10-12 minutes, flipping once, until golden and cooked through. Serve.

Cheddar-ham-corn Muffins

Servings: 8

Cooking Time: 8 Minutes

Ingredients:

- ¾ cup yellow cornmeal
- ¼ cup flour
- 1½ teaspoons baking powder
- ¼ teaspoon salt
- 1 egg, beaten
- 2 tablespoons canola oil
- ½ cup milk
- ½ cup shredded sharp Cheddar cheese
- ½ cup diced ham
- 8 foil muffin cups, liners removed and sprayed with cooking spray

Directions:

1. Preheat air fryer to 390°F (200°C).
2. In a medium bowl, stir together the cornmeal, flour, baking powder, and salt.
3. Add egg, oil, and milk to dry ingredients and mix well.
4. Stir in shredded cheese and diced ham.
5. Divide batter among the muffin cups.
6. Place 4 filled muffin cups in air fryer basket and bake for 5minutes.
7. Reduce temperature to 330°F (165°C) and bake for 1 to 2minutes or until toothpick inserted in center of muffin comes out clean.
8. Repeat steps 6 and 7 to cook remaining muffins.

Cinnamon Pumpkin Donuts

Servings: 6

Cooking Time: 30 Minutes

Ingredients:

- 1/3 cup canned pumpkin purée
- 1 cup flour
- 3 tbsp brown sugar
- ½ tsp ground cinnamon
- 1/8 tsp ground nutmeg
- 1 tsp baking powder
- 3 tbsp milk
- 2 tbsp butter, melted
- 1 large egg
- 3 tbsp powdered sugar

Directions:

1. Combine the flour, brown sugar, cinnamon, nutmeg, and baking powder in a bowl. Whisk the pumpkin, milk, butter, and egg white in another bowl. Pour the pumpkin mixture over the dry ingredients and stir. Add more milk or flour if necessary to make a soft dough.Cover your hands in flour, make 12 pieces from the dough, and form them into balls. Measure the frying basket, then cut foil or parchment paper about an inch smaller than the measurement. Poke holes in it and put it in the basket.
2. Preheat air fryer to 360°F (180°C). Set the donut holes in the basket and Air Fry for 5-7 minutes. Allow the donuts to chill for 5 minutes, then roll in powdered sugar. Serve.

Country Gravy

Servings: 2

Cooking Time: 7 Minutes

Ingredients:

- ¼ pound pork sausage, casings removed
- 1 tablespoon butter
- 2 tablespoons flour
- 2 cups whole milk
- ½ teaspoon salt
- freshly ground black pepper
- 1 teaspoon fresh thyme leaves

Directions:

1. Preheat a saucepan over medium heat. Add and brown the sausage, crumbling it into small pieces as it cooks. Add the butter and flour, stirring well to combine. Continue to cook for 2 minutes, stirring constantly.
2. Slowly pour in the milk, whisking as you do, and bring the mixture to a boil to thicken. Season with salt and freshly ground black pepper, lower the heat and simmer until the sauce has thickened to your desired consistency – about 5 minutes. Stir in the fresh thyme, season to taste and serve hot.

Holiday Breakfast Casserole

Servings:2

Cooking Time: 25 Minutes

Ingredients:

- ¼ cup cooked spicy breakfast sausage
- 5 eggs
- 2 tbsp heavy cream
- ½ tsp ground cumin
- Salt and pepper to taste
- ½ cup feta cheese crumbles
- 1 tomato, diced
- 1 can green chiles, including juice
- 1 zucchini, diced

Directions:

1. Preheat air fryer to 325°F. Mix all ingredients in a bowl and pour into a greased baking pan. Place the pan in the frying basket and Bake for 14 minutes. Let cool for 5 minutes before slicing. Serve right away.

Strawberry Streusel Muffins

Servings: 12
Cooking Time: 14 Minutes
Ingredients:
- 1¾ cups all-purpose flour
- ½ cup granulated sugar
- 2 teaspoons baking powder
- ¼ teaspoon baking soda
- ½ teaspoon salt
- ½ cup plain yogurt
- ½ cup milk
- ¼ cup vegetable oil
- 2 large eggs
- 1 teaspoon vanilla extract
- ½ cup freeze-dried strawberries
- 2 tablespoons brown sugar
- ¼ cup oats
- 2 tablespoons butter

Directions:
1. Preheat the air fryer to 330°F (165°C).
2. In a large bowl, whisk together the flour, sugar, baking powder, baking soda, and salt; set aside.
3. In a separate bowl, whisk together the yogurt, milk, vegetable oil, eggs, and vanilla extract.
4. Make a well in the dry ingredients; then pour the wet ingredients into the well of the dry ingredients. Using a rubber spatula, mix the ingredients for 1 minute or until slightly lumpy. Fold in the strawberries.
5. In a small bowl, use your fingers to mix together the brown sugar, oats, and butter until coarse crumbles appear. Divide the mixture in half.
6. Using silicone muffin liners, fill 6 muffin liners two-thirds full.
7. Crumble half of the streusel topping onto the first batch of muffins.
8. Carefully place the muffin liners in the air fryer basket and bake for 14 minutes (or until the tops are browned and a toothpick inserted in the center comes out clean). Carefully remove the muffins from the basket and repeat with the remaining batter and topping.
9. Serve warm.

Pumpkin Empanadas

Servings: 4
Cooking Time: 30 Minutes
Ingredients:
- 1 can pumpkin purée
- ¼ cup white sugar
- 2 tsp cinnamon
- 1 tbsp brown sugar
- ½ tbsp cornstarch
- ¼ tsp vanilla extract
- 2 tbsp butter
- 4 empanada dough shells

Directions:
1. Place the puree in a pot and top with white and brown sugar, cinnamon, cornstarch, vanilla extract, 1 tbsp of water and butter and stir thoroughly. Bring to a boil over medium heat. Simmer for 4-5 minutes. Allow to cool.
2. Preheat air fryer to 360°F (180°C). Lay empanada shells flat on a clean counter. Spoon the pumpkin mixture into each of the shells. Fold the empanada shells over to cover completely. Seal the edges with water and press down with a fork to secure. Place the empanadas on the greased frying basket and Bake for 15 minutes, flipping once halfway through until golden. Serve hot.

English Muffin Sandwiches

Servings: 4
Cooking Time: 15 Minutes
Ingredients:
- 4 English muffins
- 8 pepperoni slices
- 4 cheddar cheese slices
- 1 tomato, sliced

Directions:
1. Preheat air fryer to 370°F (185°C). Split open the English muffins along the crease. On the bottom half of the muffin, layer 2 slices of pepperoni and one slice of the cheese and tomato. Place the top half of the English muffin to finish the sandwich. Lightly spray with cooking oil. Place the muffin sandwiches in the air fryer. Bake for 8 minutes, flipping once. Let cool slightly before serving.

Vegetarian Quinoa Cups

Servings: 6
Cooking Time: 25 Minutes
Ingredients:
- 1 carrot, chopped
- 1 zucchini, chopped
- 4 asparagus, chopped
- ¾ cup quinoa flour
- 2 tbsp lemon juice
- ¼ cup nutritional yeast
- ¼ tsp garlic powder
- Salt and pepper to taste

Directions:

1. Preheat air fryer to 340°F (170°C). Combine the vegetables, quinoa flour, water, lemon juice, nutritional yeast, garlic powder, salt, and pepper in a medium bowl, and mix well. Divide the mixture between 6 cupcake molds. Place the filled molds into the air fryer and Bake for 20 minutes, or until the tops are lightly browned and a toothpick inserted into the center comes out clean. Serve cooled.

Crustless Broccoli, Roasted Pepper And Fontina Quiche

Servings: 4

Cooking Time: 60 Minutes

Ingredients:

- 7-inch cake pan
- 1 cup broccoli florets
- ¾ cup chopped roasted red peppers
- 1¼ cups grated Fontina cheese
- 6 eggs
- ¾ cup heavy cream
- ½ teaspoon salt
- freshly ground black pepper

Directions:

1. Preheat the air fryer to 360°F (180°C).
2. Grease the inside of a 7-inch cake pan (4 inches deep) or other oven-safe pan that will fit into your air fryer. Place the broccoli florets and roasted red peppers in the cake pan and top with the grated Fontina cheese.
3. Whisk the eggs and heavy cream together in a bowl. Season the eggs with salt and freshly ground black pepper. Pour the egg mixture over the cheese and vegetables and cover the pan with aluminum foil. Transfer the cake pan to the air fryer basket.
4. Air-fry at 360°F (180°C) for 60 minutes. Remove the aluminum foil for the last two minutes of cooking time.
5. Unmold the quiche onto a platter and cut it into slices to serve with a side salad or perhaps some air-fried potatoes.

Morning Chicken Frittata Cups

Servings: 6

Cooking Time: 30 Minutes

Ingredients:

- ¼ cup shredded cooked chicken breasts
- 3 eggs
- 2 tbsp heavy cream
- 4 tsp Tabasco sauce
- ¼ cup grated Asiago cheese
- 2 tbsp chives, chopped

Directions:

1. Preheat air fryer to 350°F. Beat all ingredients in a bowl. Divide the egg mixture between greased 6 muffin cups and place them in the frying basket. Bake for 8-10 minutes until set. Let cool slightly before serving. Enjoy!

Carrot Orange Muffins

Servings: 12

Cooking Time: 12 Minutes

Ingredients:

- 1½ cups all-purpose flour
- ½ cup granulated sugar
- ½ teaspoon ground cinnamon
- 2 teaspoons baking powder
- ¼ teaspoon baking soda
- ½ teaspoon salt
- 2 large eggs
- ¼ cup vegetable oil
- ⅓ cup orange marmalade
- 2 cups grated carrots

Directions:

1. Preheat the air fryer to 320°F (160°C).
2. In a large bowl, whisk together the flour, sugar, cinnamon, baking powder, baking soda, and salt; set aside.
3. In a separate bowl, whisk together the eggs, vegetable oil, orange marmalade, and grated carrots.
4. Make a well in the dry ingredients; then pour the wet ingredients into the well of the dry ingredients. Using a rubber spatula, mix the ingredients for 1 minute or until slightly lumpy.
5. Using silicone muffin liners, fill 6 muffin liners two-thirds full.
6. Carefully place the muffin liners in the air fryer basket and bake for 12 minutes (or until the tops are browned and a toothpick inserted in the center comes out clean). Carefully remove the muffins from the basket and repeat with remaining batter.
7. Serve warm.

Flank Steak With Caramelized Onions

Servings: 2

Cooking Time: 30 Minutes

Ingredients:

- ½ lb flank steak, cubed
- 1 tbsp mustard powder
- ½ tsp garlic powder
- 2 eggs
- 1 onion, sliced thinly
- Salt and pepper to taste

Directions:

1. Preheat air fryer to 360°F (180°C). Coat the flank steak cubes with mustard and garlic powders. Place them in the frying basket along with the onion and Bake for 3 minutes. Flip the steak over and gently stir the onions and cook for another 3 minutes. Push the steak and onions over to one side of the basket, creating space for heat-safe baking dish. Crack the eggs into a ceramic dish. Place the dish in the fryer. Cook for 15 minutes at 320°F (160°C) until the egg white are set and the onion is caramelized. Season with salt and pepper. Serve warm.

Roasted Vegetable Frittata

Servings: 1

Cooking Time: 19 Minutes

Ingredients:

- ½ red or green bell pepper, cut into ½-inch chunks
- 4 button mushrooms, sliced
- ½ cup diced zucchini
- ½ teaspoon chopped fresh oregano or thyme
- 1 teaspoon olive oil
- 3 eggs, beaten
- ½ cup grated Cheddar cheese
- salt and freshly ground black pepper, to taste
- 1 teaspoon butter
- 1 teaspoon chopped fresh parsley

Directions:

1. Preheat the air fryer to 400°F (205°C).
2. Toss the peppers, mushrooms, zucchini and oregano with the olive oil and air-fry for 6 minutes, shaking the basket once or twice during the cooking process to redistribute the ingredients.
3. While the vegetables are cooking, beat the eggs well in a bowl, stir in the Cheddar cheese and season with salt and freshly ground black pepper. Add the air-fried vegetables to this bowl when they have finished cooking.
4. Place a 6- or 7-inch non-stick metal cake pan into the air fryer basket with the butter using an aluminum sling to lower the pan into the basket. (Fold a piece of aluminum foil into a strip about 2-inches wide by 24-inches long.) Air-fry for 1 minute at 380°F (195°C) to melt the butter. Remove the cake pan and rotate the pan to distribute the butter and grease the pan. Pour the egg mixture into the cake pan and return the pan to the air fryer, using the aluminum sling.
5. Air-fry at 380°F (195°C) for 12 minutes, or until the frittata has puffed up and is lightly browned. Let the frittata sit in the air fryer for 5 minutes to cool to an edible temperature and set up. Remove the cake pan from the air fryer, sprinkle with parsley and serve immediately.

Cinnamon Banana Bread With Pecans

Servings: 6

Cooking Time: 35 Minutes

Ingredients:

- 2 ripe bananas, mashed
- 1 egg
- ¼ cup Greek yogurt
- ¼ cup olive oil
- ½ tsp peppermint extract
- 2 tbsp honey
- 1 cup flour
- ¼ tsp salt
- ¼ tsp baking soda
- ½ tsp ground cinnamon
- ¼ cup chopped pecans

Directions:

1. Preheat air fryer to 360°F (180°C). Add the bananas, egg, yogurt, olive oil, peppermint, and honey in a large bowl and mix until combined and mostly smooth.
2. Sift the flour, salt, baking soda, and cinnamon into the wet mixture, then stir until just combined. Gently fold in the pecans. Spread to distribute evenly into a greased loaf pan. Place the loaf pan in the frying basket and Bake for 23 minutes or until golden brown on top and a toothpick inserted into the center comes out clean. Allow to cool for 5 minutes. Serve.

Broccoli Cornbread

Servings: 6

Cooking Time: 18 Minutes

Ingredients:

- 1 cup frozen chopped broccoli, thawed and drained
- ¼ cup cottage cheese
- 1 egg, beaten
- 2 tablespoons minced onion
- 2 tablespoons melted butter
- ½ cup flour
- ½ cup yellow cornmeal
- 1 teaspoon baking powder
- ½ teaspoon salt
- ¼ cup milk, plus 2 tablespoons
- cooking spray

Directions:

1. Place thawed broccoli in colander and press with a spoon to squeeze out excess moisture.
2. Stir together all ingredients in a large bowl.
3. Spray 6 x 6-inch baking pan with cooking spray.
4. Spread batter in pan and cook at 330°F (165°C) for 18 minutes or until cornbread is lightly browned and loaf starts to pull away from sides of pan.

Zucchini Hash Browns

Servings: 4
Cooking Time: 20 Minutes
Ingredients:

- 2 shredded zucchinis
- 2 tbsp nutritional yeast
- 1 tsp allspice
- 1 egg white

Directions:

1. Preheat air fryer to 400°F (205°C). Combine zucchinis, nutritional yeast, allspice, and egg white in a bowl. Make 4 patties out of the mixture. Cut 4 pieces of parchment paper, put a patty on each foil, and fold in all sides to create a rectangle. Using a spatula, flatten them and spread them.
2. Then unwrap each foil and remove the hash browns onto the fryer and Air Fry for 12 minutes until golden brown and crispy, turning once. Serve right away.

Poultry Recipes

Chicken Tenders With Basil-strawberry Glaze

Servings: 4
Cooking Time: 20 Minutes
Ingredients:

- 1 lb chicken tenderloins
- ¼ cup strawberry preserves
- 3 tbsp chopped basil
- 1 tsp orange juice
- ½ tsp orange zest
- Salt and pepper to taste

Directions:

1. Combine all ingredients, except for 1 tbsp of basil, in a bowl. Marinade in the fridge covered for 30 minutes.
2. Preheat air fryer to 350°F. Place the chicken tenders in the frying basket and Air Fry for 4-6 minutes. Shake gently the basket and turn over the chicken. Cook for 5 more minutes. Top with the remaining basil to serve.

Thai Chicken Drumsticks

Servings: 4
Cooking Time: 20 Minutes
Ingredients:

- 2 tablespoons soy sauce
- ¼ cup rice wine vinegar
- 2 tablespoons chili garlic sauce
- 2 tablespoons sesame oil
- 1 teaspoon minced fresh ginger
- 2 teaspoons sugar
- ½ teaspoon ground coriander
- juice of 1 lime
- 8 chicken drumsticks (about 2½ pounds)
- ¼ cup chopped peanuts
- chopped fresh cilantro
- lime wedges

Directions:

1. Combine the soy sauce, rice wine vinegar, chili sauce, sesame oil, ginger, sugar, coriander and lime juice in a large bowl and mix together. Add the chicken drumsticks and marinate for 30 minutes.
2. Preheat the air fryer to 370°F (185°C).
3. Place the chicken in the air fryer basket. It's ok if the ends of the drumsticks overlap a little. Spoon half of the marinade over the chicken, and reserve the other half.
4. Air-fry for 10 minutes. Turn the chicken over and pour the rest of the marinade over the chicken. Air-fry for an additional 10 minutes.
5. Transfer the chicken to a plate to rest and cool to an edible temperature. Pour the marinade from the bottom of the air fryer into a small saucepan and bring it to a simmer over medium-high heat. Simmer the liquid for 2 minutes so that it thickens enough to coat the back of a spoon.
6. Transfer the chicken to a serving platter, pour the sauce over the chicken and sprinkle the chopped peanuts on top. Garnish with chopped cilantro and lime wedges.

Turkey Tenderloin With A Lemon Touch

Servings: 4
Cooking Time: 45 Minutes

Ingredients:

- 1 lb boneless, skinless turkey breast tenderloin
- Salt and pepper to taste
- ½ tsp garlic powder
- ½ tsp chili powder
- ½ tsp dried thyme
- 1 lemon, juiced
- 1 tbsp chopped cilantro

Directions:

1. Preheat air fryer to 350°F (175°C). Dry the turkey completely with a paper towel, then season with salt, pepper, garlic powder, chili powder, and thyme. Place the turkey in the frying basket. Squeeze the lemon juice over the turkey and bake for 10 minutes. Turn the turkey and bake for another 10 to 15 minutes. Allow to rest for 10 minutes before slicing. Serve sprinkled with cilantro and enjoy.

Country Chicken Hoagies

Servings: 2
Cooking Time: 30 Minutes

Ingredients:

- ¼ cup button mushrooms, sliced
- 1 hoagie bun, halved
- 1 chicken breast, cubed
- ½ white onion, sliced
- 1 cup bell pepper strips
- 2 cheddar cheese slices

Directions:

1. Preheat air fryer to 320°F (160°C). Place the chicken pieces, onions, bell pepper strips, and mushroom slices on one side of the frying basket. Lay the hoagie bun halves, crusty side up and soft side down, on the other half of the air fryer. Bake for 10 minutes. Flip the hoagie buns and cover with cheddar cheese. Stir the chicken and vegetables. Cook for another 6 minutes until the cheese is melted and the chicken is juicy on the inside and crispy on the outside. Place the cheesy hoagie halves on a serving plate and cover one half with the chicken and veggies. Close with the other cheesy hoagie half. Serve.

Parmesan Chicken Fingers

Servings: 2
Cooking Time: 19 Minutes

Ingredients:

- ½ cup flour
- 1 teaspoon salt
- freshly ground black pepper
- 2 eggs, beaten
- ¾ cup seasoned panko breadcrumbs
- ¾ cup grated Parmesan cheese
- 8 chicken tenders (about 1 pound)
- OR
- 2 to 3 boneless, skinless chicken breasts, cut into strips
- vegetable oil
- marinara sauce

Directions:

1. Set up a dredging station. Combine the flour, salt and pepper in a shallow dish. Place the beaten eggs in second shallow dish, and combine the panko breadcrumbs and Parmesan cheese in a third shallow dish.
2. Dredge the chicken tenders in the flour mixture. Then dip them into the egg, and finally place the chicken in the breadcrumb mixture. Press the coating onto both sides of the chicken tenders. Place the coated chicken tenders on a baking sheet until they are all coated. Spray both sides of the chicken fingers with vegetable oil.
3. Preheat the air fryer to 360°F (180°C).
4. Air-fry the chicken fingers in two batches. Transfer half the chicken fingers to the air fryer basket and air-fry for 9 minutes, turning the chicken over halfway through the cooking time. When the second batch of chicken fingers has finished cooking, return the first batch to the air fryer with the second batch and air-fry for one minute to heat everything through.
5. Serve immediately with marinara sauce, honey-mustard, ketchup or your favorite dipping sauce.

Indian Chicken Tandoori

Servings: 2
Cooking Time: 35 Minutes

Ingredients:

- 2 chicken breasts, cubed
- ½ cup hung curd
- 1 tsp turmeric powder
- 1 tsp red chili powder
- 1 tsp chaat masala powder
- Pinch of salt

Directions:

1. Preheat air fryer to 350°F (175°C). Mix the hung curd, turmeric, red chili powder, chaat masala powder, and salt in a mixing bowl. Stir until the mixture is free of lumps. Coat the chicken with the mixture, cover, and refrigerate for 30 minutes to marinate. Place the marinated chicken chunks in a baking pan and drizzle with the remaining marinade. Bake for 25 minutes until the chicken is juicy and spiced. Serve warm.

Cheesy Chicken Tenders

Servings: 4

Cooking Time: 25 Minutes

Ingredients:

- 1 cup grated Parmesan cheese
- ¼ cup grated cheddar
- 1 ¼ lb chicken tenders
- 1 egg, beaten
- 2 tbsp milk
- Salt and pepper to taste
- ½ tsp garlic powder
- 1 tsp dried thyme
- ¼ tsp shallot powder

Directions:

1. Preheat the air fryer to 400°F (205°C). Stir the egg and milk until combined. Mix the salt, pepper, garlic, thyme, shallot, cheddar cheese, and Parmesan cheese on a plate. Dip the chicken in the egg mix, then in the cheese mix, and press to coat. Lay the tenders in the frying basket in a single layer. Add a raised rack to cook more at one time. Spray all with oil and Bake for 12-16 minutes, flipping once halfway through cooking. Serve hot.

Hazelnut Chicken Salad With Strawberries

Servings: 4

Cooking Time: 30 Minutes

Ingredients:

- 2 chicken breasts, cubed
- Salt and pepper to taste
- ¾ cup mayonnaise
- 1 tbsp lime juice
- ½ cup chopped hazelnuts
- ½ cup chopped celery
- ½ cup diced strawberries

Directions:

1. Preheat air fryer to 350ºF. Sprinkle chicken cubes with salt and pepper. Place them in the frying basket and Air Fry for 9 minutes, shaking once. Remove to a bowl and leave it to cool. Add the mayonnaise, lime juice, hazelnuts, celery, and strawberries. Serve.

Saucy Chicken Thighs

Servings: 4

Cooking Time: 35 Minutes

Ingredients:

- 8 boneless, skinless chicken thighs
- 1 tbsp Italian seasoning
- Salt and pepper to taste
- 2 garlic cloves, minced
- ½ tsp apple cider vinegar
- ½ cup honey
- ¼ cup Dijon mustard

Directions:

1. Preheat air fryer to 400°F (205°C). Season the chicken with Italian seasoning, salt, and black pepper. Place in the greased frying basket and Bake for 15 minutes, flipping once halfway through cooking.
2. While the chicken is cooking, add garlic, honey, vinegar, and Dijon mustard in a saucepan and stir-fry over medium heat for 4 minutes or until the sauce has thickened and warmed through. Transfer the thighs to a serving dish and drizzle with honey-mustard sauce. Serve and enjoy!

Chicken Wellington

Servings: 2

Cooking Time: 31 Minutes

Ingredients:

- 2 (5-ounce) boneless, skinless chicken breasts
- ½ cup White Worcestershire sauce
- 3 tablespoons butter
- ½ cup finely diced onion (about ½ onion)
- 8 ounces button mushrooms, finely chopped
- ¼ cup chicken stock
- 2 tablespoons White Worcestershire sauce (or white wine)
- salt and freshly ground black pepper
- 1 tablespoon chopped fresh tarragon
- 2 sheets puff pastry, thawed
- 1 egg, beaten
- vegetable oil

Directions:

1. Place the chicken breasts in a shallow dish. Pour the White Worcestershire sauce over the chicken coating both sides and marinate for 30 minutes.
2. While the chicken is marinating, melt the butter in a large skillet over medium-high heat on the stovetop. Add the onion and sauté for a few minutes, until it starts to soften. Add the mushrooms and sauté for 5 minutes until the vegetables are brown and soft. Deglaze the skillet with the chicken stock, scraping up any bits from the bottom of the pan. Add the White Worcestershire sauce and simmer for 3 minutes until the mixture reduces and starts to thicken. Season with salt and freshly ground black pepper. Remove the mushroom mixture from the heat and stir in the fresh tarragon. Let the mushroom mixture cool.
3. Preheat the air fryer to 360°F (180°C).

4. Remove the chicken from the marinade and transfer it to the air fryer basket. Tuck the small end of the chicken breast under the thicker part to shape it into a circle rather than an oval. Pour the marinade over the chicken and air-fry for 10 minutes.

5. Roll out the puff pastry and cut out two 6-inch squares. Brush the perimeter of each square with the egg wash. Place half of the mushroom mixture in the center of each puff pastry square. Place the chicken breasts, top side down on the mushroom mixture. Starting with one corner of puff pastry and working in one direction, pull the pastry up over the chicken to enclose it and press the ends of the pastry together in the middle. Brush the pastry with the egg wash to seal the edges. Turn the Wellingtons over and set aside.

6. To make a decorative design with the remaining puff pastry, cut out four 10-inch strips. For each Wellington, twist two of the strips together, place them over the chicken breast wrapped in puff pastry, and tuck the ends underneath to seal it. Brush the entire top and sides of the Wellingtons with the egg wash.

7. Preheat the air fryer to 350°F (175°C).

8. Spray or brush the air fryer basket with vegetable oil. Air-fry the chicken Wellingtons for 13 minutes. Carefully turn the Wellingtons over. Air-fry for another 8 minutes. Transfer to serving plates, light a candle and enjoy!

Mexican Chicken Roll-ups

Servings: 4

Cooking Time: 35 Minutes

Ingredients:

- ½ red bell pepper, cut into strips
- ½ green bell pepper, cut into strips
- 2 chicken breasts
- ½ lime, juiced
- 2 tbsp taco seasoning
- 1 spring onion, thinly sliced

Directions:

1. Preheat air fryer to 400°F (205°C). Cut the chicken into cutlets by slicing the chicken breast in half horizontally in order to have 4 thin cutlets. Drizzle with lime juice and season with taco seasoning. Divide the red pepper, green pepper, and spring onion equally between the 4 cutlets. Roll up the cutlets. Secure with toothpicks. Place the chicken roll-ups in the air fryer and lightly spray with cooking oil. Bake for 12 minutes, turning once. Serve warm.

Mexican-inspired Chicken Breasts

Servings: 4

Cooking Time: 20 Minutes

Ingredients:

- ⅛ tsp crushed red pepper flakes
- 1 red pepper, deseeded and diced
- Salt to taste
- 4 chicken breasts
- ¾ tsp garlic powder
- ½ tsp onion powder
- ½ tsp ground cumin
- ½ tsp ancho chile powder
- ½ tsp sweet paprika
- ½ tsp Mexican oregano
- 1 tomato, chopped
- ½ diced red onion
- 3 tbsp fresh lime juice
- 10 ounces avocado, diced
- 1 tbsp chopped cilantro

Directions:

1. Preheat air fryer to 380°F (195°C). Stir together salt, garlic and onion powder, cumin, ancho chili powder, paprika, Mexican oregano, and pepper flakes in a bowl. Spray the chicken with cooking oil and rub with the spice mix. Air Fry the chicken for 10 minutes, flipping once until browned and fully cooked. Repeat for all of the chicken. Mix the onion and lime juice in a bowl. Fold in the avocado, cilantro, red pepper, salt, and tomato and coat gently. To serve, top the chicken with guacamole salsa.

Greek Gyros With Chicken & Rice

Servings: 4

Cooking Time: 25 Minutes

Ingredients:

- 1 lb chicken breasts, cubed
- ¼ cup cream cheese
- 2 tbsp olive oil
- 1 tsp dried oregano
- 1 tsp ground cumin
- 1 tsp ground cinnamon
- ¼ tsp ground nutmeg
- Salt and pepper to taste
- ¼ tsp ground turmeric
- 2 cups cooked rice
- 1 cup Tzatziki sauce

Directions:

1. Preheat air fryer to 380°F (195°C). Put all ingredients in a bowl and mix together until the chicken is coated well. Spread the chicken mixture in the frying basket, then Bake for 10 minutes. Stir the chicken mixture and Bake for an additional 5 minutes. Serve with rice and tzatziki sauce.

Southern-style Chicken Legs

Servings: 6

Cooking Time: 20 Minutes

Ingredients:

- 2 cups buttermilk
- 1 tablespoon hot sauce
- 12 chicken legs
- ½ teaspoon salt
- ½ teaspoon pepper
- 1 teaspoon paprika
- ½ teaspoon onion powder
- 1 teaspoon garlic powder
- 1 cup all-purpose flour

Directions:

1. In an airtight container, place the buttermilk, hot sauce, and chicken legs and refrigerate for 4 to 8 hours.
2. In a medium bowl, whisk together the salt, pepper, paprika, onion powder, garlic powder, and flour. Drain the chicken legs from the buttermilk and dip the chicken legs into the flour mixture, stirring to coat well.
3. Preheat the air fryer to 390°F (200°C).
4. Place the chicken legs in the air fryer basket and spray with cooking spray. Cook for 10 minutes, turn the chicken legs over, and cook for another 8 to 10 minutes. Check for an internal temperature of 165°F (75°C).

Yogurt-marinated Chicken Legs

Servings: 4

Cooking Time: 50 Minutes

Ingredients:

- 1 cup Greek yogurt
- 1 tbsp Dijon mustard
- 1 tsp smoked paprika
- 1 tbsp crushed red pepper
- 1 tsp garlic powder
- 1 tsp dried oregano
- 1 tsp dried thyme
- 1 teaspoon ground cumin
- ¼ cup lemon juice
- Salt and pepper to taste
- 1 ½ lb chicken legs
- 3 tbsp butter, melted

Directions:

1. Combine all ingredients, except chicken and butter, in a bowl. Fold in chicken legs and toss until coated. Let sit covered in the fridge for 60 minutes up to overnight.
2. Preheat air fryer at 375ºF. Shake excess marinade from chicken; place them in the greased frying basket and Air Fry for 18 minutes, brush melted butter and flip once. Let chill for 5 minutes before serving.

Chipotle Chicken Drumsticks

Servings: 4

Cooking Time: 40 Minutes

Ingredients:

- 1 can chipotle chilies packed in adobe sauce
- 2 tbsp grated Mexican cheese
- 6 chicken drumsticks
- 1 egg, beaten
- ½ cup bread crumbs
- 1 tbsp corn flakes
- Salt and pepper to taste

Directions:

1. Preheat air fryer to 350°F (175°C). Place the chilies in the sauce in your blender and pulse until a fine paste is formed. Transfer to a bowl and add the beaten egg. Combine thoroughly. Mix the breadcrumbs, Mexican cheese, corn flakes, salt, and pepper in a separate bowl, and set aside.
2. Coat the chicken drumsticks with the crumb mixture, then dip into the bowl with wet ingredients, then dip again into the dry ingredients. Arrange the chicken drumsticks on the greased frying basket in a single flat layer. Air Fry for 14-16 minutes, turning each chicken drumstick over once. Serve warm.

Enchilada Chicken Quesadillas

Servings: 4

Cooking Time: 35 Minutes

Ingredients:

- 2 cups cooked chicken breasts, shredded
- 1 can diced green chilies, including juice
- 2 cups grated Mexican cheese blend
- 3/4 cup sour cream
- 2 tsp chili powder
- 1 tsp cumin
- 1 tbsp chipotle sauce
- 1 tsp dried onion flakes
- ½ tsp salt
- 3 tbsp butter, melted
- 8 flour tortillas

Directions:

1. In a small bowl, whisk the sour cream, chipotle sauce and chili powder. Let chill in the fridge until ready to use.
2. Preheat air fryer at 350ºF. Mix the chicken, green chilies, cumin, and salt in a bowl. Set aside. Brush on one side of a tortilla lightly with melted butter. Layer with ¼ cup of chicken, onion flakes and ¼ cup of Mexican cheese. Top with a second tortilla and lightly brush with butter on top. Repeat with the remaining ingredients. Place quesadillas, butter side down, in the frying basket and Bake for 3 minutes. Cut them into 6 sections and serve with cream sauce on the side.

Buttered Chicken Thighs

Servings: 4

Cooking Time: 30 Minutes

Ingredients:

- 4 bone-in chicken thighs, skinless
- 2 tbsp butter, melted
- 1 tsp garlic powder
- 1 tsp lemon zest
- Salt and pepper to taste
- 1 lemon, sliced

Directions:

1. Preheat air fryer to 380°F (195°C). Stir the chicken thighs in the butter, lemon zest, garlic powder, and salt. Divide the chicken thighs between 4 pieces of foil and sprinkle with black pepper, and then top with slices of lemon. Bake in the air fryer for 20-22 minutes until golden. Serve.

Chicken Cordon Bleu Patties

Servings: 4

Cooking Time: 30 Minutes

Ingredients:

- 1/3 cup grated Fontina cheese
- 3 tbsp milk
- 1/3 cup bread crumbs
- 1 egg, beaten
- ½ tsp dried parsley
- Salt and pepper to taste
- 1 ¼ lb ground chicken
- ¼ cup finely chopped ham

Directions:

1. Preheat air fryer to 350°F (175°C). Mix milk, breadcrumbs, egg, parsley, salt and pepper in a bowl. Using your hands, add the chicken and gently mix until just combined. Divide into 8 portions and shape into thin patties. Place on waxed paper. On 4 of the patties, top with ham and Fontina cheese, then place another patty on top of that. Gently pinch the edges together so that none of the ham or cheese is peeking out. Arrange the burgers in the greased frying basket and Air Fry until cooked through, for 14-16 minutes. Serve and enjoy!

Pecan Turkey Cutlets

Servings: 4

Cooking Time: 12 Minutes

Ingredients:

- ¾ cup panko breadcrumbs
- ¼ teaspoon salt
- ¼ teaspoon pepper
- ¼ teaspoon dry mustard
- ¼ teaspoon poultry seasoning
- ½ cup pecans
- ¼ cup cornstarch
- 1 egg, beaten
- 1 pound turkey cutlets, ½-inch thick
- salt and pepper
- oil for misting or cooking spray

Directions:

1. Place the panko crumbs, ¼ teaspoon salt, ¼ teaspoon pepper, mustard, and poultry seasoning in food processor. Process until crumbs are finely crushed. Add pecans and process in short pulses just until nuts are finely chopped. Go easy so you don't overdo it!
2. Preheat air fryer to 360°F (180°C).
3. Place cornstarch in one shallow dish and beaten egg in another. Transfer coating mixture from food processor into a third shallow dish.
4. Sprinkle turkey cutlets with salt and pepper to taste.
5. Dip cutlets in cornstarch and shake off excess. Then dip in beaten egg and roll in crumbs, pressing to coat well. Spray both sides with oil or cooking spray.
6. Place 2 cutlets in air fryer basket in a single layer and cook for 12 minutes or until juices run clear.
7. Repeat step 6 to cook remaining cutlets.

Spiced Mexican Stir-fried Chicken

Servings: 4

Cooking Time: 30 Minutes

Ingredients:

- 1 lb chicken breasts, cubed
- 2 green onions, chopped
- 1 red bell pepper, chopped
- 1 jalapeño pepper, minced
- 2 tsp olive oil
- 2/3 cup canned black beans
- ½ cup salsa
- 2 tsp Mexican chili powder

Directions:

1. Preheat air fryer to 400°F (205°C). Combine the chicken, green onions, bell pepper, jalapeño, and olive oil in a bowl. Transfer to a bowl to the frying basket and Air Fry for 10 minutes, stirring once during cooking. When done, stir in the black beans, salsa, and chili powder. Air Fry for 7-10 minutes or until cooked through. Serve.

Spicy Black Bean Turkey Burgers With Cumin-avocado Spread

Servings: 2

Cooking Time: 20 Minutes

Ingredients:
- 1 cup canned black beans, drained and rinsed
- ¾ pound lean ground turkey
- 2 tablespoons minced red onion
- 1 Jalapeño pepper, seeded and minced
- 2 tablespoons plain breadcrumbs
- ½ teaspoon chili powder
- ¼ teaspoon cayenne pepper
- salt, to taste
- olive or vegetable oil
- 2 slices pepper jack cheese
- toasted burger rolls, sliced tomatoes, lettuce leaves
- Cumin-Avocado Spread:
- 1 ripe avocado
- juice of 1 lime
- 1 teaspoon ground cumin
- ½ teaspoon salt
- 1 tablespoon chopped fresh cilantro
- freshly ground black pepper

Directions:

1. Place the black beans in a large bowl and smash them slightly with the back of a fork. Add the ground turkey, red onion, Jalapeño pepper, breadcrumbs, chili powder and cayenne pepper. Season with salt. Mix with your hands to combine all the ingredients and then shape them into 2 patties. Brush both sides of the burger patties with a little olive or vegetable oil.
2. Preheat the air fryer to 380°F (195°C).
3. Transfer the burgers to the air fryer basket and air-fry for 20 minutes, flipping them over halfway through the cooking process. Top the burgers with the pepper jack cheese (securing the slices to the burgers with a toothpick) for the last 2 minutes of the cooking process.
4. While the burgers are cooking, make the cumin avocado spread. Place the avocado, lime juice, cumin and salt in food processor and process until smooth. (For a chunkier spread, you can mash this by hand in a bowl.) Stir in the cilantro and season with freshly ground black pepper. Chill the spread until you are ready to serve.
5. When the burgers have finished cooking, remove them from the air fryer and let them rest on a plate, covered gently with aluminum foil. Brush a little olive oil on the insides of the burger rolls. Place the rolls, cut side up, into the air fryer basket and air-fry at 400°F (205°C) for 1 minute to toast and warm them.
6. Spread the cumin-avocado spread on the rolls and build your burgers with lettuce and sliced tomatoes and any other ingredient you like. Serve warm with a side of sweet potato fries.

Maewoon Chicken Legs

Servings: 4

Cooking Time: 30 Minutes + Chilling Time

Ingredients:
- 4 scallions, sliced, whites and greens separated
- ¼ cup tamari
- 2 tbsp sesame oil
- 1 tsp sesame seeds
- ¼ cup honey
- 2 tbsp gochujang
- 2 tbsp ketchup
- 4 cloves garlic, minced
- ½ tsp ground ginger
- Salt and pepper to taste
- 1 tbsp parsley
- 1 ½ lb chicken legs

Directions:

1. Whisk all ingredients, except chicken and scallion greens, in a bowl. Reserve ¼ cup of marinade. Toss chicken legs in the remaining marinade and chill for 30 minutes.
2. Preheat air fryer at 400°F. Place chicken legs in the greased frying basket and Air Fry for 10 minutes. Turn chicken. Cook for 8 more minutes. Let sit in a serving dish for 5 minutes. Coat the cooked chicken with the reserved marinade and scatter with scallion greens, sesame seeds and parsley to serve.

Farmer's Fried Chicken

Servings: 4

Cooking Time: 55 Minutes

Ingredients:
- 3 lb whole chicken, cut into breasts, drumsticks, and thighs
- 2 cups flour
- 4 tsp salt
- 4 tsp dried basil
- 4 tsp dried thyme
- 2 tsp dried shallot powder
- 2 tsp smoked paprika
- 1 tsp mustard powder
- 1 tsp celery salt
- 1 cup kefir
- ¼ cup honey

Directions:

1. Preheat the air fryer to 370°F (185°C). Combine the flour, salt, basil, thyme, shallot, paprika, mustard powder, and celery salt in a bowl. Pour into a glass jar. Mix the kefir and honey in a large bowl and add the chicken, stir to coat. Marinate for 15 minutes at room temperature. Remove the chicken from the kefir mixture; discard the rest. Put 2/3 cup of the flour mix onto a plate and dip the chicken. Shake gently and put on a wire rack for 10 minutes. Line the frying basket with round parchment paper with holes punched in it. Place the chicken in a single layer and spray with cooking oil. Air Fry for 18-25 minutes, flipping once around minute 10. Serve hot.

Za'atar Chicken Drumsticks

Servings: 4

Cooking Time: 45 Minutes

Ingredients:

- 2 tbsp butter, melted
- 8 chicken drumsticks
- 1 ½ tbsp Za'atar seasoning
- Salt and pepper to taste
- 1 lemon, zested
- 2 tbsp parsley, chopped

Directions:

1. Preheat air fryer to 390°F (200°C). Mix the Za'atar seasoning, lemon zest, parsley, salt, and pepper in a bowl. Add the chicken drumsticks and toss to coat. Place them in the air fryer and brush them with butter. Air Fry for 18-20 minutes, flipping once until crispy. Serve and enjoy!

Granny Pesto Chicken Caprese

Servings: 4

Cooking Time: 30 Minutes

Ingredients:

- 2 tbsp grated Parmesan cheese
- 4 oz fresh mozzarella cheese, thinly sliced
- 16 grape tomatoes, halved
- 4 garlic cloves, minced
- 1 tsp olive oil
- Salt and pepper to taste
- 4 chicken cutlets
- 1 tbsp prepared pesto
- 1 large egg, beaten
- ½ cup bread crumbs
- 2 tbsp Italian seasoning
- 1 tsp balsamic vinegar
- 2 tbsp chopped fresh basil

Directions:

1. Preheat air fryer to 400°F (205°C). In a bowl, coat the tomatoes with garlic, olive oil, salt and pepper. Air Fry for 5 minutes, shaking them twice. Set aside when soft.

2. Place the cutlets between two sheets of parchment paper. Pound the chicken to ¼-inch thickness using a meat mallet. Season on both sides with salt and pepper. Spread an even coat of pesto. Put the beaten egg in a shallow bowl. Mix the crumbs, Italian seasoning, and Parmesan in a second shallow bowl. Dip the chicken in the egg bowl, and then in the crumb mix. Press the crumbs so that they stick to the chicken.

3. Place the chicken in the greased frying basket. Air Fry the chicken for 6-8 minutes, flipping once until golden and cooked through. Put 1 oz of mozzarella and ¼ of the tomatoes on top of each cutlet. When all of the cutlets are cooked, return them to the frying basket and melt the cheese for 2 minutes. Remove from the fryer, drizzle with balsamic vinegar and basil on top.

Chicken & Rice Sautée

Servings: 4

Cooking Time: 25 Minutes

Ingredients:

- 1 can pineapple chunks, drained, ¼ cup juice reserved
- 1 cup cooked long-grain rice
- 1 lb chicken breasts, cubed
- 1 red onion, chopped
- 1 tbsp peanut oil
- 1 peeled peach, cubed
- 1 tbsp cornstarch
- ½ tsp ground ginger
- ¼ tsp chicken seasoning

Directions:

1. Preheat air fryer to 400°F (205°C). Combine the chicken, red onion, pineapple, and peanut oil in a metal bowl, then put the bowl in the fryer. Air Fry for 9 minutes, remove and stir. Toss the peach in and put the bowl back into the fryer for 3 minutes. Slide out and stir again. Mix the reserved pineapple juice, corn starch, ginger, and chicken seasoning in a bowl, then pour over the chicken mixture and stir well. Put the bowl back into the fryer and cook for 3 more minutes or until the chicken is cooked through and the sauce is thick. Serve over cooked rice.

Greek Chicken Wings

Servings: 4

Cooking Time: 30 Minutes

Ingredients:

- 8 whole chicken wings
- ½ lemon, juiced
- ½ tsp garlic powder
- 1 tsp shallot powder
- ½ tsp Greek seasoning
- Salt and pepper to taste
- ¼ cup buttermilk
- ½ cup all-purpose flour

Directions:

1. Preheat air fryer to 400°F (205°C). Put the wings in a resealable bag along with lemon juice, garlic, shallot, Greek seasoning, salt and pepper. Seal the bag and shake to coat. Set up bowls large enough to fit the wings.
2. In one bowl, pour the buttermilk. In the other, add flour. Using tongs, dip the wings into the buttermilk, then dredge in flour. Transfer the wings in the greased frying basket, spraying lightly with cooking oil. Air Fry for 25 minutes, shaking twice, until golden and cooked through. Allow to cool slightly, and serve.

Air-fried Turkey Breast With Cherry Glaze

Servings: 6

Cooking Time: 54 Minutes

Ingredients:

- 1 (5-pound) turkey breast
- 2 teaspoons olive oil
- 1 teaspoon dried thyme
- ½ teaspoon dried sage
- 1 teaspoon salt
- ½ teaspoon freshly ground black pepper
- ½ cup cherry preserves
- 1 tablespoon chopped fresh thyme leaves
- 1 teaspoon soy sauce*
- freshly ground black pepper

Directions:

1. All turkeys are built differently, so depending on the turkey breast and how your butcher has prepared it, you may need to trim the bottom of the ribs in order to get the turkey to sit upright in the air fryer basket without touching the heating element. The key to this recipe is getting the right size turkey breast. Once you've managed that, the rest is easy, so make sure your turkey breast fits into the air fryer basket before you Preheat the air fryer.
2. Preheat the air fryer to 350°F (175°C).
3. Brush the turkey breast all over with the olive oil. Combine the thyme, sage, salt and pepper and rub the outside of the turkey breast with the spice mixture.
4. Transfer the seasoned turkey breast to the air fryer basket, breast side up, and air-fry at 350°F (175°C) for 25 minutes. Turn the turkey breast on its side and air-fry for another 12 minutes. Turn the turkey breast on the opposite side and air-fry for 12 more minutes. The internal temperature of the turkey breast should reach 165°F (75°C) when fully cooked.
5. While the turkey is air-frying, make the glaze by combining the cherry preserves, fresh thyme, soy sauce and pepper in a small bowl. When the cooking time is up, return the turkey breast to an upright position and brush the glaze all over the turkey. Air-fry for a final 5 minutes, until the skin is nicely browned and crispy. Let the turkey rest, loosely tented with foil, for at least 5 minutes before slicing and serving.

Yummy Maple-mustard Chicken Kabobs

Servings: 4

Cooking Time: 35 Minutes+ Chilling Time

Ingredients:

- 1 lb boneless, skinless chicken thighs, cubed
- 1 green bell pepper, chopped
- ½ cup honey mustard
- ½ yellow onion, chopped
- 8 cherry tomatoes
- 2 tbsp chopped scallions

Directions:

1. Toss chicken cubes and honey mustard in a bowl and let chill covered in the fridge for 30 minutes. Preheat air fryer to 350ºF. Thread chicken cubes, onion, cherry tomatoes, and bell peppers, alternating, onto 8 skewers. Place them on a kebab rack. Place rack in the frying basket and Air Fry for 12 minutes. Top with scallions to serve.

Peachy Chicken Chunks With Cherries

Servings: 4

Cooking Time: 16 Minutes

Ingredients:

- ⅓ cup peach preserves
- 1 teaspoon ground rosemary
- ½ teaspoon black pepper
- ½ teaspoon salt
- ½ teaspoon marjoram

- 1 teaspoon light olive oil
- 1 pound boneless chicken breasts, cut in 1½-inch chunks
- oil for misting or cooking spray
- 10-ounce package frozen unsweetened dark cherries, thawed and drained

Directions:
1. In a medium bowl, mix together peach preserves, rosemary, pepper, salt, marjoram, and olive oil.
2. Stir in chicken chunks and toss to coat well with the preserve mixture.
3. Spray air fryer basket with oil or cooking spray and lay chicken chunks in basket.
4. Cook at 390°F (200°C) for 7 minutes. Stir. Cook for 8 more minutes or until chicken juices run clear.
5. When chicken has cooked through, scatter the cherries over and cook for additional minute to heat cherries.

Mom's Chicken Wings

Servings: 4
Cooking Time: 35 Minutes

Ingredients:
- 2 lb chicken wings, split at the joint
- 1 tbsp water
- 1 tbsp sesame oil
- 2 tbsp Dijon mustard
- ¼ tsp chili powder
- 1 tbsp tamari
- 1 tsp honey
- 1 tsp white wine vinegar

Directions:
1. Preheat air fryer to 400°F. Coat the wings with sesame oil. Place them in the frying basket and Air Fry for 16-18 minutes, tossing once or twice. Whisk the remaining ingredients in a bowl. Reserve. When ready, transfer the wings to a serving bowl. Pour the previously prepared sauce over and toss to coat. Serve immediately.

Chicken Cordon Bleu

Servings: 2
Cooking Time: 16 Minutes

Ingredients:
- 2 boneless, skinless chicken breasts
- ¼ teaspoon salt
- 2 teaspoons Dijon mustard
- 2 ounces deli ham
- 2 ounces Swiss, fontina, or Gruyère cheese
- ⅓ cup all-purpose flour
- 1 egg
- ½ cup breadcrumbs

Directions:
1. Pat the chicken breasts with a paper towel. Season the chicken with the salt. Pound the chicken breasts to 1½ inches thick. Create a pouch by slicing the side of each chicken breast. Spread 1 teaspoon Dijon mustard inside the pouch of each chicken breast. Wrap a 1-ounce slice of ham around a 1-ounce slice of cheese and place into the pouch. Repeat with the remaining ham and cheese.
2. In a medium bowl, place the flour.
3. In a second bowl, whisk the egg.
4. In a third bowl, place the breadcrumbs.
5. Dredge the chicken in the flour and shake off the excess. Next, dip the chicken into the egg and then in the breadcrumbs. Set the chicken on a plate and repeat with the remaining chicken piece.
6. Preheat the air fryer to 360°F (180°C).
7. Place the chicken in the air fryer basket and spray liberally with cooking spray. Cook for 8 minutes, turn the chicken breasts over, and liberally spray with cooking spray again; cook another 6 minutes. Once golden brown, check for an internal temperature of 165°F (75°C).

Party Buffalo Chicken Drumettes

Servings: 6
Cooking Time: 30 Minutes

Ingredients:
- 16 chicken drumettes
- 1 tsp garlic powder
- 1 tbsp chicken seasoning
- Black pepper to taste
- ¼ cup Buffalo wings sauce
- 2 spring onions, sliced

Directions:
1. Preheat air fryer to 400°F (205°C). Sprinkle garlic, chicken seasoning, and black pepper on the drumettes. Place them in the fryer and spray with cooking oil. Air Fry for 10 minutes, shaking the basket once. Transfer the drumettes to a large bowl. Drizzle with Buffalo wing sauce and toss to coat. Place in the fryer and Fry for 7-8 minutes, until crispy. Allow to cool slightly. Top with spring onions and serve warm.

Crunchy Chicken Strips

Servings: 4

Cooking Time: 40 Minutes

Ingredients:
- 1 chicken breast, sliced into strips
- 1 tbsp grated Parmesan cheese
- 1 cup breadcrumbs
- 1 tbsp chicken seasoning
- 2 eggs, beaten
- Salt and pepper to taste

Directions:

1. Preheat air fryer to 350°F (175°C). Mix the breadcrumbs, Parmesan cheese, chicken seasoning, salt, and pepper in a mixing bowl. Coat the chicken with the crumb mixture, then dip in the beaten eggs. Finally, coat again with the dry ingredients. Arrange the coated chicken pieces on the greased frying basket and Air Fry for 15 minutes. Turn over halfway through cooking and cook for another 15 minutes. Serve immediately.

Daadi Chicken Salad

Servings: 2

Cooking Time: 30 Minutes

Ingredients:
- ½ cup chopped golden raisins
- 1 Granny Smith apple, grated
- 2 chicken breasts
- Salt and pepper to taste
- ¾ cup mayonnaise
- 1 tbsp lime juice
- 1 tsp curry powder
- ½ sliced avocado
- 1 scallion, minced
- 2 tbsp chopped pecans
- 1 tsp poppy seeds

Directions:

1. Preheat air fryer at 350ºF. Sprinkle chicken breasts with salt and pepper, place them in the greased frying basket, and Air Fry for 8-10 minutes, tossing once. Let rest for 5 minutes before cutting. In a salad bowl, combine chopped chicken, mayonnaise, lime juice, curry powder, raisins, apple, avocado, scallion, and pecans. Let sit covered in the fridge until ready to eat. Before serve sprinkled with the poppy seeds.

Buttered Turkey Breasts

Servings: 6

Cooking Time: 65 Minutes

Ingredients:
- ½ cup butter, melted
- 6 garlic cloves, minced
- 1 tsp dried oregano
- ½ tsp dried thyme
- ½ tsp dried rosemary
- Salt and pepper to taste
- 4 lb bone-in turkey breast
- 1 tbsp chopped cilantro

Directions:

1. Preheat air fryer to 350°F (175°C). Combine butter, garlic, oregano, salt, and pepper in a small bowl. Place the turkey breast on a plate and coat the entire turkey with the butter mixture. Put the turkey breast-side down in the frying basket and scatter with thyme and rosemary. Bake for 20 minutes. Flip the turkey so that the breast side is up, then bake for another 20-30 minutes until it has an internal temperature of 165°F (75°C). Allow to rest for 10 minutes before carving. Serve sprinkled with cilantro.

Quick Chicken For Filling

Servings: 2

Cooking Time: 8 Minutes

Ingredients:
- 1 pound chicken tenders, skinless and boneless
- ½ teaspoon ground cumin
- ½ teaspoon garlic powder
- cooking spray

Directions:

1. Sprinkle raw chicken tenders with seasonings.
2. Spray air fryer basket lightly with cooking spray to prevent sticking.
3. Place chicken in air fryer basket in single layer.
4. Cook at 390°F (200°C) for 4minutes, turn chicken strips over, and cook for an additional 4minutes.
5. Test for doneness. Thick tenders may require an additional minute or two.

Jerk Turkey Meatballs

Servings: 7

Cooking Time: 8 Minutes

Ingredients:
- 1 pound lean ground turkey
- ¼ cup chopped onion
- 1 teaspoon minced garlic
- ½ teaspoon dried thyme
- ¼ teaspoon ground cinnamon
- 1 teaspoon cayenne pepper
- ½ teaspoon paprika

- ½ teaspoon salt
- ⅛ teaspoon black pepper
- ¼ teaspoon red pepper flakes
- 2 teaspoons brown sugar
- 1 large egg, whisked
- ⅓ cup panko breadcrumbs
- 2⅓ cups cooked brown Jasmine rice
- 2 green onions, chopped
- ¾ cup sweet onion dressing

Directions:
1. Preheat the air fryer to 350°F (17°C).
2. In a medium bowl, mix the ground turkey with the onion, garlic, thyme, cinnamon, cayenne pepper, paprika, salt, pepper, red pepper flakes, and brown sugar. Add the whisked egg and stir in the breadcrumbs until the turkey starts to hold together.
3. Using a 1-ounce scoop, portion the turkey into meatballs. You should get about 28 meatballs.
4. Spray the air fryer basket with olive oil spray.
5. Place the meatballs into the air fryer basket and cook for 5 minutes, shake the basket, and cook another 2 to 4 minutes (or until the internal temperature of the meatballs reaches 165°F (75°C)).
6. Remove the meatballs from the basket and repeat for the remaining meatballs.
7. Serve warm over a bed of rice with chopped green onions and spicy Caribbean jerk dressing.

Chicken Meatballs With A Surprise

Servings: 4
Cooking Time: 35 Minutes

Ingredients:
- 1/3 cup cottage cheese crumbles
- 1 lb ground chicken
- ½ tsp onion powder
- ¼ cup chopped basil
- ½ cup bread crumbs
- ½ tsp garlic powder

Directions:
1. Preheat air fryer to 350°F. Combine the ground chicken, onion, basil, cottage cheese, bread crumbs, and garlic powder in a bowl. Form into 18 meatballs, about 2 tbsp each. Place the chicken meatballs in the greased frying basket and Air Fry for 12 minutes, shaking once. Serve.

Kale & Rice Chicken Rolls

Servings: 4
Cooking Time: 35 Minutes

Ingredients:

- 4 boneless, skinless chicken thighs
- ½ tsp ground fenugreek seeds
- 1 cup cooked wild rice
- 2 sundried tomatoes, diced
- ½ cup chopped kale
- 2 garlic cloves, minced
- 1 tsp salt
- 1 lemon, juiced
- ½ cup crumbled feta
- 1 tbsp olive oil

Directions:
1. Preheat air fryer to 380°F (195°C). Put the chicken thighs between two pieces of plastic wrap, and using a meat mallet or a rolling pin, pound them out to about ¼-inch thick. Combine the rice, tomatoes, kale, garlic, salt, fenugreek seeds and lemon juice in a bowl and mix well.
2. Divide the rice mixture among the chicken thighs and sprinkle with feta. Fold the sides of the chicken thigh over the filling, and then gently place each of them seam-side down into the greased air frying basket. Drizzle the stuffed chicken thighs with olive oil. Roast the stuffed chicken thighs for 12 minutes, then turn them over and cook for an additional 10 minutes. Serve and enjoy!

Chicken Salad With Roasted Vegetables

Servings: 4
Cooking Time: 25 Minutes

Ingredients:
- 4 tbsp honey-mustard salad dressing
- 3 chicken breasts, cubed
- 1 red onion, sliced
- 1 orange bell pepper, sliced
- 1 cup sliced zucchini
- ½ tsp dried thyme
- ½ cup mayonnaise
- 2 tbsp lemon juice

Directions:
1. Preheat air fryer to 400°F (205°C). Add chicken, onion, pepper, and zucchini to the fryer. Drizzle with 1 tbsp of the salad dressing and sprinkle with thyme. Toss to coat. Bake for 5-6 minutes. Shake the basket, then continue cooking for another 5-6 minutes. In a bowl, combine the rest of the dressing, mayonnaise, and lemon juice. Transfer the chicken and vegetables and toss to coat. Serve and enjoy!

Buttery Chicken Legs

Servings: 4
Cooking Time: 50 Minutes
Ingredients:
- 1 tsp baking powder
- 1 tsp dried mustard
- 1 tsp smoked paprika
- 1 tsp garlic powder
- 1 tsp dried thyme
- Salt and pepper to taste
- 1 ½ lb chicken legs
- 3 tbsp butter, melted

Directions:
1. Preheat air fryer to 370ºF. Combine all ingredients, except for butter, in a bowl until coated. Place the chicken legs in the greased frying basket. Air Fry for 18 minutes, flipping once and brushing with melted butter on both sides. Let chill onto a serving plate for 5 minutes before serving.

Gruyère Asparagus & Chicken Quiche

Servings: 4
Cooking Time: 30 Minutes
Ingredients:
- 1 grilled chicken breasts, diced
- ½ cup shredded Gruyère cheese
- 1 premade pie crust
- 2 eggs, beaten
- ¼ cup milk
- Salt and pepper to taste
- ½ lb asparagus, sliced
- 1 lemon, zested

Directions:
1. Preheat air fryer to 360°F (180°C). Carefully press the crust into a baking dish, trimming the edges. Prick the dough with a fork a few times. Add the eggs, milk, asparagus, salt, pepper, chicken, lemon zest, and half of Gruyère cheese to a mixing bowl and stir until completely blended. Pour the mixture into the pie crust. Bake in the air fryer for 15 minutes. Sprinkle the remaining Gruyère cheese on top of the quiche filling. Bake for 5 more minutes until the quiche is golden brown. Remove and allow to cool for a few minutes before cutting. Serve sliced and enjoy!

Tortilla Crusted Chicken Breast

Servings: 2
Cooking Time: 12 Minutes
Ingredients:
- ⅓ cup flour
- 1 teaspoon salt
- 1½ teaspoons chili powder
- 1 teaspoon ground cumin
- freshly ground black pepper
- 1 egg, beaten
- ¾ cup coarsely crushed yellow corn tortilla chips
- 2 (3- to 4-ounce) boneless chicken breasts
- vegetable oil
- ½ cup salsa
- ½ cup crumbled queso fresco
- fresh cilantro leaves
- sour cream or guacamole (optional)

Directions:
1. Set up a dredging station with three shallow dishes. Combine the flour, salt, chili powder, cumin and black pepper in the first shallow dish. Beat the egg in the second shallow dish. Place the crushed tortilla chips in the third shallow dish.
2. Dredge the chicken in the spiced flour, covering all sides of the breast. Then dip the chicken into the egg, coating the chicken completely. Finally, place the chicken into the tortilla chips and press the chips onto the chicken to make sure they adhere to all sides of the breast. Spray the coated chicken breasts on both sides with vegetable oil.
3. Preheat the air fryer to 380°F (195°C).
4. Air-fry the chicken for 6 minutes. Then turn the chicken breasts over and air-fry for another 6 minutes. (Increase the cooking time if you are using chicken breasts larger than 3 to 4 ounces.)
5. When the chicken has finished cooking, serve each breast with a little salsa, the crumbled queso fresco and cilantro as the finishing touch. Serve some sour cream and/or guacamole at the table, if desired.

German Chicken Frikadellen

Servings: 6
Cooking Time: 20 Minutes
Ingredients:
- 1 lb ground chicken
- 1 egg
- 3/4 cup bread crumbs
- ¼ cup diced onions
- 1 grated carrot
- 1 tsp yellow mustard
- Salt and pepper to taste
- ¼ cup chopped parsley

Directions:
1. Preheat air fryer at 350ºF. In a bowl, combine the ground chicken, egg, crumbs, onions, carrot, parsley, salt, and pepper. Mix well with your hands. Form mixture into meatballs. Place them in the frying basket and Air Fry for 8-10 minutes, tossing once until golden. Serve right away.

Bacon & Chicken Flatbread

Servings: 2

Cooking Time: 35 Minutes

Ingredients:

- 1 flatbread dough
- 1 chicken breast, cubed
- 1 cup breadcrumbs
- 2 eggs, beaten
- Salt and pepper to taste
- 2 tsp dry rosemary
- 1 tsp fajita seasoning
- 1 tsp onion powder
- 3 bacon strips
- ½ tbsp ranch sauce

Directions:

1. Preheat air fryer to 360°F (180°C). Place the breadcrumbs, onion powder, rosemary, salt, and pepper in a mixing bowl. Coat the chicken with the mixture, dip into the beaten eggs, then roll again into the dry ingredients. Arrange the coated chicken pieces on one side of the greased frying basket. On the other side of the basket, lay the bacon strips. Air Fry for 6 minutes. Turn the bacon pieces over and flip the chicken and cook for another 6 minutes.

2. Roll the flatbread out and spread the ranch sauce all over the surface. Top with the bacon and chicken and sprinkle with fajita seasoning. Close the bread to contain the filling and place it in the air fryer. Cook for 10 minutes, flipping the flatbread once until golden brown. Let it cool for a few minutes. Then slice and serve.

Sweet Chili Spiced Chicken

Servings: 4

Cooking Time: 43 Minutes

Ingredients:

- Spice Rub:
- 2 tablespoons brown sugar
- 2 tablespoons paprika
- 1 teaspoon dry mustard powder
- 1 teaspoon chili powder
- 2 tablespoons coarse sea salt or kosher salt
- 2 teaspoons coarsely ground black pepper
- 1 tablespoon vegetable oil
- 1 (3½-pound) chicken, cut into 8 pieces

Directions:

1. Prepare the spice rub by combining the brown sugar, paprika, mustard powder, chili powder, salt and pepper. Rub the oil all over the chicken pieces and then rub the spice mix onto the chicken, covering completely. This is done very easily in a zipper sealable bag. You can do this ahead of time and let the chicken marinate in the refrigerator, or just proceed with cooking right away.

2. Preheat the air fryer to 370°F (185°C).

3. Air-fry the chicken in two batches. Place the two chicken thighs and two drumsticks into the air fryer basket. Air-fry at 370°F (185°C) for 10 minutes. Then, gently turn the chicken pieces over and air-fry for another 10 minutes. Remove the chicken pieces and let them rest on a plate while you cook the chicken breasts. Air-fry the chicken breasts, skin side down for 8 minutes. Turn the chicken breasts over and air-fry for another 12 minutes.

4. Lower the temperature of the air fryer to 340°F (170°C). Place the first batch of chicken on top of the second batch already in the basket and air-fry for a final 3 minutes.

5. Let the chicken rest for 5 minutes and serve warm with some mashed potatoes and a green salad or vegetables.

Chicken Breasts Wrapped In Bacon

Servings: 4

Cooking Time: 35 Minutes

Ingredients:

- ¼ cup mayonnaise
- ¼ cup sour cream
- 3 tbsp ketchup
- 1 tbsp yellow mustard
- 1 tbsp light brown sugar
- 1 lb chicken tenders
- 1 tsp dried parsley
- 8 bacon slices

Directions:

1. Preheat the air fryer to 370°F (185°C). Combine the mayonnaise, sour cream, ketchup, mustard, and brown sugar in a bowl and mix well, then set aside. Sprinkle the chicken with the parsley and wrap each one in a slice of bacon. Put the wrapped chicken in the frying basket in a single layer and Air Fry for 18-20 minutes, flipping once until the bacon is crisp. Serve with sauce.

Mushroom & Turkey Bread Pizza

Servings: 4

Cooking Time: 35 Minutes

Ingredients:

- 10 cooked turkey sausages, sliced
- 1 cup shredded mozzarella cheese
- 1 cup shredded Cheddar cheese
- 1 French loaf bread
- 2 tbsp butter, softened
- 1 tsp garlic powder
- 1 1/3 cups marinara sauce
- 1 tsp Italian seasoning
- 2 scallions, chopped
- 1 cup mushrooms, sliced

Directions:

1. Preheat the air fryer to 370°F (185°C). Cut the bread in half crosswise, then split each half horizontally. Combine butter and garlic powder, then spread on the cut sides of the bread. Bake the halves in the fryer for 3-5 minutes or until the leaves start to brown. Set the toasted bread on a work surface and spread marinara sauce over the top. Sprinkle the Italian seasoning, then top with sausages, scallions, mushrooms, and cheeses. Set the pizzas in the air fryer and Bake for 8-12 minutes or until the cheese is melted and starting to brown. Serve hot.

Fish And Seafood Recipes

Timeless Garlic-lemon Scallops

Servings: 2

Cooking Time: 15 Minutes

Ingredients:

- 2 tbsp butter, melted
- 1 garlic clove, minced
- 1 tbsp lemon juice
- 1 lb jumbo sea scallops

Directions:

1. Preheat air fryer to 400ºF. Whisk butter, garlic, and lemon juice in a bowl. Roll scallops in the mixture to coat all sides. Place scallops in the frying basket and Air Fry for 4 minutes, flipping once. Brush the tops of each scallop with butter mixture and cook for 4 more minutes, flipping once. Serve and enjoy!

Catalan-style Crab Samfaina

Servings: 4

Cooking Time: 30 Minutes

Ingredients:

- 1 peeled eggplant, cubed
- 1 zucchini, cubed
- 1 onion, chopped
- 1 red bell pepper, chopped
- 2 large tomatoes, chopped
- 1 tbsp olive oil
- ½ tsp dried thyme
- ½ tsp dried basil
- Salt and pepper to taste
- 1 ½ cups cooked crab meat

Directions:

1. Preheat air fryer to 400°F (205°C). In a pan, mix together all ingredients, except the crabmeat. Place the pan in the air fryer and Bake for 9 minutes. Remove the bowl and stir in the crabmeat. Return to the air fryer and roast for another 2-5 minutes until the vegetables are tender and ratatouille bubbling. Serve hot.

Herb-rubbed Salmon With Avocado

Servings: 4

Cooking Time: 30 Minutes

Ingredients:

- 1 tbsp sweet paprika
- ½ tsp cayenne pepper
- 1 tsp garlic powder
- 1 tsp dried oregano
- ½ tsp dried coriander
- 1 tsp dried thyme
- ½ tsp dried dill
- Salt and pepper to taste

- 4 wild salmon fillets
- 2 tbsp chopped red onion
- 1½ tbsp fresh lemon juice
- 1 tsp olive oil
- 2 tbsp cilantro, chopped
- 1 avocado, diced

Directions:

1. Mix paprika, cayenne, garlic powder, oregano, thyme, dill, coriander, salt, and pepper in a small bowl. Spray and rub cooking oil on both sides of the fish, then cover with the spices. Add red onion, lemon juice, olive oil, cilantro, salt, and pepper in a bowl. Set aside for 5 minutes, then carefully add avocado.
2. Preheat air fryer to 400°F (205°C). Place the salmon skin-side down in the greased frying basket and Bake for 5-7 minutes or until the fish flakes easily with a fork. Transfer to a plate and top with the avocado salsa.

Caribbean Skewers

Servings: 4

Cooking Time: 25 Minutes

Ingredients:

- 1 ½ lb large shrimp, peeled and deveined
- 1 can pineapple chunks, drained, liquid reserved
- 1 red bell pepper, chopped
- 3 scallions, chopped
- 1 tbsp lemon juice
- 1 tbsp olive oil
- ½ tsp jerk seasoning
- ⅛ tsp cayenne pepper
- 2 tbsp cilantro, chopped

Directions:

1. Preheat the air fryer to 37-°F (5°C). Thread the shrimp, pineapple, bell pepper, and scallions onto 8 bamboo skewers. Mix 3 tbsp of pineapple juice with lemon juice, olive oil, jerk seasoning, and cayenne pepper. Brush every bit of the mix over the skewers. Place 4 kebabs in the frying basket, add a rack, and put the rest of the skewers on top. Bake for 6-9 minutes and rearrange at about 4-5 minutes. Cook until the shrimp curl and pinken. Sprinkle with freshly chopped cilantro and serve.

Family Fish Nuggets With Tartar Sauce

Servings:4

Cooking Time: 30 Minutes

Ingredients:

- ½ cup mayonnaise
- 1 tbsp yellow mustard
- ½ cup diced dill pickles
- Salt and pepper to taste
- 1 egg, beaten
- ¼ cup cornstarch
- ¼ cup flour
- 1 lb cod, cut into sticks

Directions:

1. In a bowl, whisk the mayonnaise, mustard, pickles, salt, and pepper. Set aside the resulting tarter sauce.
2. Preheat air fryer to 350ºF. Add the beaten egg to a bowl. In another bowl, combine cornstarch, flour, salt, and pepper. Dip fish nuggets in the egg and roll them in the flour mixture. Place fish nuggets in the lightly greased frying basket and Air Fry for 10 minutes, flipping once. Serve with the sauce on the side.

Chili Blackened Shrimp

Servings: 4

Cooking Time: 15 Minutes

Ingredients:

- 1 lb peeled shrimp, deveined
- 1 tsp paprika
- ½ tsp dried dill
- ½ tsp red chili flakes
- ½ lemon, juiced
- Salt and pepper to taste

Directions:

1. Preheat air fryer to 400°F (205°C). In a resealable bag, add shrimp, paprika, dill, red chili flakes, lemon juice, salt and pepper. Seal and shake well. Place the shrimp in the greased frying basket and Air Fry for 7-8 minutes, shaking the basket once until blackened. Let cool slightly and serve.

Breaded Parmesan Perch

Servings: 5

Cooking Time: 15 Minutes

Ingredients:

- ¼ cup grated Parmesan
- ½ tsp salt
- ¼ tsp paprika
- 1 tbsp chopped dill
- 1 tsp dried thyme
- 2 tsp Dijon mustard
- 2 tbsp bread crumbs
- 4 ocean perch fillets
- 1 lemon, quartered
- 2 tbsp chopped cilantro

Directions:

1. Preheat air fryer to 400°F (205°C). Combine salt, paprika, pepper, dill, mustard, thyme, Parmesan, and bread crumbs in a wide bowl. Coat all sides of the fillets in the breading, then transfer to the greased frying basket. Air Fry for 8 minutes until outside is golden and the inside is cooked through. Garnish with lemon wedges and sprinkle with cilantro. Serve and enjoy!

Maple Balsamic Glazed Salmon

Servings: 4

Cooking Time: 10 Minutes

Ingredients:

- 4 (6-ounce) fillets of salmon
- salt and freshly ground black pepper
- vegetable oil
- ¼ cup pure maple syrup
- 3 tablespoons balsamic vinegar
- 1 teaspoon Dijon mustard

Directions:

1. Preheat the air fryer to 400°F (205°C).
2. Season the salmon well with salt and freshly ground black pepper. Spray or brush the bottom of the air fryer basket with vegetable oil and place the salmon fillets inside. Air-fry the salmon for 5 minutes.
3. While the salmon is air-frying, combine the maple syrup, balsamic vinegar and Dijon mustard in a small saucepan over medium heat and stir to blend well. Let the mixture simmer while the fish is cooking. It should start to thicken slightly, but keep your eye on it so it doesn't burn.
4. Brush the glaze on the salmon fillets and air-fry for an additional 5 minutes. The salmon should feel firm to the touch when finished and the glaze should be nicely browned on top. Brush a little more glaze on top before removing and serving with rice and vegetables, or a nice green salad.

Salmon Croquettes

Servings: 4

Cooking Time: 8 Minutes

Ingredients:

- 1 tablespoon oil
- ½ cup breadcrumbs
- 1 14.75-ounce can salmon, drained and all skin and fat removed
- 1 egg, beaten
- ⅓ cup coarsely crushed saltine crackers (about 8 crackers)
- ½ teaspoon Old Bay Seasoning
- ½ teaspoon onion powder
- ½ teaspoon Worcestershire sauce

Directions:

1. Preheat air fryer to 390°F (200°C).
2. In a shallow dish, mix oil and breadcrumbs until crumbly.
3. In a large bowl, combine the salmon, egg, cracker crumbs, Old Bay, onion powder, and Worcestershire. Mix well and shape into 8 small patties about ½-inch thick.
4. Gently dip each patty into breadcrumb mixture and turn to coat well on all sides.
5. Cook at 390°F (200°C) for 8minutes or until outside is crispy and browned.

Fish Tacos With Hot Coleslaw

Servings: 4

Cooking Time: 25 Minutes

Ingredients:

- 2 cups shredded green cabbage
- ½ red onion, thinly sliced
- 1 jalapeño, thinly sliced
- 1 tsp lemon juice
- 1 tbsp chives, chopped
- 3 tbsp mayonnaise
- 1 tbsp hot sauce
- 2 tbsp chopped cilantro
- 1 tbsp apple cider vinegar
- Salt to taste
- 1 large egg, beaten
- 1 cup crushed tortilla chips
- 1 lb cod fillets, cubed
- 8 corn tortillas

Directions:

1. Mix the lemon juice, chives, mayonnaise, and hot sauce in a bowl until blended. Add the cabbage to a large bowl. Then add onion, jalapeño, cilantro, vinegar and salt. Toss until well mixed. Put in the fridge until ready to serve.
2. Preheat air fryer to 360°F (180°C). In one shallow bowl, add the beaten egg. In another shallow bowl, add the crushed tortilla chips. Salt the cod, then dip into the egg mixture. Allow excess to drip off. Next, dip into the crumbs, gently pressing into the crumbs. Place the fish in the greased frying basket and Air Fry for 6 minutes, flipping once until crispy and completely cooked. Place 2 warm tortillas on each plate. Top with cod cubes, ¼ cup of slaw, and drizzle with spicy mayo. Serve and enjoy!

Cheesy Tuna Tower

Servings: 2

Cooking Time: 15 Minutes

Ingredients:

- ½ cup grated mozzarella
- 1 can tuna in water
- ¼ cup mayonnaise
- 2 tsp yellow mustard
- 1 tbsp minced dill pickle
- 1 tbsp minced celery
- 1 tbsp minced green onion
- Salt and pepper to taste
- 4 tomato slices
- 8 avocado slices

Directions:

1. Preheat air fryer to 350ºF. In a bowl, combine tuna, mayonnaise, mustard, pickle, celery, green onion, salt, and pepper. Cut a piece of parchment paper to fit the bottom of the frying basket. Place tomato slices on paper in a single layer and top with 2 avocado slices. Share tuna salad over avocado slices and top with mozzarella cheese. Place the towers in the frying basket and Bake for 4 minutes until the cheese starts to brown. Serve warm.

King Prawns Al Ajillo

Servings: 4

Cooking Time: 15 Minutes

Ingredients:

- 1 ¼ lb peeled king prawns, deveined
- ½ cup grated Parmesan
- 1 tbsp olive oil
- 1 tbsp lemon juice
- ½ tsp garlic powder
- 2 garlic cloves, minced

Directions:

1. Preheat the air fryer to 350°F (175°C). In a large bowl, add the prawns and sprinkle with olive oil, lemon juice, and garlic powder. Toss in the minced garlic and Parmesan, then toss to coat. Put the prawns in the frying basket and Air Fry for 10-15 minutes or until the prawns cook through. Shake the basket once while cooking. Serve immediately.

Fried Shrimp

Servings: 3

Cooking Time: 7 Minutes

Ingredients:

- 1 Large egg white
- 2 tablespoons Water
- 1 cup Plain dried bread crumbs (gluten-free, if a concern)
- ¼ cup All-purpose flour or almond flour
- ¼ cup Yellow cornmeal
- 1 teaspoon Celery salt
- 1 teaspoon Mild paprika
- Up to ½ teaspoon Cayenne (optional)
- ¾ pound Large shrimp (20–25 per pound), peeled and deveined
- Vegetable oil spray

Directions:

1. Preheat the air fryer to 400°F (205°C).

2. Set two medium or large bowls on your counter. In the first, whisk the egg white and water until foamy. In the second, stir the bread crumbs, flour, cornmeal, celery salt, paprika, and cayenne (if using) until well combined.

3. Pour all the shrimp into the egg white mixture and stir gently until all the shrimp are coated. Use kitchen tongs to pick them up one by one and transfer them to the bread-crumb mixture. Turn each in the bread-crumb mixture to coat it evenly and thoroughly on all sides before setting it on a cutting board. When you're done coating the shrimp, coat them all on both sides with the vegetable oil spray.

4. Set the shrimp in as close to one layer in the basket as you can. Some may overlap. Air-fry for 7 minutes, gently rearranging the shrimp at the 4-minute mark to get covered surfaces exposed, until golden brown and firm but not hard.

5. Use kitchen tongs to gently transfer the shrimp to a wire rack. Cool for only a minute or two before serving.

Holliday Lobster Salad

Servings: 2

Cooking Time: 20 Minutes

Ingredients:

- 2 lobster tails
- ¼ cup mayonnaise
- 2 tsp lemon juice
- 1 stalk celery, sliced
- 2 tsp chopped chives
- 2 tsp chopped tarragon
- Salt and pepper to taste
- 2 tomato slices
- 4 cucumber slices
- 1 avocado, diced

Directions:

1. Preheat air fryer to 400ºF. Using kitchen shears, cut down the middle of each lobster tail on the softer side. Carefully run your finger between the lobster meat and the shell to loosen meat. Place lobster tails, cut sides up, in the frying basket, and Air Fry for 8 minutes. Transfer to a large plate and let cool for 3 minutes until easy to handle, then

pull lobster meat from the shell and roughly chop it. Combine chopped lobster, mayonnaise, lemon juice, celery, chives, tarragon, salt, and pepper in a bowl. Divide between 2 medium plates and top with tomato slices, cucumber and avocado cubes. Serve immediately.

Southeast Asian-style Tuna Steaks

Servings: 4

Cooking Time: 20 Minutes

Ingredients:
- 1 stalk lemongrass, bent in half
- 4 tuna steaks
- 2 tbsp soy sauce
- 2 tsp sesame oil
- 2 tsp rice wine vinegar
- 1 tsp grated fresh ginger
- ⅛ tsp pepper
- 3 tbsp lemon juice
- 2 tbsp chopped cilantro
- 1 sliced red chili

Directions:
1. Preheat air fryer to 390°F (200°C). Place the tuna steak on a shallow plate. Mix together soy sauce, sesame oil, rice wine vinegar, and ginger in a small bowl. Pour over the tuna, rubbing the marinade gently into both sides of the fish. Marinate for about 10 minutes. Then sprinkle with pepper. Place the lemongrass in the frying basket and top with tuna steaks. Add the remaining lemon juice and 1 tablespoon of water in the pan below the basket. Bake until the tuna is cooked through, 8-10 minutes. Discard the lemongrass before topping with cilantro and red chili. Serve and enjoy!

Shrimp Patties

Servings: 4

Cooking Time: 10 Minutes

Ingredients:
- ½ pound shelled and deveined raw shrimp
- ¼ cup chopped red bell pepper
- ¼ cup chopped green onion
- ¼ cup chopped celery
- 2 cups cooked sushi rice
- ½ teaspoon garlic powder
- ½ teaspoon Old Bay Seasoning
- ½ teaspoon salt
- 2 teaspoons Worcestershire sauce
- ½ cup plain breadcrumbs
- oil for misting or cooking spray

Directions:

1. Finely chop the shrimp. You can do this in a food processor, but it takes only a few pulses. Be careful not to overprocess into mush.
2. Place shrimp in a large bowl and add all other ingredients except the breadcrumbs and oil. Stir until well combined.
3. Preheat air fryer to 390°F (200°C).
4. Shape shrimp mixture into 8 patties, no more than ½-inch thick. Roll patties in breadcrumbs and mist with oil or cooking spray.
5. Place 4 shrimp patties in air fryer basket and cook at 390°F (200°C) for 10 minutes, until shrimp cooks through and outside is crispy.
6. Repeat step 5 to cook remaining shrimp patties.

Fish Tacos With Jalapeño-lime Sauce

Servings: 4

Cooking Time: 7 Minutes

Ingredients:
- Fish Tacos
- 1 pound fish fillets
- ¼ teaspoon cumin
- ¼ teaspoon coriander
- ⅛ teaspoon ground red pepper
- 1 tablespoon lime zest
- ¼ teaspoon smoked paprika
- 1 teaspoon oil
- cooking spray
- 6–8 corn or flour tortillas (6-inch size)
- Jalapeño-Lime Sauce
- ½ cup sour cream
- 1 tablespoon lime juice
- ¼ teaspoon grated lime zest
- ½ teaspoon minced jalapeño (flesh only)
- ¼ teaspoon cumin
- Napa Cabbage Garnish
- 1 cup shredded Napa cabbage
- ¼ cup slivered red or green bell pepper
- ¼ cup slivered onion

Directions:

1. Slice the fish fillets into strips approximately ½-inch thick.
2. Put the strips into a sealable plastic bag along with the cumin, coriander, red pepper, lime zest, smoked paprika, and oil. Massage seasonings into the fish until evenly distributed.
3. Spray air fryer basket with nonstick cooking spray and place seasoned fish inside.
4. Cook at 390°F (200°C) for approximately 5minutes. Shake basket to distribute fish. Cook an additional 2 minutes, until fish flakes easily.

5. While the fish is cooking, prepare the Jalapeño-Lime Sauce by mixing the sour cream, lime juice, lime zest, jalapeño, and cumin together to make a smooth sauce. Set aside.
6. Mix the cabbage, bell pepper, and onion together and set aside.
7. To warm refrigerated tortillas, wrap in damp paper towels and microwave for 30 to 60 seconds.
8. To serve, spoon some of fish into a warm tortilla. Add one or two tablespoons Napa Cabbage Garnish and drizzle with Jalapeño-Lime Sauce.

Fish Cakes

Servings: 4
Cooking Time: 10 Minutes

Ingredients:
- ¾ cup mashed potatoes (about 1 large russet potato)
- 12 ounces cod or other white fish
- salt and pepper
- oil for misting or cooking spray
- 1 large egg
- ¼ cup potato starch
- ½ cup panko breadcrumbs
- 1 tablespoon fresh chopped chives
- 2 tablespoons minced onion

Directions:
1. Peel potatoes, cut into cubes, and cook on stovetop till soft.
2. Salt and pepper raw fish to taste. Mist with oil or cooking spray, and cook in air fryer at 360°F (180°C) for 6 to 8 minutes, until fish flakes easily. If fish is crowded, rearrange halfway through cooking to ensure all pieces cook evenly.
3. Transfer fish to a plate and break apart to cool.
4. Beat egg in a shallow dish.
5. Place potato starch in another shallow dish, and panko crumbs in a third dish.
6. When potatoes are done, drain in colander and rinse with cold water.
7. In a large bowl, mash the potatoes and stir in the chives and onion. Add salt and pepper to taste, then stir in the fish.
8. If needed, stir in a tablespoon of the beaten egg to help bind the mixture.
9. Shape into 8 small, fat patties. Dust lightly with potato starch, dip in egg, and roll in panko crumbs. Spray both sides with oil or cooking spray.
10. Cook at 360°F (180°C) for 10 minutes, until golden brown and crispy.

Mediterranean Salmon Burgers

Servings: 4
Cooking Time: 30 Minutes

Ingredients:
- 1 lb salmon fillets
- 1 scallion, diced
- 4 tbsp mayonnaise
- 1 egg
- 1 tsp capers, drained
- Salt and pepper to taste
- ¼ tsp paprika
- 1 lemon, zested
- 1 lemon, sliced
- 1 tbsp chopped dill
- ¼ cup bread crumbs
- 4 buns, toasted
- 4 tsp whole-grain mustard
- 4 lettuce leaves
- 1 small tomato, sliced

Directions:
1. Preheat air fryer to 400°F (205°C). Divide salmon in half. Cut one of the halves into chunks and transfer the chunks to the food processor. Also, add scallion, 2 tablespoons mayonnaise, egg, capers, dill, salt, pepper, paprika, and lemon zest. Pulse to puree. Dice the rest of the salmon into ¼-inch chunks. Combine chunks and puree along with bread crumbs in a large bowl. Shape the fish into 4 patties and transfer to the frying basket. Air Fry for 5 minutes, then flip the patties. Air Fry for another 5 to 7 minutes. Place the patties each on a bun along with 1 teaspoon mustard, mayonnaise, lettuce, lemon slices, and a slice of tomato. Serve and enjoy.

Blackened Red Snapper

Servings: 4
Cooking Time: 8 Minutes

Ingredients:
- 1½ teaspoons black pepper
- ¼ teaspoon thyme
- ¼ teaspoon garlic powder
- ⅛ teaspoon cayenne pepper
- 1 teaspoon olive oil
- 4 4-ounce red snapper fillet portions, skin on
- 4 thin slices lemon
- cooking spray

Directions:
1. Mix the spices and oil together to make a paste. Rub into both sides of the fish.
2. Spray air fryer basket with nonstick cooking spray and lay snapper steaks in basket, skin-side down.
3. Place a lemon slice on each piece of fish.
4. Cook at 390°F (200°C) for 8 minutes. The fish will not flake when done, but it should be white through the center.

Shrimp & Grits

Servings: 4

Cooking Time: 5 Minutes

Ingredients:

- 1 pound raw shelled shrimp, deveined (26–30 count or smaller)
- Marinade
- 2 tablespoons lemon juice
- 2 tablespoons Worcestershire sauce
- 1 tablespoon olive oil
- 1 teaspoon Old Bay Seasoning
- ½ teaspoon hot sauce
- Grits
- ¾ cup quick cooking grits (not instant)
- 3 cups water
- ½ teaspoon salt
- 1 tablespoon butter
- ½ cup chopped green bell pepper
- ½ cup chopped celery
- ½ cup chopped onion
- ½ teaspoon oregano
- ¼ teaspoon Old Bay Seasoning
- 2 ounces sharp Cheddar cheese, grated

Directions:

1. Stir together all marinade ingredients. Pour marinade over shrimp and set aside.
2. For grits, heat water and salt to boil in saucepan on stovetop. Stir in grits, lower heat to medium-low, and cook about 5minutes or until thick and done.
3. Place butter, bell pepper, celery, and onion in air fryer baking pan. Cook at 390°F (200°C) for 2minutes and stir. Cook 6 or 7minutes longer, until crisp tender.
4. Add oregano and 1 teaspoon Old Bay to cooked vegetables. Stir in grits and cheese and cook at 390°F (200°C) for 1 minute. Stir and cook 1 to 2minutes longer to melt cheese.
5. Remove baking pan from air fryer. Cover with plate to keep warm while shrimp cooks.
6. Drain marinade from shrimp. Place shrimp in air fryer basket and cook at 360°F (180°C) for 3minutes. Stir or shake basket. Cook 2 more minutes, until done.
7. To serve, spoon grits onto plates and top with shrimp.

Sriracha Salmon Melt Sandwiches

Servings: 4

Cooking Time: 20 Minutes

Ingredients:

- 2 tbsp butter, softened
- 2 cans pink salmon
- 2 English muffins
- 1/3 cup mayonnaise
- 2 tbsp Dijon mustard
- 1 tbsp fresh lemon juice
- 1/3 cup chopped celery
- ½ tsp sriracha sauce
- 4 slices tomato
- 4 slices Swiss cheese

Directions:

1. Preheat the air fryer to 370°F (185°C). Split the English muffins with a fork and spread butter on the 4 halves. Put the halves in the basket and Bake for 3-5 minutes, or until toasted. Remove and set aside. Combine the salmon, mayonnaise, mustard, lemon juice, celery, and sriracha in a bowl. Divide among the English muffin halves. Top each sandwich with tomato and cheese and put in the frying basket. Bake for 4-6 minutes or until the cheese is melted and starts to brown. Serve hot.

Restaurant-style Breaded Shrimp

Servings: 2

Cooking Time: 35 Minutes

Ingredients:

- ½ lb fresh shrimp, peeled
- 2 eggs, beaten
- ½ cup breadcrumbs
- ½ onion, finely chopped
- ½ tsp ground ginger
- ½ tsp garlic powder
- ½ tsp turmeric
- ½ tsp red chili powder
- Salt and pepper to taste
- ½ tsp amchur powder

Directions:

1. Preheat air fryer to 350°F (175°C). Place the beaten eggs in a bowl and dip in the shrimp. Blend the bread crumbs with all the dry ingredients in another bowl. Add in the shrimp and toss to coat. Place the coated shrimp in the greased frying basket. Air Fry for 12-14 minutes until the breaded crust of the shrimp is golden brown. Toss the basket two or three times during the cooking time. Serve.

Fish Goujons With Tartar Sauce

Servings: 4

Cooking Time: 20 Minutes

Ingredients:

- ¼ cup flour
- Salt and pepper to taste
- ¼ tsp smoked paprika
- ¼ tsp dried oregano
- 1 tsp dried thyme
- 1 egg
- 4 haddock fillets
- 1 lemon, thinly sliced
- ½ cup tartar sauce

Directions:

1. Preheat air fryer to 400°F (205°C). Combine flour, salt, pepper, paprika, thyme, and oregano in a wide bowl. Whisk egg and 1 teaspoon water in another wide bowl. Slice each fillet into 4 strips. Dip the strips in the egg mixture. Then roll them in the flour mixture and coat completely. Arrange the fish strips on the greased frying basket. Air Fry for 4 minutes. Flip the fish and Air Fry for another 4 to 5 minutes until crisp. Serve warm with lemon slices and tartar sauce on the side and enjoy.

Horseradish Tuna Croquettes

Servings: 4

Cooking Time: 40 Minutes

Ingredients:

- 1 can tuna in water, drained
- 1/3 cup mayonnaise
- 1 tbsp minced celery
- 1 green onion, sliced
- 2 tsp dried dill
- 1 tsp lime juice
- 1 cup bread crumbs
- 1 egg
- 1 tsp prepared horseradish

Directions:

1. Preheat air fryer to 370°F. Add the tuna, mayonnaise, celery, green onion, dill, lime juice, ¼ cup bread crumbs, egg, and horseradish in a bowl and mix to combine. Mold the mixture into 12 rectangular mound shapes. Roll each croquette in a shallow dish with 3/4 cup of bread crumbs. Place croquettes in the lightly greased frying basket and Air Fry for 12 minutes on all sides. Serve.

Catalan Sardines With Romesco Sauce

Servings: 2

Cooking Time: 15 Minutes

Ingredients:

- 2 cans skinless, boneless sardines in oil, drained
- ½ cup warmed romesco sauce
- ½ cup bread crumbs

Directions:

1. Preheat air fryer to 350°F. In a shallow dish, add bread crumbs. Roll in sardines to coat. Place sardines in the greased frying basket and Air Fry for 6 minutes, turning once. Serve with romesco sauce.

Crunchy Clam Strips

Servings: 3

Cooking Time: 8 Minutes

Ingredients:

- ½ pound Clam strips, drained
- 1 Large egg, well beaten
- ½ cup All-purpose flour
- ½ cup Yellow cornmeal
- 1½ teaspoons Table salt
- 1½ teaspoons Ground black pepper
- Up to ¾ teaspoon Cayenne
- Vegetable oil spray

Directions:

1. Preheat the air fryer to 400°F (205°C).
2. Toss the clam strips and beaten egg in a bowl until the clams are well coated.
3. Mix the flour, cornmeal, salt, pepper, and cayenne in a large zip-closed plastic bag until well combined. Using a flatware fork or small kitchen tongs, lift the clam strips one by one out of the egg, letting any excess egg slip back into the rest. Put the strips in the bag with the flour mixture. Once all the strips are in the bag, seal it and shake gently until the strips are well coated.
4. Use kitchen tongs to pick out the clam strips and lay them on a cutting board (leaving any extra flour mixture in the bag to be discarded). Coat the strips on both sides with vegetable oil spray.
5. When the machine is at temperature, spread the clam strips in the basket in one layer. They may touch in places, but try to leave as much air space as possible around them. Air-fry undisturbed for 8 minutes, or until brown and crunchy.
6. Gently dump the contents of the basket onto a serving platter. Cool for just a minute or two before serving hot.

Saucy Shrimp

Servings: 4

Cooking Time: 30 Minutes

Ingredients:
- 1 lb peeled shrimp, deveined
- ½ cup grated coconut
- ¼ cup bread crumbs
- ¼ cup flour
- ¼ tsp smoked paprika
- Salt and pepper to taste
- 1 egg
- 2 tbsp maple syrup
- ½ tsp rice vinegar
- 1 tbsp hot sauce
- ⅛ tsp red pepper flakes
- ¼ cup orange juice
- 1 tsp cornstarch
- ½ cup banana ketchup
- 1 lemon, sliced

Directions:

1. Preheat air fryer to 350°F (175°C). Combine coconut, bread crumbs, flour, paprika, black pepper, and salt in a bowl. In a separate bowl, whisk egg and 1 teaspoon water. Dip one shrimp into the egg bowl and shake off excess drips. Dip the shrimp in the bread crumb mixture and coat it completely. Continue the process for all of the shrimp. Arrange the shrimp on the greased frying basket. Air Fry for 5 minutes, then use tongs to flip the shrimp. Cook for another 2-3 minutes.
2. To make the sauce, add maple syrup, banana ketchup, hot sauce, vinegar, and red pepper flakes in a small saucepan over medium heat. Make a slurry in a small bowl with orange juice and cornstarch. Stir in slurry and continue stirring. Bring the sauce to a boil and cook for 5 minutes. When the sauce begins to thicken, remove from heat and allow to sit for 5 minutes. Serve shrimp warm along with sauce and lemon slices on the side.

Tuna Nuggets In Hoisin Sauce

Servings: 4

Cooking Time: 7 Minutes

Ingredients:
- ½ cup hoisin sauce
- 2 tablespoons rice wine vinegar
- 2 teaspoons sesame oil
- 1 teaspoon garlic powder
- 2 teaspoons dried lemongrass
- ¼ teaspoon red pepper flakes
- ½ small onion, quartered and thinly sliced
- 8 ounces fresh tuna, cut into 1-inch cubes
- cooking spray
- 3 cups cooked jasmine rice

Directions:

1. Mix the hoisin sauce, vinegar, sesame oil, and seasonings together.
2. Stir in the onions and tuna nuggets.
3. Spray air fryer baking pan with nonstick spray and pour in tuna mixture.
4. Cook at 390°F (200°C) for 3minutes. Stir gently.
5. Cook 2minutes and stir again, checking for doneness. Tuna should be barely cooked through, just beginning to flake and still very moist. If necessary, continue cooking and stirring in 1-minute intervals until done.
6. Serve warm over hot jasmine rice.

Beer-battered Cod

Servings: 3

Cooking Time: 12 Minutes

Ingredients:
- 1½ cups All-purpose flour
- 3 tablespoons Old Bay seasoning
- 1 Large egg(s)
- ¼ cup Amber beer, pale ale, or IPA
- 3 4-ounce skinless cod fillets
- Vegetable oil spray

Directions:

1. Preheat the air fryer to 400°F (205°C).
2. Set up and fill two shallow soup plates or small pie plates on your counter: one with the flour, whisked with the Old Bay until well combined; and one with the egg(s), whisked with the beer until foamy and uniform.
3. Dip a piece of cod in the flour mixture, turning it to coat on all sides (not just the top and bottom). Gently shake off any excess flour and dip the fish in the egg mixture, turning it to coat. Let any excess egg mixture slip back into the rest, then set the fish back in the flour mixture and coat it again, then back in the egg mixture for a second wash, then back in the flour mixture for a third time. Coat the fish on all sides with vegetable oil spray and set it aside. "Batter" the remaining piece(s) of cod in the same way.
4. Set the coated cod fillets in the basket with as much space between them as possible. They should not touch. Air-fry undisturbed for 12 minutes, or until brown and crisp.
5. Use kitchen tongs to gently transfer the fish to a wire rack. Cool for only a couple of minutes before serving.

British Fish & Chips

Servings: 4

Cooking Time: 40 Minutes

Ingredients:

- 2 peeled russet potatoes, thinly sliced
- 1 egg white
- 1 tbsp lemon juice
- 1/3 cup ground almonds
- 2 bread slices, crumbled
- ½ tsp dried basil
- 4 haddock fillets

Directions:

1. Preheat air fryer to 390°F (200°C). Lay the potato slices in the frying basket and Air Fry for 11-15 minutes. Turn the fries a couple of times while cooking. While the fries are cooking, whisk the egg white and lemon juice together in a bowl. On a plate, combine the almonds, breadcrumbs, and basil. First, one at a time, dip the fillets into the egg mix and then coat in the almond/breadcrumb mix. Lay the fillets on a wire rack until the fries are done. Preheat the oven to 350°F (175°C). After the fries are done, move them to a pan and place in the oven to keep warm. Put the fish in the frying basket and Air Fry for 10-14 minutes or until cooked through, golden, and crispy. Serve with the fries.

Black Olive & Shrimp Salad

Servings: 4

Cooking Time: 15 Minutes

Ingredients:

- 1 lb cleaned shrimp, deveined
- ½ cup olive oil
- 4 garlic cloves, minced
- 1 tbsp balsamic vinegar
- ¼ tsp cayenne pepper
- ¼ tsp dried basil
- ¼ tsp salt
- ¼ tsp onion powder
- 1 tomato, diced
- ¼ cup black olives

Directions:

1. Preheat air fryer to 380°F (195°C). Place the olive oil, garlic, balsamic, cayenne, basil, onion powder and salt in a bowl and stir to combine. Divide the tomatoes and black olives between 4 small ramekins. Top with shrimp and pour a quarter of the oil mixture over the shrimp. Bake for 6-8 minutes until the shrimp are cooked through. Serve.

Fried Scallops

Servings: 3

Cooking Time: 6 Minutes

Ingredients:

- ½ cup All-purpose flour or tapioca flour
- 1 Large egg(s), well beaten
- 2 cups Corn flake crumbs (gluten-free, if a concern)
- Up to 2 teaspoons Cayenne
- 1 teaspoon Celery seeds
- 1 teaspoon Table salt
- 1 pound Sea scallops
- Vegetable oil spray

Directions:

1. Preheat the air fryer to 400°F (205°C).
2. Set up and fill three shallow soup plates or small pie plates on your counter: one for the flour; one for the beaten egg(s); and one for the corn flake crumbs, stirred with the cayenne, celery seeds, and salt until well combined.
3. One by one, dip a scallop in the flour, turning it every way to coat it thoroughly. Gently shake off any excess flour, then dip the scallop in the egg(s), turning it again to coat all sides. Let any excess egg slip back into the rest, then set the scallop in the corn flake mixture. Turn it several times, pressing gently to get an even coating on the scallop all around. Generously coat the scallop with vegetable oil spray, then set it aside on a cutting board. Coat the remaining scallops in the same way.
4. Set the scallops in the basket with as much air space between them as possible. They should not touch. Air-fry undisturbed for 6 minutes, or until lightly browned and firm.
5. Use kitchen tongs to gently transfer the scallops to a wire rack. Cool for only a minute or two before serving.

Chinese Fish Noodle Bowls

Servings: 4

Cooking Time: 40 Minutes

Ingredients:

- 1 can crushed pineapple, drained
- 1 shallot, minced
- 2 tbsp chopped cilantro
- 2 ½ tsp lime juice
- 1 tbsp honey
- Salt and pepper to taste
- 1 ½ cups grated red cabbage
- ¼ chopped green beans
- 2 grated baby carrots
- ½ tsp granulated sugar
- 2 tbsp mayonnaise

- 1 clove garlic, minced
- 8 oz cooked rice noodles
- 2 tsp sesame oil
- 1 tsp sesame seeds
- 4 cod fillets
- 1 tsp Chinese five-spice

Directions:

1. Preheat air fryer at 350ºF. Combine the pineapple, shallot, 1 tbsp of cilantro, honey, 2 tsp of lime juice, salt, and black pepper in a bowl. Let chill the salsa covered in the fridge until ready to use. Mix the cabbage, green beans, carrots, sugar, remaining lime juice, mayonnaise, garlic, salt, and pepper in a bowl. Let chill covered in the fridge until ready to use. In a bowl, toss cooked noodles and sesame oil, stirring occasionally to avoid sticking.

2. Sprinkle cod fillets with salt and five-spice. Place them in the greased frying basket and Air Fry for 10 minutes until the fish is opaque and flakes easily with a fork. Divide noodles into 4 bowls, top each with salsa, slaw, and fish. Serve right away sprinkled with another tbsp of cilantro and sesame seeds.

Catfish Nuggets

Servings: 4

Cooking Time: 7 Minutes Per Batch

Ingredients:

- 2 medium catfish fillets, cut in chunks (approximately 1 x 2 inch)
- salt and pepper
- 2 eggs
- 2 tablespoons skim milk
- ½ cup cornstarch
- 1 cup panko breadcrumbs, crushed
- oil for misting or cooking spray

Directions:

1. Season catfish chunks with salt and pepper to your liking.
2. Beat together eggs and milk in a small bowl.
3. Place cornstarch in a second small bowl.
4. Place breadcrumbs in a third small bowl.
5. Dip catfish chunks in cornstarch, dip in egg wash, shake off excess, then roll in breadcrumbs.
6. Spray all sides of catfish chunks with oil or cooking spray.
7. Place chunks in air fryer basket in a single layer, leaving space between for air circulation.
8. Cook at 390ºF (200ºC) for 4minutes, turn, and cook an additional 3 minutes, until fish flakes easily and outside is crispy brown.
9. Repeat steps 7 and 8 to cook remaining catfish nuggets.

Hot Calamari Rings

Servings: 4

Cooking Time: 25 Minutes

Ingredients:

- ½ cup all-purpose flour
- 2 tsp hot chili powder
- 2 eggs
- 1 tbsp milk
- 1 cup bread crumbs
- Salt and pepper to taste
- 1 lb calamari rings
- 1 lime, quartered
- ½ cup aioli sauce

Directions:

1. Preheat air fryer at 400ºF. In a shallow bowl, add flour and hot chili powder. In another bowl, mix the eggs and milk. In a third bowl, mix the breadcrumbs, salt and pepper. Dip calamari rings in flour mix first, then in eggs mix and shake off excess. Then, roll ring through breadcrumb mixture. Place calamari rings in the greased frying basket and Air Fry for 4 minutes, tossing once. Squeeze lime quarters over calamari. Serve with aioli sauce.

Parmesan Fish Bites

Servings: 2

Cooking Time: 30 Minutes

Ingredients:

- 1 haddock fillet, cut into bite-sized pieces
- 1 tbsp shredded cheddar
- 2 tbsp shredded Parmesan
- 2 eggs, beaten
- ½ cup breadcrumbs
- Salt and pepper to taste
- ½ cup mayoracha sauce

Directions:

1. Preheat air fryer to 350°F (175°C). Dip the strips in the beaten eggs. Place the bread crumbs, Parmesan, cheddar, salt and pepper in a bowl and mix well. Coat the fish strips in the dry mixture and place them on the foil-lined frying basket. Air Fry for 14-16 minutes. Halfway through the cooking time, shake the basket. When the cooking time is over, the fish will be cooked through and crust golden brown. Serve with mayoracha sauce (mixed mayo with sriracha) for dipping and enjoy!

Coconut Shrimp

Servings: 4

Cooking Time: 12 Minutes

Ingredients:
- 1 pound large shrimp (about 16 to 20), peeled and deveined
- ½ cup flour
- salt and freshly ground black pepper
- 2 egg whites
- ½ cup fine breadcrumbs
- ½ cup shredded unsweetened coconut
- zest of one lime
- ½ teaspoon salt
- ⅛ to ¼ teaspoon ground cayenne pepper
- vegetable or canola oil
- sweet chili sauce or duck sauce (for serving)

Directions:

1. Set up a dredging station. Place the flour in a shallow dish and season well with salt and freshly ground black pepper. Whisk the egg whites in a second shallow dish. In a third shallow dish, combine the breadcrumbs, coconut, lime zest, salt and cayenne pepper.
2. Preheat the air fryer to 400°F (205°C).
3. Dredge each shrimp first in the flour, then dip it in the egg mixture, and finally press it into the breadcrumb-coconut mixture to coat all sides. Place the breaded shrimp on a plate or baking sheet and spray both sides with vegetable oil.
4. Air-fry the shrimp in two batches, being sure not to over-crowd the basket. Air-fry for 5 minutes, turning the shrimp over for the last minute or two. Repeat with the second batch of shrimp.
5. Lower the temperature of the air fryer to 340°F (170°C). Return the first batch of shrimp to the air fryer basket with the second batch and air-fry for an additional 2 minutes, just to re-heat everything.
6. Serve with sweet chili sauce, duck sauce or just eat them plain!

Buttered Swordfish Steaks

Servings: 4

Cooking Time: 30 Minutes

Ingredients:
- 4 swordfish steaks
- 2 eggs, beaten
- 3 oz melted butter
- ½ cup breadcrumbs
- Black pepper to taste
- 1 tsp dried rosemary
- 1 tsp dried marjoram
- 1 lemon, cut into wedges

Directions:

1. Preheat air fryer to 350°F (175°C). Place the eggs and melted butter in a bowl and stir thoroughly. Combine the breadcrumbs, rosemary, marjoram, and black pepper in a separate bowl. Dip the swordfish steaks in the beaten eggs, then coat with the crumb mixture. Place the coated fish in the frying basket. Air Fry for 12-14 minutes, turning once until the fish is cooked through and the crust is toasted and crispy. Serve with lemon wedges.

Fish Nuggets With Broccoli Dip

Servings: 4

Cooking Time: 40 Minutes

Ingredients:
- 1 lb cod fillets, cut into chunks
- 1 ½ cups broccoli florets
- ¼ cup grated Parmesan
- 3 garlic cloves, peeled
- 3 tbsp sour cream
- 2 tbsp lemon juice
- 2 tbsp olive oil
- 2 egg whites
- 1 cup panko bread crumbs
- 1 tsp dried dill
- Salt and pepper to taste

Directions:

1. Preheat the air fryer to 400°F (205°C). Put the broccoli and garlic in the greased frying basket and Air Fry for 5-7 minutes or until tender. Remove to a blender and add sour cream, lemon juice, olive oil, and ½ tsp of salt and process until smooth. Set the sauce aside. Beat the egg whites until frothy in a shallow bowl. On a plate, combine the panko, Parmesan, dill, pepper, and the remaining ½ tsp of salt. Dip the cod fillets in the egg whites, then the breadcrumbs, pressing to coat. Put half the cubes in the frying basket and spray with cooking oil. Air Fry for 6-8 minutes or until the fish is cooked through. Serve the fish with the sauce and enjoy!

Lime Bay Scallops

Servings: 4

Cooking Time: 10 Minutes

Ingredients:
- 2 tbsp butter, melted
- 1 lime, juiced
- ¼ tsp salt
- 1 lb bay scallops
- 2 tbsp chopped cilantro

Directions:

1. Preheat air fryer to 350°F. Combine all ingredients in a bowl, except for the cilantro. Place scallops in the frying basket and Air Fry for 5 minutes, tossing once. Serve immediately topped with cilantro.

Maple-crusted Salmon

Servings: 2

Cooking Time: 8 Minutes

Ingredients:

- 12 ounces salmon filets
- ⅓ cup maple syrup
- 1 teaspoon Worcestershire sauce
- 2 teaspoons Dijon mustard or brown mustard
- ½ cup finely chopped walnuts
- ½ teaspoon sea salt
- ½ lemon
- 1 tablespoon chopped parsley, for garnish

Directions:

1. Place the salmon in a shallow baking dish. Top with maple syrup, Worcestershire sauce, and mustard. Refrigerate for 30 minutes.
2. Preheat the air fryer to 350°F (175°C).
3. Remove the salmon from the marinade and discard the marinade.
4. Place the chopped nuts on top of the salmon filets, and sprinkle salt on top of the nuts. Place the salmon, skin side down, in the air fryer basket. Cook for 6 to 8 minutes or until the fish flakes in the center.
5. Remove the salmon and plate on a serving platter. Squeeze fresh lemon over the top of the salmon and top with chopped parsley. Serve immediately.

Californian Tilapia

Servings: 4

Cooking Time: 15 Minutes

Ingredients:

- Salt and pepper to taste
- ¼ tsp garlic powder
- ¼ tsp chili powder
- ¼ tsp dried oregano
- ¼ tsp smoked paprika
- 1 tbsp butter, melted
- 4 tilapia fillets
- 2 tbsp lime juice
- 1 lemon, sliced

Directions:

1. Preheat air fryer to 400°F (205°C). Combine salt, pepper, oregano, garlic powder, chili powder, and paprika in a small bowl. Place tilapia in a pie pan, then pour lime juice and butter over the fish. Season both sides of the fish with the spice blend. Arrange the tilapia in a single layer of the parchment-lined frying basket without touching each other. Air Fry for 4 minutes, then carefully flip the fish. Air Fry for another 4 to 5 minutes until the fish is cooked and the outside is crispy. Serve immediately with lemon slices on the side and enjoy.

Lemon-dill Salmon Burgers

Servings: 4

Cooking Time: 8 Minutes

Ingredients:

- 2 (6-ounce) fillets of salmon, finely chopped by hand or in a food processor
- 1 cup fine breadcrumbs
- 1 teaspoon freshly grated lemon zest
- 2 tablespoons chopped fresh dill weed
- 1 teaspoon salt
- freshly ground black pepper
- 2 eggs, lightly beaten
- 4 brioche or hamburger buns
- lettuce, tomato, red onion, avocado, mayonnaise or mustard, to serve

Directions:

1. Preheat the air fryer to 400°F (205°C).
2. Combine all the ingredients in a bowl. Mix together well and divide into four balls. Flatten the balls into patties, making an indentation in the center of each patty with your thumb (this will help the burger stay flat as it cooks) and flattening the sides of the burgers so that they fit nicely into the air fryer basket.
3. Transfer the burgers to the air fryer basket and air-fry for 4 minutes. Flip the burgers over and air-fry for another 3 to 4 minutes, until nicely browned and firm to the touch.
4. Serve on soft brioche buns with your choice of topping – lettuce, tomato, red onion, avocado, mayonnaise or mustard.

Honey Pecan Shrimp

Servings: 4

Cooking Time: 10 Minutes

Ingredients:

- ¼ cup cornstarch
- ¾ teaspoon sea salt, divided
- ¼ teaspoon pepper
- 2 egg whites
- ⅔ cup finely chopped pecans
- 1 pound raw, peeled, and deveined shrimp
- ¼ cup honey
- 2 tablespoons mayonnaise

Directions:

1. In a small bowl, whisk together the cornstarch, ½ teaspoon of the salt, and the pepper.
2. In a second bowl, whisk together the egg whites until soft and foamy. (They don't need to be whipped to peaks or even soft peaks, just frothy.)

3. In a third bowl, mix together the pecans and the remaining ¼ teaspoon of sea salt.
4. Pat the shrimp dry with paper towels. Working in small batches, dip the shrimp into the cornstarch, then into the egg whites, and then into the pecans until all the shrimp are coated with pecans.
5. Preheat the air fryer to 330°F (165°C).
6. Place the coated shrimp inside the air fryer basket and spray with cooking spray. Cook for 5 minutes, toss the shrimp, and cook another 5 minutes.
7. Meanwhile, place the honey in a microwave-safe bowl and microwave for 30 seconds. Whisk in the mayonnaise until smooth and creamy. Pour the honey sauce into a serving bowl. Add the cooked shrimp to the serving bowl while hot and toss to coat. Serve immediately.

Hazelnut-crusted Fish

Servings: 4
Cooking Time: 30 Minutes

Ingredients:
- ½ cup hazelnuts, ground
- 1 scallion, finely chopped
- 1 lemon, juiced and zested
- ½ tbsp olive oil
- Salt and pepper to taste
- 3 skinless sea bass fillets
- 1 tsp Dijon mustard

Directions:
1. Place the hazelnuts in a small bowl along with scallion, lemon zest, olive oil, salt and pepper. Mix everything until combined. Spray only the top of the fish with cooking oil, then squeeze lemon juice onto the fish. Coat the top of the fish with mustard. Spread with hazelnuts and press gently so that it stays on the fish.
2. Preheat air fryer to 375°F (190°C). Air Fry the fish in the greased frying basket for 7-8 minutes or it starts browning and the fish is cooked through. Serve hot.

Super Crunchy Flounder Fillets

Servings: 2
Cooking Time: 6 Minutes

Ingredients:
- ½ cup All-purpose flour or tapioca flour
- 1 Large egg white(s)
- 1 tablespoon Water
- ¾ teaspoon Table salt
- 1 cup Plain panko bread crumbs (gluten-free, if a concern)
- 2 4-ounce skinless flounder fillet(s)
- Vegetable oil spray

Directions:

1. Preheat the air fryer to 400°F (205°C).
2. Set up and fill three shallow soup plates or small pie plates on your counter: one for the flour; one for the egg white(s), beaten with the water and salt until foamy; and one for the bread crumbs.
3. Dip one fillet in the flour, turning it to coat both sides. Gently shake off any excess flour, then dip the fillet in the egg white mixture, turning it to coat. Let any excess egg white mixture slip back into the rest, then set the fish in the bread crumbs. Turn it several times, gently pressing it into the crumbs to create an even crust. Generously coat both sides of the fillet with vegetable oil spray. If necessary, set it aside and continue coating the remaining fillet(s) in the same way.
4. Set the fillet(s) in the basket. If working with more than one fillet, they should not touch, although they may be quite close together, depending on the basket's size. Air-fry undisturbed for 6 minutes, or until lightly browned and crunchy.
5. Use a nonstick-safe spatula to transfer the fillet(s) to a wire rack. Cool for only a minute or two before serving.

Tex-mex Fish Tacos

Servings: 3
Cooking Time: 7 Minutes

Ingredients:
- ¾ teaspoon Chile powder
- ¼ teaspoon Ground cumin
- ¼ teaspoon Dried oregano
- 3 5-ounce skinless mahi-mahi fillets
- Vegetable oil spray
- 3 Corn or flour tortillas
- 6 tablespoons Diced tomatoes
- 3 tablespoons Regular, low-fat, or fat-free sour cream

Directions:
1. Preheat the air fryer to 400°F (205°C).
2. Stir the chile powder, cumin, and oregano in a small bowl until well combined.
3. Coat each piece of fish all over (even the sides and ends) with vegetable oil spray. Sprinkle the spice mixture evenly over all sides of the fillets. Lightly spray them again.
4. When the machine is at temperature, set the fillets in the basket with as much air space between them as possible. Air-fry undisturbed for 7 minutes, until lightly browned and firm but not hard.
5. Use a nonstick-safe spatula to transfer the fillets to a wire rack. Microwave the tortillas on high for a few seconds, until supple. Put a fillet in each tortilla and top each with 2 tablespoons diced tomatoes and 1 tablespoon sour cream.

Quick Shrimp Scampi

Servings: 2

Cooking Time: 5 Minutes

Ingredients:

- 16 to 20 raw large shrimp, peeled, deveined and tails removed
- ½ cup white wine
- freshly ground black pepper
- ¼ cup + 1 tablespoon butter, divided
- 1 clove garlic, sliced
- 1 teaspoon olive oil
- salt, to taste
- juice of ½ lemon, to taste
- ¼ cup chopped fresh parsley

Directions:

1. Start by marinating the shrimp in the white wine and freshly ground black pepper for at least 30 minutes, or as long as 2 hours in the refrigerator.
2. Preheat the air fryer to 400°F (205°C).
3. Melt ¼ cup of butter in a small saucepan on the stovetop. Add the garlic and let the butter simmer, but be sure to not let it burn.
4. Pour the shrimp and marinade into the air fryer, letting the marinade drain through to the bottom drawer. Drizzle the olive oil on the shrimp and season well with salt. Air-fry at 400°F (205°C) for 3 minutes. Turn the shrimp over (don't shake the basket because the marinade will splash around) and pour the garlic butter over the shrimp. Air-fry for another 2 minutes.
5. Remove the shrimp from the air fryer basket and transfer them to a bowl. Squeeze lemon juice over all the shrimp and toss with the chopped parsley and remaining tablespoon of butter. Season to taste with salt and serve immediately.

Spiced Shrimp Empanadas

Servings: 5

Cooking Time: 30 Minutes

Ingredients:

- ½ lb peeled and deveined shrimp, chopped
- 2 tbsp diced red bell peppers
- 1 shallot, minced
- 1 scallion, chopped
- 2 garlic cloves, minced
- 2 tbsp chopped cilantro
- ½ tbsp lemon juice
- ¼ tsp sweet paprika
- ⅛ tsp salt
- ⅛ tsp red pepper flakes
- ¼ tsp ground nutmeg
- 1 large egg, beaten
- 10 empanada discs

Directions:

1. Combine all ingredients, except the egg and empanada discs, in a bowl. Toss to coat. Beat the 1 egg with 1 tsp of water in a small bowl until blended. Set aside.
2. On your work board, place one empanada disc. Add 2 tbsp of shrimp mixture in the middle. Brush the edges of the disc with the egg mixture. Fold the disc in half and seal the edges. Crimp with a fork by pressing around the edges. Brush the tops with the egg mixture. Preheat air fryer to 380°F (195°C). Put the empanadas in the greased frying basket and Air Fry for 9 minutes, flipping once until golden and crispy. Serve hot.

Beef, pork & Lamb Recipes

Sausage-cheese Calzone

Servings: 8
Cooking Time: 8 Minutes
Ingredients:
- Crust
- 2 cups white wheat flour, plus more for kneading and rolling
- 1 package (¼ ounce) RapidRise yeast
- 1 teaspoon salt
- ½ teaspoon dried basil
- 1 cup warm water (115°F (45°C) to 125°F (50°C))
- 2 teaspoons olive oil
- Filling
- ¼ pound Italian sausage
- ½ cup ricotta cheese
- 4 ounces mozzarella cheese, shredded
- ¼ cup grated Parmesan cheese
- oil for misting or cooking spray
- marinara sauce for serving

Directions:
1. Crumble Italian sausage into air fryer baking pan and cook at 390°F (200°C) for 5minutes. Stir, breaking apart, and cook for 3 to 4minutes, until well done. Remove and set aside on paper towels to drain.
2. To make dough, combine flour, yeast, salt, and basil. Add warm water and oil and stir until a soft dough forms. Turn out onto lightly floured board and knead for 3 or 4minutes. Let dough rest for 10minutes.
3. To make filling, combine the three cheeses in a medium bowl and mix well. Stir in the cooked sausage.
4. Cut dough into 8 pieces.
5. Working with 4 pieces of the dough, press each into a circle about 5 inches in diameter. Top each dough circle with 2 heaping tablespoons of filling. Fold over to create a half-moon shape and press edges firmly together. Be sure that edges are firmly sealed to prevent leakage. Spray both sides with oil or cooking spray.
6. Place 4 calzones in air fryer basket and cook at 360°F (180°C) for 5minutes. Mist with oil and cook for 3 minutes, until crust is done and nicely browned.
7. While the first batch is cooking, press out the remaining dough, fill, and shape into calzones.
8. Spray both sides with oil and cook for 5minutes. If needed, mist with oil and continue cooking for 3 minutes longer. This second batch will cook a little faster than the first because your air fryer is already hot.
9. Serve with marinara sauce on the side for dipping.

Crispy Steak Subs

Servings: 2
Cooking Time: 30 Minutes
Ingredients:
- 1 hoagie bun baguette, halved
- 6 oz flank steak, sliced
- ½ white onion, sliced
- ½ red pepper, sliced
- 2 mozzarella cheese slices

Directions:
1. Preheat air fryer to 320°F (160°C). Place the flank steak slices, onion, and red pepper on one side of the frying basket. Add the hoagie bun halves, crusty side up, to the other half of the air fryer. Bake for 10 minutes. Flip the hoagie buns. Cover both sides with one slice of mozzarella cheese. Gently stir the steak, onions, and peppers. Cook for 6 more minutes until the cheese is melted and the steak is juicy on the inside and crispy on the outside.
2. Remove the cheesy hoagie halves to a serving plate. Cover one side with the steak, and top with the onions and peppers. Close with the other cheesy hoagie half, slice into two pieces, and enjoy!

Greek Pork Chops

Servings: 4
Cooking Time: 30 Minutes
Ingredients:
- 3 tbsp grated Halloumi cheese
- 4 pork chops
- 1 tsp Greek seasoning
- Salt and pepper to taste
- ¼ cup all-purpose flour
- 2 tbsp bread crumbs

Directions:
1. Preheat air fryer to 380°F (195°C). Season the pork chops with Greek seasoning, salt and pepper. In a shallow bowl, add flour. In another shallow bowl, combine the crumbs and Halloumi. Dip the chops in the flour, then in the bread crumbs. Place them in the fryer and spray with cooking oil. Bake for 12-14 minutes, flipping once. Serve warm.

Lemon-garlic Strip Steak

Servings: 2

Cooking Time: 15 Minutes

Ingredients:

- 3 cloves garlic, minced
- 1 tbsp lemon juice
- 1 tbsp olive oil
- Salt and pepper to taste
- 1 tbsp chopped parsley
- ½ tsp chopped rosemary
- ½ tsp chopped sage
- 1 strip steak

Directions:

1. In a small bowl, whisk all ingredients. Brush mixture over strip steak and let marinate covered in the fridge for 30 minutes. Preheat air fryer at 400ºF. Place strip steak in the greased frying basket and Bake for 8 minutes until rare, turning once. Let rest onto a cutting board for 5 minutes before serving.

Mustard And Rosemary Pork Tenderloin With Fried Apples

Servings: 2

Cooking Time: 26 Minutes

Ingredients:

- 1 pork tenderloin (about 1-pound)
- 2 tablespoons coarse brown mustard
- salt and freshly ground black pepper
- 1½ teaspoons finely chopped fresh rosemary, plus sprigs for garnish
- 2 apples, cored and cut into 8 wedges
- 1 tablespoon butter, melted
- 1 teaspoon brown sugar

Directions:

1. Preheat the air fryer to 370°F (185°C).
2. Cut the pork tenderloin in half so that you have two pieces that fit into the air fryer basket. Brush the mustard onto both halves of the pork tenderloin and then season with salt, pepper and the fresh rosemary. Place the pork tenderloin halves into the air fryer basket and air-fry for 10 minutes. Turn the pork over and air-fry for an additional 8 minutes or until the internal temperature of the pork registers 155°F (70°C) on an instant read thermometer. If your pork tenderloin is especially thick, you may need to add a minute or two, but it's better to check the pork and add time, than to overcook it.
3. Let the pork rest for 5 minutes. In the meantime, toss the apple wedges with the butter and brown sugar and air-fry at 400°F (205°C) for 8 minutes, shaking the basket once or twice during the cooking process so the apples cook and brown evenly.
4. Slice the pork on the bias. Serve with the fried apples scattered over the top and a few sprigs of rosemary as garnish.

Beef Al Carbon (street Taco Meat)

Servings: 6

Cooking Time: 8 Minutes

Ingredients:

- 1½ pounds sirloin steak, cut into ½-inch cubes
- ¾ cup lime juice
- ½ cup extra-virgin olive oil
- 1 teaspoon ground cumin
- 2 teaspoons garlic powder
- 1 teaspoon salt

Directions:

1. In a large bowl, toss together the steak, lime juice, olive oil, cumin, garlic powder, and salt. Allow the meat to marinate for 30 minutes. Drain off all the marinade and pat the meat dry with paper towels.
2. Preheat the air fryer to 400°F (205°C).
3. Place the meat in the air fryer basket and spray with cooking spray. Cook the meat for 5 minutes, toss the meat, and continue cooking another 3 minutes, until slightly crispy.

Flank Steak With Roasted Peppers And Chimichurri

Servings: 4

Cooking Time: 22 Minutes

Ingredients:

- 2 cups flat-leaf parsley leaves
- ¼ cup fresh oregano leaves
- 3 cloves garlic
- ½ cup olive oil
- ¼ cup red wine vinegar
- ½ teaspoon salt
- freshly ground black pepper
- ¼ teaspoon crushed red pepper flakes
- ½ teaspoon ground cumin
- 1 pound flank steak
- 1 red bell pepper, cut into strips
- 1 yellow bell pepper, cut into strips

Directions:

1. Make the chimichurri sauce by chopping the parsley, oregano and garlic in a food processor. Add the olive oil, vinegar and seasonings and process again. Pour half of the

sauce into a shallow dish with the flank steak and set the remaining sauce aside. Pierce the flank steak with a needle-style meat tenderizer or a paring knife and marinate the steak for 2 to 24 hours in the refrigerator. When you are ready to cook, remove the steak from the refrigerator and let it sit at room temperature for 30 minutes.

2. Preheat the air fryer to 400°F (205°C).

3. Cut the flank steak in half so that it fits more easily into the air fryer and transfer both pieces to the air fryer basket. Air-fry for 14 minutes, depending on how you like your steak cooked (10 minutes will give you medium for a 1-inch thick flank steak). Flip the steak over halfway through the cooking time.

4. When the flank steak is cooked to your liking, transfer it to a cutting board, loosely tent with foil and let it rest while you cook the peppers.

5. Toss the peppers in a little olive oil, salt and freshly ground black pepper and transfer them to the air fryer basket. Air-fry at 400°F (205°C) for 8 minutes, shaking the basket once or twice throughout the cooking process. To serve, slice the flank steak against the grain of the meat and top with the roasted peppers. Drizzle the reserved chimichurri sauce on top, thinning the sauce with another tablespoon of olive oil if desired.

Herby Lamb Chops

Servings: 2

Cooking Time: 25 Minutes

Ingredients:

- 3 lamb chops
- 1 cup breadcrumbs
- 2 eggs, beaten
- Salt and pepper to taste
- ½ tbsp thyme
- ½ tbsp mint, chopped
- ½ tsp garlic powder
- ½ tsp ground rosemary
- ½ tsp cayenne powder
- ½ tsp ras el hanout

Directions:

1. Preheat air fryer to 320°F (160°C). Mix the breadcrumbs, thyme, mint, garlic, rosemary, cayenne, ras el hanout, salt, and pepper in a bowl. Dip the lamb chops in the beaten eggs, then coat with the crumb mixture. Air Fry for 14-16 minutes, turning once. Serve and enjoy!

Italian Sausage Rolls

Servings: 4

Cooking Time: 20 Minutes

Ingredients:

- 1 red bell pepper, cut into strips
- 4 Italian sausages
- 1 zucchini, cut into strips
- ½ onion, cut into strips
- 1 tsp dried oregano
- ½ tsp garlic powder
- 5 Italian rolls

Directions:

1. Preheat air fryer to 360°F (180°C). Place all sausages in the air fryer. Bake for 10 minutes. While the sausages are cooking, season the bell pepper, zucchini and onion with oregano and garlic powder. When the time is up, flip the sausages, then add the peppers and onions. Cook for another 5 minutes or until the vegetables are soft and the sausages are cooked through. Put the sausage on Italian rolls, then top with peppers and onions. Serve.

Paprika Fried Beef

Servings: 4

Cooking Time: 30 Minutes

Ingredients:

- Celery salt to taste
- 4 beef cube steaks
- ½ cup milk
- 1 cup flour
- 2 tsp paprika
- 1 egg
- 1 cup bread crumbs
- 2 tbsp olive oil

Directions:

1. Preheat air fryer to 350°F (175°C). Place the cube steaks in a zipper sealed bag or between two sheets of cling wrap. Gently pound the steaks until they are slightly thinner. Set aside. In a bowl, mix together milk, flour, paprika, celery salt, and egg until just combined. In a separate bowl, mix together the crumbs and olive oil. Take the steaks and dip them into the buttermilk batter, shake off some of the excess, and return to a plate for 5 minutes. Next, dip the steaks in the bread crumbs, patting the crumbs into both sides. Air Fry the steaks until the crust is crispy and brown, 12-16 minutes. Serve warm.

Italian Sausage & Peppers

Servings: 6
Cooking Time: 25 Minutes

Ingredients:

- 1 6-ounce can tomato paste
- ⅔ cup water
- 1 8-ounce can tomato sauce
- 1 teaspoon dried parsley flakes
- ½ teaspoon garlic powder
- ⅛ teaspoon oregano
- ½ pound mild Italian bulk sausage
- 1 tablespoon extra virgin olive oil
- ½ large onion, cut in 1-inch chunks
- 4 ounces fresh mushrooms, sliced
- 1 large green bell pepper, cut in 1-inch chunks
- 8 ounces spaghetti, cooked
- Parmesan cheese for serving

Directions:

1. In a large saucepan or skillet, stir together the tomato paste, water, tomato sauce, parsley, garlic, and oregano. Heat on stovetop over very low heat while preparing meat and vegetables.
2. Break sausage into small chunks, about ½-inch pieces. Place in air fryer baking pan.
3. Cook at 390°F (200°C) for 5minutes. Stir. Cook 7 minutes longer or until sausage is well done. Remove from pan, drain on paper towels, and add to the sauce mixture.
4. If any sausage grease remains in baking pan, pour it off or use paper towels to soak it up. (Be careful handling that hot pan!)
5. Place olive oil, onions, and mushrooms in pan and stir. Cook for 5minutes or just until tender. Using a slotted spoon, transfer onions and mushrooms from baking pan into the sauce and sausage mixture.
6. Place bell pepper chunks in air fryer baking pan and cook for 8 minutes or until tender. When done, stir into sauce with sausage and other vegetables.
7. Serve over cooked spaghetti with plenty of Parmesan cheese.

Calzones South Of The Border

Servings: 8
Cooking Time: 8 Minutes

Ingredients:

- Filling
- ¼ pound ground pork sausage
- ½ teaspoon chile powder
- ¼ teaspoon ground cumin
- ⅛ teaspoon garlic powder
- ⅛ teaspoon onion powder
- ⅛ teaspoon oregano
- ½ cup ricotta cheese
- 1 ounce sharp Cheddar cheese, shredded
- 2 ounces Pepper Jack cheese, shredded
- 1 4-ounce can chopped green chiles, drained
- oil for misting or cooking spray
- salsa, sour cream, or guacamole
- Crust
- 2 cups white wheat flour, plus more for kneading and rolling
- 1 package (¼ ounce) RapidRise yeast
- 1 teaspoon salt
- ½ teaspoon chile powder
- ½ teaspoon ground cumin
- 1 cup warm water (45°C to 50°C))
- 2 teaspoons olive oil

Directions:

1. Crumble sausage into air fryer baking pan and stir in the filling seasonings: chile powder, cumin, garlic powder, onion powder, and oregano. Cook at 390°F (200°C) for 2minutes. Stir, breaking apart, and cook for 3 to 4minutes, until well done. Remove and set aside on paper towels to drain.
2. To make dough, combine flour, yeast, salt, chile powder, and cumin. Stir in warm water and oil until soft dough forms. Turn out onto lightly floured board and knead for 3 or 4minutes. Let dough rest for 10minutes.
3. Place the three cheeses in a medium bowl. Add cooked sausage and chiles and stir until well mixed.
4. Cut dough into 8 pieces.
5. Working with 4 pieces of the dough, press each into a circle about 5 inches in diameter. Top each dough circle with 2 heaping tablespoons of filling. Fold over into a half-moon shape and press edges together. Seal edges firmly to prevent leakage. Spray both sides with oil or cooking spray.
6. Place 4 calzones in air fryer basket and cook at 360°F (180°C) for 5minutes. Mist with oil or spray and cook for 3minutes, until crust is done and nicely browned.
7. While the first batch is cooking, press out the remaining dough, fill, and shape into calzones.
8. Spray both sides with oil or cooking spray and cook for 5minutes. If needed, mist with oil and continue cooking for 3 minutes longer. This second batch will cook a little faster than the first because your air fryer is already hot.
9. Serve plain or with salsa, sour cream, or guacamole.

Meat Loaves

Servings: 4
Cooking Time: 19 Minutes
Ingredients:
- Sauce
- ¼ cup white vinegar
- ¼ cup brown sugar
- 2 tablespoons Worcestershire sauce
- ½ cup ketchup
- Meat Loaves
- 1 pound very lean ground beef
- ⅔ cup dry bread (approx. 1 slice torn into small pieces)
- 1 egg
- ⅓ cup minced onion
- 1 teaspoon salt
- 2 tablespoons ketchup

Directions:
1. In a small saucepan, combine all sauce ingredients and bring to a boil. Remove from heat and stir to ensure that brown sugar dissolves completely.
2. In a large bowl, combine the beef, bread, egg, onion, salt, and ketchup. Mix well.
3. Divide meat mixture into 4 portions and shape each into a thick, round patty. Patties will be about 3 to 3½ inches in diameter, and all four should fit easily into the air fryer basket at once.
4. Cook at 360°F (180°C) for 18 minutes, until meat is well done. Baste tops of mini loaves with a small amount of sauce, and cook 1 minute.
5. Serve hot with additional sauce on the side.

Rosemary Lamb Chops

Servings: 4
Cooking Time: 6 Minutes
Ingredients:
- 8 lamb chops
- 1 tablespoon extra-virgin olive oil
- 1 teaspoon dried rosemary, crushed
- 2 cloves garlic, minced
- 1 teaspoon sea salt
- ¼ teaspoon black pepper

Directions:
1. In a large bowl, mix together the lamb chops, olive oil, rosemary, garlic, salt, and pepper. Let sit at room temperature for 10 minutes.
2. Meanwhile, preheat the air fryer to 380°F (195°C).
3. Cook the lamb chops for 3 minutes, flip them over, and cook for another 3 minutes.

Provençal Grilled Rib-eye

Servings: 4
Cooking Time: 25 Minutes
Ingredients:
- 4 ribeye steaks
- 1 tbsp herbs de Provence
- Salt and pepper to taste

Directions:
1. Preheat air fryer to 360°F (180°C). Season the steaks with herbs, salt and pepper. Place them in the greased frying basket and cook for 8-12 minutes, flipping once. Use a thermometer to check for doneness and adjust time as needed. Let the steak rest for a few minutes and serve.

Balsamic London Broil

Servings: 4
Cooking Time: 25 Minutes
Ingredients:
- 2 ½ lb top round London broil steak
- ¼ cup coconut aminos
- 1 tbsp balsamic vinegar
- 1 tbsp olive oil
- 1 tbsp mustard
- 2 tsp maple syrup
- 2 garlic cloves, minced
- 1 tsp dried oregano
- Salt and pepper to taste
- ¼ tsp smoked paprika
- 2 tbsp red onions, chopped

Directions:
1. Whisk coconut aminos, mustard, vinegar, olive oil, maple oregano, syrup, oregano garlic, red onions, salt, pepper, and paprika in a small bowl. Put the steak in a shallow container and pour the marinade over the steak. Cover and let sit for 20 minutes.
2. Preheat air fryer to 400°F (205°C). Transfer the steak to the frying basket and bake for 5 minutes. Flip the steak and bake for another 4 to 6 minutes. Allow sitting for 5 minutes before slicing. Serve warm and enjoy.

Lazy Mexican Meat Pizza

Servings: 4
Cooking Time: 35 Minutes
Ingredients:
- 1 ¼ cups canned refried beans
- 2 cups shredded cheddar
- ½ cup chopped cilantro
- 2/3 cup salsa
- 1 red bell pepper, chopped

- 1 sliced jalapeño
- 1 pizza crust
- 16 meatballs, halved

Directions:

1. Preheat the air fryer to 375°F (190°C). Combine the refried beans, salsa, jalapeño, and bell pepper in a bowl and spread on the pizza crust. Top with meatball halves and sprinkle with cheddar cheese. Put the pizza in the greased frying basket and Bake for 7-10 minutes until hot and the cheese is brown. Sprinkle with the fresh cilantro and serve.

Perfect Pork Chops

Servings: 3
Cooking Time: 10 Minutes

Ingredients:

- ¾ teaspoon Mild paprika
- ¾ teaspoon Dried thyme
- ¾ teaspoon Onion powder
- ¼ teaspoon Garlic powder
- ¼ teaspoon Table salt
- ¼ teaspoon Ground black pepper
- 3 6-ounce boneless center-cut pork loin chops
- Vegetable oil spray

Directions:

1. Preheat the air fryer to 400°F (205°C).
2. Mix the paprika, thyme, onion powder, garlic powder, salt, and pepper in a small bowl until well combined. Massage this mixture into both sides of the chops. Generously coat both sides of the chops with vegetable oil spray.
3. When the machine is at temperature, set the chops in the basket with as much air space between them as possible. Air-fry undisturbed for 10 minutes, or until an instant-read meat thermometer inserted into the thickest part of a chop registers 145°F (60°C).
4. Use kitchen tongs to transfer the chops to a cutting board or serving plates. Cool for 5 minutes before serving.

Red Curry Flank Steak

Servings: 4
Cooking Time: 18 Minutes

Ingredients:

- 3 tablespoons red curry paste
- ¼ cup olive oil
- 2 teaspoons grated fresh ginger
- 2 tablespoons soy sauce
- 2 tablespoons rice wine vinegar
- 3 scallions, minced
- 1½ pounds flank steak
- fresh cilantro (or parsley) leaves

Directions:

1. Mix the red curry paste, olive oil, ginger, soy sauce, rice vinegar and scallions together in a bowl. Place the flank steak in a shallow glass dish and pour half the marinade over the steak. Pierce the steak several times with a fork or meat tenderizer to let the marinade penetrate the meat. Turn the steak over, pour the remaining marinade over the top and pierce the steak several times again. Cover and marinate the steak in the refrigerator for 6 to 8 hours.
2. When you are ready to cook, remove the steak from the refrigerator and let it sit at room temperature for 30 minutes.
3. Preheat the air fryer to 400°F (205°C).
4. Cut the flank steak in half so that it fits more easily into the air fryer and transfer both pieces to the air fryer basket. Pour the marinade over the steak. Air-fry for 18 minutes, depending on your preferred degree of doneness of the steak (12 minutes = medium rare). Flip the steak over halfway through the cooking time.
5. When your desired degree of doneness has been reached, remove the steak to a cutting board and let it rest for 5 minutes before slicing. Thinly slice the flank steak against the grain of the meat. Transfer the slices to a serving platter, pour any juice from the bottom of the air fryer over the sliced flank steak and sprinkle the fresh cilantro on top.

Greek Pita Pockets

Servings: 4
Cooking Time: 7 Minutes

Ingredients:

- Dressing
- 1 cup plain yogurt
- 1 tablespoon lemon juice
- 1 teaspoon dried dill weed, crushed
- 1 teaspoon ground oregano
- ½ teaspoon salt
- Meatballs
- ½ pound ground lamb
- 1 tablespoon diced onion
- 1 teaspoon dried parsley
- 1 teaspoon dried dill weed, crushed
- ¼ teaspoon oregano
- ¼ teaspoon coriander
- ¼ teaspoon ground cumin
- ¼ teaspoon salt
- 4 pita halves
- Suggested Toppings
- red onion, slivered
- seedless cucumber, thinly sliced
- crumbled Feta cheese
- sliced black olives
- chopped fresh peppers

Directions:
1. Stir dressing ingredients together and refrigerate while preparing lamb.
2. Combine all meatball ingredients in a large bowl and stir to distribute seasonings.
3. Shape meat mixture into 12 small meatballs, rounded or slightly flattened if you prefer.
4. Cook at 390°F (200°C) for 7 minutes, until well done. Remove and drain on paper towels.
5. To serve, pile meatballs and your choice of toppings in pita pockets and drizzle with dressing.

German-style Pork Patties

Servings: 6
Cooking Time: 35 Minutes

Ingredients:
- 1 lb ground pork
- ¼ cup diced fresh pear
- 1 tbsp minced sage leaves
- 1 garlic clove, minced
- 2 tbsp chopped chives
- Salt and pepper to taste

Directions:
1. Preheat the air fryer to 375°F (190°C). Combine the pork, pear, sage, chives, garlic, salt, and pepper in a bowl and mix gently but thoroughly with your hands, then make 8 patties about ½ inch thick. Lay the patties in the frying basket in a single layer and Air Fry for 15-20 minutes, flipping once halfway through. Remove and drain on paper towels, then serve. Serve and enjoy!

Beef And Spinach Braciole

Servings: 4
Cooking Time: 92 Minutes

Ingredients:
- 7-inch oven-safe baking pan or casserole
- ½ onion, finely chopped
- 1 teaspoon olive oil
- ⅓ cup red wine
- 2 cups crushed tomatoes
- 1 teaspoon Italian seasoning
- ½ teaspoon garlic powder
- ¼ teaspoon crushed red pepper flakes
- 2 tablespoons chopped fresh parsley
- 2 top round steaks (about 1½ pounds)
- salt and freshly ground black pepper
- 2 cups fresh spinach, chopped
- 1 clove minced garlic
- ½ cup roasted red peppers, julienned
- ½ cup grated pecorino cheese
- ¼ cup pine nuts, toasted and rough chopped
- 2 tablespoons olive oil

Directions:
1. Preheat the air fryer to 400°F (205°C).
2. Toss the onions and olive oil together in a 7-inch metal baking pan or casserole dish. Air-fry at 400°F (205°C) for 5 minutes, stirring a couple times during the cooking process. Add the red wine, crushed tomatoes, Italian seasoning, garlic powder, red pepper flakes and parsley and stir. Cover the pan tightly with aluminum foil, lower the air fryer temperature to 350°F (175°C) and continue to air-fry for 15 minutes.
3. While the sauce is simmering, prepare the beef. Using a meat mallet, pound the beef until it is ¼-inch thick. Season both sides of the beef with salt and pepper. Combine the spinach, garlic, red peppers, pecorino cheese, pine nuts and olive oil in a medium bowl. Season with salt and freshly ground black pepper. Spread the mixture evenly over the steaks. Starting at one of the short ends, roll the beef around the filling, tucking in the sides as you roll to ensure the filling is completely enclosed. Secure the beef rolls with toothpicks.
4. Remove the baking pan with the sauce from the air fryer and set it aside. Preheat the air fryer to 400°F (205°C).
5. Brush or spray the beef rolls with a little olive oil and air-fry at 400°F (205°C) for 12 minutes, rotating the beef during the cooking process for even browning. When the beef is browned, submerge the rolls into the sauce in the baking pan, cover the pan with foil and return it to the air fryer. Air-fry at 250°F (120°C) for 60 minutes.
6. Remove the beef rolls from the sauce. Cut each roll into slices and serve with pasta, ladling some of the sauce overtop.

Seedy Rib Eye Steak Bites

Servings: 4
Cooking Time: 20 Minutes

Ingredients:
- 1 lb rib eye steak, cubed
- 2 garlic cloves, minced
- 2 tbsp olive oil
- 1 tbsp thyme, chopped
- 1 tsp ground fennel seeds
- Salt and pepper to taste
- 1 onion, thinly sliced

Directions:
1. Preheat air fryer to 380°F (195°C). Place the steak, garlic, olive oil, thyme, fennel seeds, salt, pepper, and onion in a bowl. Mix until all of the beef and onion are well coated. Put the seasoned steak mixture into the frying basket. Roast for 10 minutes, stirring once. Let sit for 5 minutes. Serve.

Beef & Barley Stuffed Bell Peppers

Servings: 4

Cooking Time: 30 Minutes

Ingredients:

- 1 cup pulled cooked roast beef
- 4 bell peppers, tops removed
- 1 onion, chopped
- ½ cup grated carrot
- 2 tsp olive oil
- 2 tomatoes, chopped
- 1 cup cooked barley
- 1 tsp dried marjoram

Directions:

1. Preheat air fryer to 400°F (205°C). Cut the tops of the bell peppers, then remove the stems. Put the onion, carrots, and olive oil in a baking pan and cook for 2-4 minutes. The veggies should be crispy but soft. Put the veggies in a bowl, toss in the tomatoes, barley, roast beef, and marjoram, and mix to combine. Spoon the veggie mix into the cleaned bell peppers and put them in the frying basket. Bake for 12-16 minutes or until the peppers are tender. Serve warm.

Sloppy Joes

Servings: 4

Cooking Time: 17 Minutes

Ingredients:

- oil for misting or cooking spray
- 1 pound very lean ground beef
- 1 teaspoon onion powder
- ⅓ cup ketchup
- ¼ cup water
- ½ teaspoon celery seed
- 1 tablespoon lemon juice
- 1½ teaspoons brown sugar
- 1¼ teaspoons low-sodium Worcestershire sauce
- ½ teaspoon salt (optional)
- ½ teaspoon vinegar
- ⅛ teaspoon dry mustard
- hamburger or slider buns

Directions:

1. Spray air fryer basket with nonstick cooking spray or olive oil.
2. Break raw ground beef into small chunks and pile into basket.
3. Cook at 390°F (200°C) for 5minutes. Stir to break apart and cook 3minutes. Stir and cook 4 minutes longer or until meat is well done.
4. Remove meat from air fryer, drain, and use a knife and fork to crumble into small pieces.
5. Give your air fryer basket a quick rinse to remove any bits of meat.
6. Place all the remaining ingredients except the buns in a 6 x 6-inch baking pan and mix together.
7. Add meat and stir well.
8. Cook at 330°F (165°C) for 5minutes. Stir and cook for 2minutes.
9. Scoop onto buns.

Friendly Bbq Baby Back Ribs

Servings: 4

Cooking Time: 35 Minutes

Ingredients:

- 1 rack baby back ribs, halved
- 1 tsp onion powder
- 1 tsp garlic powder
- 1 tsp brown sugar
- 1 tsp dried oregano
- 1 tsp ancho chili powder
- 1 tsp mustard powder
- Salt and pepper to taste
- ½ cup barbecue sauce

Directions:

1. Mix the onion powder, garlic powder, brown sugar, oregano, salt, mustard, ancho chili and pepper in a small bowl. Rub the seasoning all over the meat of the ribs. Cover the ribs in plastic wrap or foil. Sit for 30 minutes.
2. Preheat air fryer to 360°F (180°C). Place all of the ribs in the air fryer. Bake for 15 minutes, then use tongs to flip the ribs. Cook for another 15 minutes. Transfer to a serving dish and drizzle with barbecue sauce. Serve and enjoy!

Smokehouse-style Beef Ribs

Servings: 3

Cooking Time: 25 Minutes

Ingredients:

- ¼ teaspoon Mild smoked paprika
- ¼ teaspoon Garlic powder
- ¼ teaspoon Onion powder
- ¼ teaspoon Table salt
- ¼ teaspoon Ground black pepper
- 3 10- to 12-ounce beef back ribs (not beef short ribs)

Directions:

1. Preheat the air fryer to 350°F (175°C).
2. Mix the smoked paprika, garlic powder, onion powder, salt, and pepper in a small bowl until uniform. Massage and pat this mixture onto the ribs.

3. When the machine is at temperature, set the ribs in the basket in one layer, turning them on their sides if necessary, sort of like they're spooning but with at least ¼ inch air space between them. Air-fry for 25 minutes, turning once, until deep brown and sizzling.

4. Use kitchen tongs to transfer the ribs to a wire rack. Cool for 5 minutes before serving.

Easy Carnitas

Servings: 3

Cooking Time: 25 Minutes

Ingredients:

- 1½ pounds Boneless country-style pork ribs, cut into 2-inch pieces
- ¼ cup Orange juice
- 2 tablespoons Brine from a jar of pickles, any type, even pickled jalapeño rings (gluten-free, if a concern)
- 2 teaspoons Minced garlic
- 2 teaspoons Minced fresh oregano leaves
- ¾ teaspoon Ground cumin
- ¾ teaspoon Table salt
- ¾ teaspoon Ground black pepper

Directions:

1. Mix the country-style pork rib pieces, orange juice, pickle brine, garlic, oregano, cumin, salt, and pepper in a large bowl. Cover and refrigerate for at least 2 hours or up to 10 hours, stirring the mixture occasionally.

2. Preheat the air fryer to 400°F (205°C). Set the rib pieces in their bowl on the counter as the machine heats.

3. Use kitchen tongs to transfer the rib pieces to the basket, arranging them in one layer. Some may touch. Air-fry for 25 minutes, turning and rearranging the pieces at the 10- and 20-minute marks to make sure all surfaces have been exposed to the air currents, until browned and sizzling.

4. Use clean kitchen tongs to transfer the rib pieces to a wire rack. Cool for a couple of minutes before serving.

Cheeseburger Sliders With Pickle Sauce

Servings: 4

Cooking Time: 20 Minutes

Ingredients:

- 4 iceberg lettuce leaves, each halved lengthwise
- 2 red onion slices, rings separated
- ¼ cup shredded Swiss cheese
- 1 lb ground beef
- 1 tbsp Dijon mustard
- Salt and pepper to taste
- ¼ tsp shallot powder
- 2 tbsp mayonnaise
- 2 tsp ketchup
- ½ tsp mustard powder
- ½ tsp dill pickle juice
- ⅛ tsp onion powder
- ⅛ tsp garlic powder
- ⅛ tsp sweet paprika
- 8 tomato slices
- ½ cucumber, thinly sliced

Directions:

1. In a large bowl, use your hands to mix beef, Swiss cheese, mustard, salt, shallot, and black pepper. Do not overmix. Form 8 patties ½-inch thick. Mix together mayonnaise, ketchup, mustard powder, pickle juice, onion and garlic powder, and paprika in a medium bowl. Stir until smooth.

2. Preheat air fryer to 400°F (205°C). Place the sliders in the greased frying basket and Air Fry for about 8-10 minutes, flipping once until preferred doneness. Serve on top of lettuce halves with a slice of tomato, a slider, onion, a smear of special sauce, and cucumber.

Spanish-style Meatloaf With Manzanilla Olives

Servings: 6

Cooking Time: 35 Minutes

Ingredients:

- 2 oz Manchego cheese, grated
- 1 lb lean ground beef
- 2 eggs
- 2 tomatoes, diced
- ½ white onion, diced
- ½ cup bread crumbs
- 1 tsp garlic powder
- 1 tsp dried oregano
- 1 tsp dried thyme
- Salt and pepper to taste
- 4 Manzanilla olives, minced
- 1 tbsp olive oil
- 2 tbsp chopped parsley

Directions:

1. Preheat the oven to 380°F (195°C). Combine the ground beef, eggs, tomatoes, onion, bread crumbs, garlic powder, oregano, thyme, salt, pepper, olives and cheese in a bowl and mix well. Form into a loaf, flattening to 1-inch thick. Lightly brush the top with olive oil, then place the meatloaf into the frying basket. Bake for 25 minutes. Allow to rest for 5 minutes. Top with parsley and slice. Serve warm.

Stuffed Pork Chops

Servings: 4

Cooking Time: 12 Minutes

Ingredients:

- 4 boneless pork chops
- ½ teaspoon salt
- ½ teaspoon black pepper
- ¼ teaspoon paprika
- 1 cup frozen spinach, defrosted and squeezed dry
- 2 cloves garlic, minced
- 2 ounces cream cheese
- ¼ cup grated Parmesan cheese
- 1 tablespoon extra-virgin olive oil

Directions:

1. Pat the pork chops with a paper towel. Make a slit in the side of each pork chop to create a pouch.
2. Season the pork chops with the salt, pepper, and paprika.
3. In a small bowl, mix together the spinach, garlic, cream cheese, and Parmesan cheese.
4. Divide the mixture into fourths and stuff the pork chop pouches. Secure the pouches with toothpicks.
5. Preheat the air fryer to 400°F (205°C).
6. Place the stuffed pork chops in the air fryer basket and spray liberally with cooking spray. Cook for 6 minutes, flip and coat with more cooking spray, and cook another 6 minutes. Check to make sure the meat is cooked to an internal temperature of 145°F (60°C). Cook the pork chops in batches, as needed.

Marinated Rib-eye Steak With Herb Roasted Mushrooms

Servings: 2

Cooking Time: 10-15 Minutes

Ingredients:

- 2 tablespoons Worcestershire sauce
- ¼ cup red wine
- 2 (8-ounce) boneless rib-eye steaks
- coarsely ground black pepper
- 8 ounces baby bella (cremini) mushrooms, stems trimmed and caps halved
- 2 tablespoons olive oil
- 1 teaspoon dried parsley
- 1 teaspoon fresh thyme leaves
- salt and freshly ground black pepper
- chopped fresh chives or parsley

Directions:

1. Combine the Worcestershire sauce and red wine in a shallow baking dish. Add the steaks to the marinade, pierce them several times with the tines of a fork or a meat tenderizer and season them generously with the coarsely ground black pepper. Flip the steaks over and pierce the other side in a similar fashion, seasoning again with the coarsely ground black pepper. Marinate the steaks for 2 hours.
2. Preheat the air fryer to 400°F (205°C).
3. Toss the mushrooms in a bowl with the olive oil, dried parsley, thyme, salt and freshly ground black pepper. Transfer the steaks from the marinade to the air fryer basket, season with salt and scatter the mushrooms on top.
4. Air-fry the steaks for 10 minutes for medium-rare, 12 minutes for medium, or 15 minutes for well-done, flipping the steaks once halfway through the cooking time.
5. Serve the steaks and mushrooms together with the chives or parsley sprinkled on top. A good steak sauce or some horseradish would be a nice accompaniment.

Pepperoni Pockets

Servings: 4

Cooking Time: 8 Minutes

Ingredients:

- 4 bread slices, 1-inch thick
- olive oil for misting
- 24 slices pepperoni (about 2 ounces)
- 1 ounce roasted red peppers, drained and patted dry
- 1 ounce Pepper Jack cheese cut into 4 slices
- pizza sauce (optional)

Directions:

1. Spray both sides of bread slices with olive oil.
2. Stand slices upright and cut a deep slit in the top to create a pocket—almost to the bottom crust but not all the way through.
3. Stuff each bread pocket with 6 slices of pepperoni, a large strip of roasted red pepper, and a slice of cheese.
4. Place bread pockets in air fryer basket, standing up. Cook at 360°F (180°C) for 8 minutes, until filling is heated through and bread is lightly browned. Serve while hot as is or with pizza sauce for dipping.

Minted Lamb Chops

Servings: 4

Cooking Time: 20 Minutes

Ingredients:

- 8 lamb chops
- 2 tsp olive oil
- 1 ½ tsp chopped mint leaves
- 1 tsp ground coriander
- 1 lemon, zested
- ½ tsp baharat seasoning

- 1 garlic clove, minced
- Salt and pepper to taste

Directions:
1. Preheat air fryer to 390°F (200°C). Coat the lamb chops with olive oil. Set aside. Mix mint, coriander, baharat, zest, garlic, salt and pepper in a bowl. Rub the seasoning onto both sides of the chops. Place the chops in the greased frying basket and Air Fry for 10 minutes. Flip the lamb chops and cook for another 5 minutes. Let the lamb chops rest for a few minutes. Serve right away.

Pork Chops

Servings: 2
Cooking Time: 16 Minutes

Ingredients:
- 2 bone-in, centercut pork chops, 1-inch thick (10 ounces each)
- 2 teaspoons Worcestershire sauce
- salt and pepper
- cooking spray

Directions:
1. Rub the Worcestershire sauce into both sides of pork chops.
2. Season with salt and pepper to taste.
3. Spray air fryer basket with cooking spray and place the chops in basket side by side.
4. Cook at 360°F (180°C) for 16 minutes or until well done. Let rest for 5minutes before serving.

French-style Steak Salad

Servings: 4
Cooking Time: 25 Minutes

Ingredients:
- 1 cup sliced strawberries
- 4 tbsp crumbled blue cheese
- ¼ cup olive oil
- Salt and pepper to taste
- 1 flank steak
- ¼cup balsamic vinaigrette
- 1 tbsp Dijon mustard
- 2 tbsp lemon juice
- 8 cups baby arugula
- ½ red onion, sliced
- 4 tbsp pecan pieces
- 4 tbsp sunflower seeds
- 1 sliced kiwi
- 1 sliced orange

Directions:

1. In a bowl, whisk olive oil, salt, lemon juice and pepper. Toss in flank steak and let marinate covered in the fridge for 30 minutes up to overnight. Preheat air fryer at 325°F. Place flank steak in the greased frying basket and Bake for 18-20 minutes until rare, flipping once. Let rest for 5 minutes before slicing thinly against the grain.
2. In a salad bowl, whisk balsamic vinaigrette and mustard. Stir in arugula, salt, and pepper. Divide between 4 serving bowls. Top each salad with blue cheese, onion, pecan, sunflower seeds, strawberries, kiwi, orange and sliced steak. Serve immediately.

Hungarian Pork Burgers

Servings: 4
Cooking Time: 30 Minutes

Ingredients:
- 8 sandwich buns, halved
- ½ cup mayonnaise
- 2 tbsp mustard
- 1 tbsp lemon juice
- ¼ cup sliced red cabbage
- ¼ cup grated carrots
- 1 lb ground pork
- ½ tsp Hungarian paprika
- 1 cup lettuce, torn
- 2 tomatoes, sliced

Directions:
1. Mix the mayonnaise, 1 tbsp of mustard, lemon juice, cabbage, and carrots in a bowl. Refrigerate for 10 minutes.
2. Preheat air fryer to 400°F (205°C). Toss the pork, remaining mustard, and paprika in a bowl, mix, then make 8 patties. Place them in the air fryer and Air Fry for 7-9 minutes, flipping once until cooked through. Put some lettuce on one bottom bun, then top with a tomato slice, one burger, and some cabbage mix. Put another bun on top and serve. Repeat for all burgers. Serve and enjoy!

Steak Fajitas

Servings: 4
Cooking Time: 20 Minutes

Ingredients:
- 1 lb beef flank steak, cut into strips
- 1 red bell pepper, cut into strips
- 1 green bell pepper, cut into strips
- ½ cup sweet corn
- 1 shallot, cut into strips
- 2 tbsp fajita seasoning
- Salt and pepper to taste
- 2 tbsp olive oil

- 8 flour tortillas

Directions:

1. Preheat air fryer to 380°F (195°C). Combine beef, bell peppers, corn, shallot, fajita seasoning, salt, pepper, and olive oil in a large bowl until well mixed.

2. Pour the beef and vegetable mixture into the air fryer. Air Fry for 9-11 minutes, shaking the basket once halfway through. Spoon a portion of the beef and vegetables in each of the tortillas and top with favorite toppings. Serve.

Beef Brazilian Empanadas

Servings: 6

Cooking Time: 40 Minutes

Ingredients:

- 1 cup shredded Pepper Jack cheese
- 1/3 minced green bell pepper
- 1 cup shredded mozzarella
- 2 garlic cloves, chopped
- 1/3 onion, chopped
- 8 oz ground beef
- 1 tsp allspice
- ½ tsp paprika
- ½ teaspoon chili powder
- Salt and pepper to taste
- 15 empanada wrappers
- 1 tbsp butter

Directions:

1. Spray a skillet with cooking oil. Over medium heat, stir-fry garlic, green pepper, and onion for 2 minutes or until aromatic. Add beef, allspice, chili, paprika, salt and pepper. Use a spoon to break up the beef. Cook until brown. Drain the excess fat. On a clean work surface, glaze each empanada wrapper edge with water using a basting brush to soften the crust. Mound 2-3 tbsp of meat onto each wrapper. Top with mozzarella and pepper Jack cheese. Fold one side of the wrapper to the opposite side. Press the edges with the back of a fork to seal.

2. Preheat air fryer to 400°F (205°C). Place the empanadas in the air fryer and spray with cooking oil. Bake for 8 minutes, then flip the empanadas. Cook for another 4 minutes. Melt butter in a microwave-safe bowl for 20 seconds. Brush melted butter over the top of each empanada. Serve warm.

Sirloin Steak Bites With Gravy

Servings: 4

Cooking Time: 20 Minutes

Ingredients:

- 1 ½ lb sirloin steak, cubed
- 1 tbsp olive oil
- 2 tbsp cornstarch, divided
- 2 tbsp soy sauce
- 2 tbsp Worcestershire sauce
- 2 garlic cloves, minced
- Salt and pepper to taste
- ½ tsp smoked paprika
- ½ cup sliced red onion
- 2 fresh thyme sprigs
- ½ cup sliced mushrooms
- 1 cup beef broth
- 1 tbsp butter

Directions:

1. Preheat air fryer to 400°F (205°C). Combine beef, olive oil, 1 tablespoon of cornstarch, garlic, pepper, Worcestershire sauce, soy sauce, thyme, salt, and paprika. Arrange the beef on the greased baking dish, then top with onions and mushrooms. Place the dish in the frying basket and bake for 4 minutes. While the beef is baking, whisk beef broth and the rest of the cornstarch in a small bowl. When the beef is ready, add butter and beef broth to the baking dish. Bake for another 5 minutes. Allow resting for 5 minutes. Serve and enjoy.

Greek-style Pork Stuffed Jalapeño Poppers

Servings:6

Cooking Time: 30 Minutes

Ingredients:

- 6 jalapeños, halved lengthwise
- 3 tbsp diced Kalamata olives
- 3 tbsp olive oil
- ¼ lb ground pork
- 2 tbsp feta cheese
- 1 oz cream cheese, softened
- ½ tsp dried mint
- ½ cup Greek yogurt

Directions:

1. Warm 2 tbsp of olive oil in a skillet over medium heat. Stir in ground pork and cook for 6 minutes until no longer pink. Preheat air fryer to 350ºF. Mix the cooked pork, olives, feta cheese, and cream cheese in a bowl. Divide the pork mixture between the peppers. Place them in the frying basket and Air Fry for 6 minutes. Mix the Greek yogurt with the remaining olive oil and mint in a small bowl. Serve with the poppers.

Tarragon Pork Tenderloin

Servings: 4

Cooking Time: 25 Minutes

Ingredients:

- ½ tsp dried tarragon
- 1 lb pork tenderloin, sliced
- Salt and pepper to taste
- 2 tbsp Dijon mustard
- 1 clove garlic, minced
- 1 cup bread crumbs
- 2 tbsp olive oil

Directions:

1. Preheat air fryer to 390°F (200°C). Using a rolling pin, pound the pork slices until they are about ¾ inch thick. Season both sides with salt and pepper. Coat the pork with mustard and season with garlic and tarragon. In a shallow bowl, mix bread crumbs and olive oil. Dredge the pork with the bread crumbs, pressing firmly, so that it adheres. Put the pork in the frying basket and Air Fry until the pork outside is brown and crisp, 12-14 minutes. Serve warm.

Beef Meatballs With Herbs

Servings: 6

Cooking Time: 30 Minutes

Ingredients:

- 1 medium onion, minced
- 2 garlic cloves, minced
- 1 tsp olive oil
- 1 bread slice, crumbled
- 3 tbsp milk
- 1 tsp dried sage
- 1 tsp dried thyme
- 1 lb ground beef

Directions:

1. Preheat air fryer to 380°F (195°C). Toss the onion, garlic, and olive oil in a baking pan, place it in the air fryer, and Air Fry for 2-4 minutes. The veggies should be crispy but tender. Transfer the veggies to a bowl and add in the breadcrumbs, milk, thyme, and sage, then toss gently to combine. Add in the ground beef and mix with your hands. Shape the mixture into 24 meatballs. Put them in the frying basket and Air Fry for 12-16 minutes or until the meatballs are browned on all sides. Serve and enjoy!

Rosemary T-bone

Servings: 2

Cooking Time: 20 Minutes

Ingredients:

- 2 tbsp butter, softened
- ¼ tsp lemon juice
- 2 cloves garlic, minced
- 1 tsp minced fresh rosemary
- 1 beef T-bone steak
- Salt and pepper to taste
- ¼ tsp onion powder

Directions:

1. In a small bowl, whisk butter, lemon juice, onion powder, garlic, and rosemary. Transfer the butter mixture onto parchment paper. Roll into a log and spin ends to tighten. Let chill in the fridge for 2 hours. Remove the steak from the fridge 30 minutes before cooking. Season.

2. Preheat air fryer to 400ºF. Add the steak to the greased frying basket and Air Fry for 10 minutes, flipping once. Transfer steak to a cutting board and let sit for 5 minutes. Cut butter mixture into slices and top the steak. Let the butter melts over before serving. Enjoy!

Bourbon Bacon Burgers

Servings: 2

Cooking Time: 23-28 Minutes

Ingredients:

- 1 tablespoon bourbon
- 2 tablespoons brown sugar
- 3 strips maple bacon, cut in half
- ¾ pound ground beef (80% lean)
- 1 tablespoon minced onion
- 2 tablespoons BBQ sauce
- ½ teaspoon salt
- freshly ground black pepper
- 2 slices Colby Jack cheese (or Monterey Jack)
- 2 Kaiser rolls
- lettuce and tomato, for serving
- Zesty Burger Sauce:
- 2 tablespoons BBQ sauce
- 2 tablespoons mayonnaise
- ¼ teaspoon ground paprika
- freshly ground black pepper

Directions:

1. Preheat the air fryer to 390°F (200°C) and pour a little water into the bottom of the air fryer drawer. (This will help prevent the grease that drips into the bottom drawer from burning and smoking.)

2. Combine the bourbon and brown sugar in a small bowl. Place the bacon strips in the air fryer basket and brush with the brown sugar mixture. Air-fry at 390°F (200°C) for 4 minutes. Flip the bacon over, brush with more brown sugar

and air-fry at 390°F (200°C) for an additional 4 minutes until crispy.

3. While the bacon is cooking, make the burger patties. Combine the ground beef, onion, BBQ sauce, salt and pepper in a large bowl. Mix together thoroughly with your hands and shape the meat into 2 patties.

4. Transfer the burger patties to the air fryer basket and air-fry the burgers at 370°F (185°C) for 15 to 20 minutes, depending on how you like your burger cooked (15 minutes for rare to medium-rare; 20 minutes for well-done). Flip the burgers over halfway through the cooking process.

5. While the burgers are air-frying, make the burger sauce by combining the BBQ sauce, mayonnaise, paprika and freshly ground black pepper in a bowl.

6. When the burgers are cooked to your liking, top each patty with a slice of Colby Jack cheese and air-fry for an additional minute, just to melt the cheese. (You might want to pin the cheese slice to the burger with a toothpick to prevent it from blowing off in your air fryer.) Spread the sauce on the inside of the Kaiser rolls, place the burgers on the rolls, top with the bourbon bacon, lettuce and tomato and enjoy!

Homemade Pork Gyoza

Servings: 4

Cooking Time: 50 Minutes

Ingredients:

- 8 wonton wrappers
- 4 oz ground pork, browned
- 1 green apple
- 1 tsp rice vinegar
- 1 tbsp vegetable oil
- ½ tbsp oyster sauce
- 1 tbsp soy sauce
- A pinch of white pepper

Directions:

1. Preheat air fryer to 350°F (175°C). Combine the oyster sauce, soy sauce, rice vinegar, and white pepper in a small bowl. Add in the pork and stir thoroughly. Peel and core the apple, and slice into small cubes. Add the apples to the meat mixture, and combine thoroughly. Divide the filling between the wonton wrappers. Wrap the wontons into triangles and seal with a bit of water. Brush the wrappers with vegetable oil. Place them in the greased frying basket. Bake for 25 minutes until crispy golden brown on the outside and juicy and delicious on the inside. Serve.

Tender Steak With Salsa Verde

Servings:4

Cooking Time: 20 Minutes

Ingredients:

- 1 flank steak, halved
- 1 ½ cups salsa verde
- ½ tsp black pepper

Directions:

1. Toss steak and 1 cup of salsa verde in a bowl and refrigerate covered for 2 hours. Preheat air fryer to 400°F. Add steaks to the lightly greased frying basket and Air Fry for 10-12 minutes or until you reach your desired doneness, flipping once. Let sit onto a cutting board for 5 minutes. Thinly slice against the grain and divide between 4 plates. Spoon over the remaining salsa verde and serve sprinkled with black pepper to serve.

Fried Spam

Servings: 2

Cooking Time: 12 Minutes

Ingredients:

- ½ cup All-purpose flour or gluten-free all-purpose flour
- 1 Large egg(s)
- 1 tablespoon Wasabi paste
- 1⅓ cups Plain panko bread crumbs (gluten-free, if a concern)
- 4 ½-inch-thick Spam slices
- Vegetable oil spray

Directions:

1. Preheat the air fryer to 400°F (205°C).

2. Set up and fill three shallow soup plates or small pie plates on your counter: one for the flour; one for the egg(s), whisked with the wasabi paste until uniform; and one for the bread crumbs.

3. Dip a slice of Spam in the flour, coating both sides. Slip it into the egg mixture and turn to coat on both sides, even along the edges. Let any excess egg mixture slip back into the rest, then set the slice in the bread crumbs. Turn it several times, pressing gently to make an even coating on both sides. Generously coat both sides of the slice with vegetable oil spray. Set aside so you can dip, coat, and spray the remaining slice(s).

4. Set the slices in the basket in a single layer so that they don't touch (even if they're close together). Air-fry undisturbed for 12 minutes, or until very brown and quite crunchy.

5. Use kitchen tongs to transfer the slices to a wire rack. Cool for a minute or two before serving.

Jerk Meatballs

Servings: 6

Cooking Time: 30 Minutes

Ingredients:

- 1 tsp minced habanero
- 1 tsp Jamaican jerk seasoning
- 1 sandwich bread slice, torn
- 2 tbsp whole milk
- 1 lb ground beef
- 1 egg
- 2 tbsp diced onion
- 1 tsp smoked paprika
- 1 tsp black pepper
- 1 tbsp chopped parsley
- ½ lime

Directions:

1. Preheat air fryer at 350°F. In a bowl, combine bread pieces with milk. Add in ground beef, egg, onion, smoked paprika, black pepper, habanero, and jerk seasoning, and using your hands, squeeze ingredients together until fully combined. Form mixture into meatballs. Place meatballs in the greased frying basket and Air Fry for 8 minutes, flipping once. Squeeze lime and sprinkle the parsley over.

Bacon, Blue Cheese And Pear Stuffed Pork Chops

Servings: 3

Cooking Time: 24 Minutes

Ingredients:

- 4 slices bacon, chopped
- 1 tablespoon butter
- ½ cup finely diced onion
- ⅓ cup chicken stock
- 1½ cups seasoned stuffing cubes
- 1 egg, beaten
- ½ teaspoon dried thyme
- ½ teaspoon salt
- ⅛ teaspoon black pepper
- 1 pear, finely diced
- ⅓ cup crumbled blue cheese
- 3 boneless center-cut pork chops (2-inch thick)
- olive oil
- salt and freshly ground black pepper

Directions:

1. Preheat the air fryer to 400°F (205°C).
2. Place the bacon into the air fryer basket and air-fry for 6 minutes, stirring halfway through the cooking time. Remove the bacon and set it aside on a paper towel. Pour out the grease from the bottom of the air fryer.
3. To make the stuffing, melt the butter in a medium saucepan over medium heat on the stovetop. Add the onion and sauté for a few minutes, until it starts to soften. Add the chicken stock and simmer for 1 minute. Remove the pan from the heat and add the stuffing cubes. Stir until the stock has been absorbed. Add the egg, dried thyme, salt and freshly ground black pepper, and stir until combined. Fold in the diced pear and crumbled blue cheese.
4. Place the pork chops on a cutting board. Using the palm of your hand to hold the chop flat and steady, slice into the side of the pork chop to make a pocket in the center of the chop. Leave about an inch of chop uncut and make sure you don't cut all the way through the pork chop. Brush both sides of the pork chops with olive oil and season with salt and freshly ground black pepper. Stuff each pork chop with a third of the stuffing, packing the stuffing tightly inside the pocket.
5. Preheat the air fryer to 360°F (180°C).
6. Spray or brush the sides of the air fryer basket with oil. Place the pork chops in the air fryer basket with the open stuffed edge of the pork chop facing the outside edges of the basket.
7. Air-fry the pork chops for 18 minutes, turning the pork chops over halfway through the cooking time. When the chops are done, let them rest for 5 minutes and then transfer to a serving platter.

Canadian-style Rib Eye Steak

Servings: 2

Cooking Time: 15 Minutes

Ingredients:

- 2 tsp Montreal steak seasoning
- 1 ribeye steak
- 1 tbsp butter, halved
- 1 tsp chopped parsley
- ½ tsp fresh rosemary

Directions:

1. Preheat air fryer at 400°F. Sprinkle ribeye with steak seasoning and rosemary on both sides. Place it in the basket and Bake for 10 minutes, turning once. Remove it to a cutting board and top with butter halves. Let rest for 5 minutes and scatter with parsley. Serve immediately.

Steak Fingers

Servings: 4

Cooking Time: 8 Minutes

Ingredients:
- 4 small beef cube steaks
- salt and pepper
- ½ cup flour
- oil for misting or cooking spray

Directions:
1. Cut cube steaks into 1-inch-wide strips.
2. Sprinkle lightly with salt and pepper to taste.
3. Roll in flour to coat all sides.
4. Spray air fryer basket with cooking spray or oil.
5. Place steak strips in air fryer basket in single layer, very close together but not touching. Spray top of steak strips with oil or cooking spray.
6. Cook at 390°F (200°C) for 4minutes, turn strips over, and spray with oil or cooking spray.
7. Cook 4 more minutes and test with fork for doneness. Steak fingers should be crispy outside with no red juices inside. If needed, cook an additional 4 minutes or until well done. (Don't eat beef cube steak rare.)
8. Repeat steps 5 through 7 to cook remaining strips.

Crispy Five-spice Pork Belly

Servings: 6

Cooking Time: 60-75 Minutes

Ingredients:
- 1½ pounds Pork belly with skin
- 3 tablespoons Shaoxing (Chinese cooking rice wine), dry sherry, or white grape juice
- 1½ teaspoons Granulated white sugar
- ¾ teaspoon Five-spice powder (see the headnote)
- 1¼ cups Coarse sea salt or kosher salt

Directions:
1. Preheat the air fryer to 350°F (175°C).
2. Set the pork belly skin side up on a cutting board. Use a meat fork to make dozens and dozens of tiny holes all across the surface of the skin. You can hardly make too many holes. These will allow the skin to bubble up and keep it from becoming hard as it roasts.
3. Turn the pork belly over so that one of its longer sides faces you. Make four evenly spaced vertical slits in the meat. The slits should go about halfway into the meat toward the fat.
4. Mix the Shaoxing or its substitute, sugar, and five-spice powder in a small bowl until the sugar dissolves. Massage this mixture across the meat and into the cuts.
5. Turn the pork belly over again. Blot dry any moisture on the skin. Make a double-thickness aluminum foil tray by setting two 10-inch-long pieces of foil on top of another. Set the pork belly skin side up in the center of this tray. Fold the sides of the tray up toward the pork, crimping the foil as you work to make a high-sided case all around the pork belly. Seal the foil to the meat on all sides so that only the skin is exposed.
6. Pour the salt onto the skin and pat it down and in place to create a crust. Pick up the foil tray with the pork in it and set it in the basket.
7. Air-fry undisturbed for 35 minutes for a small batch, 45 minutes for a medium batch, or 50 minutes for a large batch.
8. Remove the foil tray with the pork belly still in it. Warning: The foil tray is full of scalding-hot fat. Discard the fat in the tray (not down the drain!), as well as the tray itself. Transfer the pork belly to a cutting board.
9. Raise the air fryer temperature to 190°C (or 195°C or 200°C, if one of these is the closest setting). Brush the salt crust off the pork, removing any visible salt from the sides of the meat, too.
10. When the machine is at temperature, return the pork belly skin side up to the basket. Air-fry undisturbed for 25 minutes, or until crisp and very well browned. If the machine is at 390°F (200°C), you may be able to shave 5 minutes off the cooking time so that the skin doesn't blacken.
11. Use a nonstick-safe spatula, and perhaps a silicone baking mitt, to transfer the pork belly to a wire rack. Cool for 10 minutes before serving.

Tacos Norteños

Servings: 4

Cooking Time: 25 Minutes

Ingredients:
- ½ cup minced purple onions
- 5 radishes, julienned
- 2 tbsp white wine vinegar
- ½ tsp granulated sugar
- Salt and pepper to taste
- ¼ cup olive oil
- ½ tsp ground cumin
- 1 flank steak
- 10 mini flour tortillas
- 1 cup shredded red cabbage
- ½ cup cucumber slices
- ½ cup fresh radish slices

Directions:
1. Combine the radishes, vinegar, sugar, and salt in a bowl. Let sit covered in the fridge until ready to use. Whisk the

olive oil, salt, black pepper and cumin in a bowl. Toss in flank steak and let marinate in the fridge for 30 minutes.
2. Preheat air fryer at 325ºF. Place flank steak in the frying basket and Bake for 18-20 minutes, tossing once. Let rest onto a cutting board for 5 minutes before slicing thinly against the grain. Add steak slices to flour tortillas along with red cabbage, chopped purple onions, cucumber slices, radish slices and fresh radish slices. Serve warm.

Vietnamese Beef Lettuce Wraps

Servings: 4
Cooking Time: 12 Minutes
Ingredients:
- ⅓ cup low-sodium soy sauce*
- 2 teaspoons fish sauce*
- 2 teaspoons brown sugar
- 1 tablespoon chili paste
- juice of 1 lime
- 2 cloves garlic, minced
- 2 teaspoons fresh ginger, minced
- 1 pound beef sirloin
- Sauce
- ⅓ cup low-sodium soy sauce*
- juice of 2 limes
- 1 tablespoon mirin wine
- 2 teaspoons chili paste
- Serving
- 1 head butter lettuce
- ½ cup julienned carrots
- ½ cup julienned cucumber
- ½ cup sliced radishes, sliced into half moons
- 2 cups cooked rice noodles
- ⅓ cup chopped peanuts

Directions:
1. Combine the soy sauce, fish sauce, brown sugar, chili paste, lime juice, garlic and ginger in a bowl. Slice the beef into thin slices, then cut those slices in half. Add the beef to the marinade and marinate for 1 to 3 hours in the refrigerator. When you are ready to cook, remove the steak from the refrigerator and let it sit at room temperature for 30 minutes.
2. Preheat the air fryer to 400°F (205°C).
3. Transfer the beef and marinade to the air fryer basket. Air-fry at 400°F (205°C) for 12 minutes, shaking the basket a few times during the cooking process.
4. While the beef is cooking, prepare a wrap-building station. Combine the soy sauce, lime juice, mirin wine and chili paste in a bowl and transfer to a little pouring vessel. Separate the lettuce leaves from the head of lettuce and put them in a serving bowl. Place the carrots, cucumber, radish, rice noodles and chopped peanuts all in separate serving bowls.
5. When the beef has finished cooking, transfer it to another serving bowl and invite your guests to build their wraps. To build the wraps, place some beef in a lettuce leaf and top with carrots, cucumbers, some rice noodles and chopped peanuts. Drizzle a little sauce over top, fold the lettuce around the ingredients and enjoy!

RECIPE INDEX

A

Air-fried Potato Salad ... 23
Air-fried Turkey Breast With Cherry Glaze ... 80
Almond-crusted Zucchini Fries ... 18
Apple Crisp ... 44
Artichoke Samosas ... 34
Asparagus Fries ... 15
Authentic Mexican Esquites ... 56
Avocado Fries ... 26

B

Bacon & Chicken Flatbread ... 85
Bacon, Blue Cheese And Pear Stuffed Pork Chops ... 115
Baked Caramelized Peaches ... 46
Baked Shishito Peppers ... 24
Balsamic Grape Dip ... 29
Balsamic London Broil ... 105
Barbecue Chicken Nachos ... 28
Basil Feta Crostini ... 29
Bbq Chips ... 33
Beef & Barley Stuffed Bell Peppers ... 108
Beef Al Carbon (street Taco Meat) ... 102
Beef And Spinach Braciole ... 107
Beef Brazilian Empanadas ... 112
Beef Meatballs With Herbs ... 113
Beef Steak Sliders ... 31
Beer-battered Cod ... 94
Bell Pepper & Lentil Tacos ... 56
Bite-sized Blooming Onions ... 60
Black And Blue Clafoutis ... 49
Black Bean Veggie Burgers ... 40
Black Olive & Shrimp Salad ... 95
Blackened Red Snapper ... 91
Blueberry Crisp ... 43
Bourbon Bacon Burgers ... 113
Bread Boat Eggs ... 67
Breaded Artichoke Hearts ... 16
Breaded Parmesan Perch ... 87
Breakfast Sausage Bites ... 67
Brie-currant & Bacon Spread ... 32
British Fish & Chips ... 95
Broccoli Cornbread ... 71
Broccoli Tots ... 14
Buffalo Bites ... 26
Buttered Chicken Thighs ... 77
Buttered Garlic Broccolini ... 11
Buttered Swordfish Steaks ... 97
Buttered Turkey Breasts ... 82
Buttery Chicken Legs ... 84

C

Californian Tilapia ... 98
Calzones South Of The Border ... 104
Canadian-style Rib Eye Steak ... 115
Caribbean Skewers ... 87
Carrot Orange Muffins ... 70
Catalan Sardines With Romesco Sauce ... 93
Catalan-style Crab Samfaina ... 86
Catfish Nuggets ... 96
Cauliflower "tater" Tots ... 32
Cauliflower Steaks Gratin ... 59
Cayenne-spiced Roasted Pecans ... 32
Cheddar Bean Taquitos ... 61
Cheddar-ham-corn Muffins ... 68
Cheese Blintzes ... 41
Cheese Sage Cauliflower ... 18
Cheeseburger Sliders With Pickle Sauce ... 109
Cheesy Chicken Tenders ... 74
Cheesy Eggplant Rounds ... 52
Cheesy Potato Pot ... 17
Cheesy Spinach Dip(2) ... 28
Cheesy Tuna Tower ... 89
Chicken & Rice Sautée ... 79
Chicken Breasts Wrapped In Bacon ... 85
Chicken Club Sandwiches ... 36
Chicken Cordon Bleu Patties ... 77
Chicken Cordon Bleu ... 81
Chicken Gyros ... 37
Chicken Meatballs With A Surprise ... 83
Chicken Salad With Roasted Vegetables ... 83

Chicken Spiedies 39
Chicken Tenders With Basil-strawberry Glaze 72
Chicken Wellington 74
Chili Blackened Shrimp 87
Chili Cheese Dogs 36
Chinese Fish Noodle Bowls 95
Chipotle Chicken Drumsticks 76
Chorizo Sausage & Cheese Balls 66
Cinnamon Banana Bread With Pecans 71
Cinnamon Pumpkin Donuts 68
Coconut Cream Roll-ups 43
Coconut Shrimp 97
Coconut-custard Pie 49
Colorful Vegetable Medley 53
Country Chicken Hoagies 73
Country Gravy 68
Crispy Apple Fries With Caramel Sauce 63
Crispy Cauliflower Puffs 21
Crispy Five-spice Pork Belly 116
Crispy Noodle Salad 15
Crispy Steak Subs 101
Crispy, Cheesy Leeks 17
Crunchy Chicken Strips 82
Crunchy Clam Strips 93
Crunchy Spicy Chickpeas 33
Crustless Broccoli, Roasted Pepper And Fontina Quiche ... 70
Curried Potato, Cauliflower And Pea Turnovers 57

D

Daadi Chicken Salad 82
Dauphinoise (potatoes Au Gratin) 23
Dijon Thyme Burgers 39
Donut Holes 47

E

Easy Carnitas 109
Easy Cheese & Spinach Lasagna 59
Effortless Mac 'n' Cheese 57
Egg Muffins 64
Egg Rolls 54
Enchilada Chicken Quesadillas 76
English Muffin Sandwiches 69
English Scones 64

F

Fall Pumpkin Cake 41

Family Fish Nuggets With Tartar Sauce 87
Famous Chocolate Lava Cake 47
Farfalle With White Sauce 55
Farmer's Fried Chicken 78
Fast Brownies 44
Favorite Blueberry Muffins 65
Fennel Tofu Bites 58
Fish Cakes 91
Fish Goujons With Tartar Sauce 93
Fish Nuggets With Broccoli Dip 97
Fish Tacos With Hot Coleslaw 88
Fish Tacos With Jalapeño-lime Sauce 90
Five-spice Roasted Sweet Potatoes 21
Flank Steak With Caramelized Onions 70
Flank Steak With Roasted Peppers And Chimichurri 102
French-style Steak Salad 111
Fried Apple Wedges 29
Fried Pineapple Chunks 48
Fried Scallops 95
Fried Shrimp 89
Fried Spam 114
Fried Twinkies 42
Friendly Bbq Baby Back Ribs 108
Fruit Turnovers 47

G

Garlic Wings 25
Garlicky Bell Pepper Mix 13
German Chicken Frikadellen 84
German-style Pork Patties 107
Goat Cheese Stuffed Portobellos 11
Golden Breaded Mushrooms 54
Granny Pesto Chicken Caprese 79
Greek Chicken Wings 80
Greek Gyros With Chicken & Rice 75
Greek Pita Pockets 106
Greek Pork Chops 101
Greek-style Pork Stuffed Jalapeño Poppers 112
Green Bean Sautée 51
Green Dip With Pine Nuts 21
Grilled Lime Scallions 24
Gruyère Asparagus & Chicken Quiche 84
Guilty Chocolate Cookies 49

H

Hasselbacks 13
Hazelnut Chicken Salad With Strawberries 74
Hazelnut-crusted Fish 99
Herb Roasted Jicama 20
Herb-rubbed Salmon With Avocado 86
Herby Lamb Chops 103
Holiday Breakfast Casserole 68
Holiday Peppermint Cake 48
Holliday Lobster Salad 89
Homemade Pork Gyoza 114
Homemade Potato Puffs 21
Home-style Cinnamon Rolls 52
Honey Pear Chips 50
Honey Pecan Shrimp 98
Honey-lemon Chicken Wings 30
Horseradish Tuna Croquettes 93
Hot Calamari Rings 96
Hungarian Pork Burgers 111

I

Indian Chicken Tandoori 73
Inside Out Cheeseburgers 35
Inside-out Cheeseburgers 40
Italian Breaded Eggplant Rounds 19
Italian Sausage & Peppers 104
Italian Sausage Rolls 103
Italian-style Fried Cauliflower 62

J

Jalapeño & Mozzarella Stuffed Mushrooms 25
Jerk Meatballs 115
Jerk Turkey Meatballs 82

K

Kale & Rice Chicken Rolls 83
King Prawns Al Ajillo 89

L

Lazy Mexican Meat Pizza 105
Lemon-dill Salmon Burgers 98
Lemon-garlic Strip Steak 102
Lemony Green Bean Sautée 22
Lime Bay Scallops 97

M

Maewoon Chicken Legs 78

Maple Balsamic Glazed Salmon 88
Maple-crusted Salmon 98
Marinated Rib-eye Steak With Herb Roasted Mushrooms 110
Meat Loaves 105
Meatless Kimchi Bowls 54
Mediterranean Salmon Burgers 91
Mexican Cheeseburgers 38
Mexican Chicken Roll-ups 75
Mexican-inspired Chicken Breasts 75
Minted Lamb Chops 110
Mixed Berry Pie 43
Mom's Chicken Wings 81
Morning Chicken Frittata Cups 70
Morning Potato Cakes 67
Mouth-watering Vegetable Casserole 26
Mozzarella Sticks 29
Muffuletta Sliders 25
Mushroom & Turkey Bread Pizza 86
Mushroom Bolognese Casserole 59
Mustard And Rosemary Pork Tenderloin With Fried Apples 102

N

Nutty Cookies 43

O

Oat & Nut Granola 64
Oatmeal Blackberry Crisp 41
Onion Ring Nachos 34
Orange-glazed Cinnamon Rolls 66
Oreo-coated Peanut Butter Cups 42

P

Paprika Fried Beef 103
Parmesan Chicken Fingers 73
Parmesan Fish Bites 96
Parsnip Fries With Romesco Sauce 20
Party Buffalo Chicken Drumettes 81
Peach Fritters 65
Peachy Chicken Chunks With Cherries 80
Pecan Turkey Cutlets 77
Pecorino Dill Muffins 14
Peppered Maple Bacon Knots 64
Pepperoni Pockets 110
Perfect Broccolini 24
Perfect Burgers 36
Perfect French Fries 16

Perfect Pork Chops	106
Philly Cheesesteak Sandwiches	35
Pineapple & Veggie Souvlaki	56
Pizza Portobello Mushrooms	50
Plantain Chips	33
Polenta	19
Pork Chops	111
Pork Tenderloin Salad	19
Prosciutto Mozzarella Bites	26
Provençal Grilled Rib-eye	105
Pumpkin Brownies	44
Pumpkin Empanadas	69

Q
Quick Chicken For Filling	82
Quick Shrimp Scampi	100
Quick-to-make Quesadillas	55
Quinoa & Black Bean Stuffed Peppers	61

R
Red Curry Flank Steak	106
Restaurant-style Breaded Shrimp	92
Rich Clam Spread	31
Rich Egg-fried Cauliflower Rice	27
Ricotta & Broccoli Cannelloni	13
Rigatoni With Roasted Onions, Fennel, Spinach And Lemon Pepper Ricotta	52
Roast Sweet Potatoes With Parmesan	17
Roasted Bell Peppers With Garlic & Dill	14
Roasted Broccoli And Red Bean Salad	15
Roasted Brussels Sprouts	11
Roasted Heirloom Carrots With Orange And Thyme	13
Roasted Jalapeño Salsa Verde	32
Roasted Pears	47
Roasted Peppers With Balsamic Vinegar And Basil	16
Roasted Red Pepper Dip	33
Roasted Vegetable Frittata	71
Roasted Vegetable, Brown Rice And Black Bean Burrito	63
Roasted Veggie Bowls	61
Roman Artichokes	22
Rosemary Lamb Chops	105
Rosemary T-bone	113

S
Salmon Burgers	38
Salmon Croquettes	88
Salt And Pepper Baked Potatoes	22
Saucy Chicken Thighs	74
Saucy Shrimp	94
Sausage And Pepper Heros	37
Sausage-cheese Calzone	101
Savory Brussels Sprouts	12
Seedy Rib Eye Steak Bites	107
Shakshuka-style Pepper Cups	66
Shrimp & Grits	92
Shrimp Egg Rolls	30
Shrimp Patties	90
Sicilian-style Vegetarian Pizza	62
Sirloin Steak Bites With Gravy	112
Skinny Fries	31
Sloppy Joes	108
Smoked Avocado Wedges	18
Smoked Salmon Croissant Sandwich	65
Smokehouse-style Beef Ribs	108
Smoky Roasted Veggie Chips	19
Smooth & Silky Cauliflower Purée	11
Southeast Asian-style Tuna Steaks	90
Southern-style Chicken Legs	76
Southwestern Sweet Potato Wedges	12
Spaghetti Squash And Kale Fritters With Pomodoro Sauce	53
Spanish Churro Bites	49
Spanish-style Meatloaf With Manzanilla Olives	109
Speedy Baked Caprese With Avocado	12
Spiced Fruit Skewers	48
Spiced Mexican Stir-fried Chicken	77
Spiced Shrimp Empanadas	100
Spicy Bean Patties	55
Spicy Black Bean Turkey Burgers With Cumin-avocado Spread	78
Spicy Chicken And Pepper Jack Cheese Bites	27
Spicy Fried Green Beans	18
Spicy Pearl Onion Dip	28
Spicy Vegetable And Tofu Shake Fry	61
Spinach And Cheese Calzone	57
Spring Vegetable Omelet	67
Spring Veggie Empanadas	60
Sriracha Salmon Melt Sandwiches	92
Steak Fajitas	111
Steak Fingers	116
Steak Fries	16

Steamboat Shrimp Salad 14
Strawberry Pastry Rolls 46
Strawberry Streusel Muffins 69
Struffoli 50
Stuffed Avocados 18
Stuffed Onions 23
Stuffed Pork Chops 110
Stunning Apples & Onions 12
Sugared Pizza Dough Dippers With Raspberry Cream Cheese Dip 45
Super Crunchy Flounder Fillets 99
Sushi-style Deviled Eggs 55
Sweet Chili Spiced Chicken 85
Sweet Potato Donut Holes 41
Sweet Roasted Carrots 62

T

Tacos Norteños 116
Tarragon Pork Tenderloin 113
Tasty Roasted Black Olives & Tomatoes 30
Tender Steak With Salsa Verde 114
Tex-mex Fish Tacos 99
Tex-mex Potatoes With Avocado Dressing 60
Tex-mex Stuffed Sweet Potatoes 58
Thai Chicken Drumsticks 72
Thanksgiving Turkey Sandwiches 37
The Ultimate Mac`n´cheese 22
Timeless Garlic-lemon Scallops 86
Tofu & Broccoli Salad 24
Tomato & Squash Stuffed Mushrooms 57
Tortilla Crusted Chicken Breast 84

Tortilla Pizza Margherita 52
Tropical Salsa 51
Tuna Nuggets In Hoisin Sauce 94
Turkey Tenderloin With A Lemon Touch 73
Turkish Mutabal (eggplant Dip) 12

V

Vanilla Butter Cake 46
Vegetable Roast 20
Vegetarian Eggplant "pizzas" 56
Vegetarian Fritters With Green Dip 27
Vegetarian Paella 53
Vegetarian Quinoa Cups 69
Veggie Burgers 51
Veggie-stuffed Bell Peppers 62
Vietnamese Beef Lettuce Wraps 117

W

Warm And Salty Edamame 28
White Bean Veggie Burgers 35
Wild Blueberry Sweet Empanadas 45

Y

Yogurt-marinated Chicken Legs 76
Yukon Gold Potato Purée 20
Yummy Maple-mustard Chicken Kabobs 80

Z

Za'atar Chicken Drumsticks 79
Za'atar Garbanzo Beans 31
Zucchini Hash Browns 72

Printed in Great Britain
by Amazon